Katzman, Nicholson and Corman

Shaping Hollywood's Future

MARK THOMAS MCGEE

Published in the USA by:
BearManor Media
P O Box 71426
Albany, Georgia 31708
www.bearmanormedia.com

Printed in the United States of America
ISBN   978-1-59393-191-9 (paperback)
              978-1-59393-192-6 (hardcover)

Book & cover design and layout by Darlene Swanson • www.van-garde.com

This book is dedicated to

Denetia Arellanas, Ace Mask,

Bob Villard and Bobbie Wenrick,

my Wednesday night pals

Foreword

Back in 1997 I was briefly (and *very* peripherally) involved with a movie called *Starship Troopers*. It was still in the preproduction stage when a friend brought me on board as a go-for, and I was flabbergasted to learn that Sony Pictures had already spent over $40 million on the damn thing. Crazier still, there was some question as to whether or not they were going through with it. It seemed that Sony and the director couldn't agree on a budget. The director insisted that he needed $105 million to make the picture and Sony wanted to hold the line at $95 million. Jesus H. Christ! If you can't make a giant bug movie for $95 million it's time to pack up your stuff and call it a day.

Jon Davison was one of the producers of this epic. He called me into his office one afternoon after he heard me whistling the song from *The Innocents*. To my surprise he knew who I was. He'd read a couple of my books. Hanging on the wall was a poster from *Attack of the Crab Monsters* (1957). I would have expected a poster from one of his productions instead of some old Roger Corman movie, but Jon used to work for Roger and he's a fan. With a nod at the poster he looked at me and said with a smile, "Basically, *this* is what we're making." The irony is *The Crab Monsters* cost around $100,000 and proved to be a lot more entertaining than *Starship Troopers*.

When I was a kid a movie like *Starship Troopers* would have been made for pocket change by guys like Sam Katzman, Jim Nicholson and Roger Corman, because in those days science fiction was dime store entertainment and they were the kings of the dime stores. Katzman worked for Columbia, which gave him an edge on Nicholson and Corman because he had access to Columbia's standing sets, props and personnel. His films had more production value than the stuff Nicholson and Corman were cranking out.

Katzman had worked for every fly-by-night outfit in Hollywood during the 1930s and 40s, learning everything there was to know about making pictures from the ground up. Nicholson was a down-on-his luck exhibitor who borrowed $3,000 to start his own production and distribution company at a time when television was taking a big bite out of studio profits and over 3,000 theatres had closed their doors. His marketing know-how turned American International Pictures (affectionately known as The Jolly Green Giant) into the biggest little motion picture company in Hollywood history. Corman made movies for Nicholson. He was AIP's most energetic and dependable producer-director.

Throughout the 1950s and 60s these three guys ruled the exploitation film business. While the major studios were making movies for an audience that was home watching television, Katzman, Nicholson and Corman had the good sense to cater to children and teenagers, the only ticket-buyers you could count on. Not that the young crowd didn't watch television but they wanted to get away from their parents, and when they were looking for entertainment they weren't interested in lavish Biblical spectacles or splashy MGM musicals, and they certainly didn't want to see some old bag like Joan Crawford whine her way through some dreary melodrama. They wanted action pictures, hot-rod pictures, rock 'n' roll pictures, monster pictures; movies they could relate to. Katzman, Nicholson and Corman gave them what they wanted. Teenpix.

Bob Walker warned his fellow exhibitors that they'd "better get behind Sam Katzman and let him continue to make the things the young set wants to see." Exhibitor Jerry Drew agreed with him. He complained that he'd "played a lot of so-called 'epics' and those nice 'family' pictures that they don't come to see. Then we play the AIP stuff to pay the bills." Astounded by the business that one of Corman's films was generating, Arthur Stein of the Central States Theatre Corporation remarked: "[It] is easily the outstanding grosser of the summer season and has far exceeded any expectations that we held for it. The results have been astounding and, frankly, we are flabbergasted on the business that we are doing."

The five major studios were having a hard time of it in the 1950s. The Supreme Court had put an end to their stranglehold on exhibition by forcing them to sell off their theatres to comply with the Sherman Antitrust Act. The court also put a stop to their practice of block booking, whereby exhibitors were forced to buy films by the truckload, sight unseen. Studio heads were still reeling when television hit them like an A-Bomb. TV sets were leaving showrooms at an alarming rate and by 1954 theatre attendance had dropped to less than half of what it had been. In desperation the majors spent more money on fewer, bigger movies. They made movies in CinemaScope and color and 3-D, hoping to lure people away from their TV sets. None of these gimmicks proved to be more effective than the banners hanging beneath the marquee that promised air conditioning.

The small town exhibitors changed their programs two or three times a week. When the studios cut back on production, they were left with nothing to play. Katzman, Nicholson and Corman were a godsend to these people.

Twenty years later the big-wigs at the major studios were *still* ignoring the major shift in their audience when the box office returns on *Easy Rider* shook them to their foundations. In his funny and insightful book, *Adventures in the Screen Trade,* William Goldman made a remark that hit the nail on the head when he wrote that none of the people who were running the studios knew *anything. Easy Rider* forced them to admit it, if only temporarily. In desperation they turned to younger filmmakers, guys who'd grown up in the 1950s, their heads filled with B-movie images. George Lucas was responsible for the first big surprise when his nostalgic *American Graffiti,* with its non-stop rock 'n' roll soundtrack, had them lining up around the block, a film that had a lot in common with AIP's beach films, better made of course. Universal refused to back it until Francis Ford Coppola agreed to put his name on it. Not having learned their lesson, Universal turned down Lucas's next project, the ground-breaking, record-breaking *Star Wars,* inspired by the studio's own *Flash Gordon* serials.

With *Creature from the Black Lagoon* serving as his blueprint, Steven Spielberg made *Jaws,* with an opening that was a lift from *The Monster that*

Challenged the World. It was the biggest hit that summer. His next film, *Close Encounters of the Third Kind* was another smash hit. Spielberg told author Ray Bradbury he would have never made it if he hadn't seen *It Came From Outer Space* six times when he was a kid.

In 1981 Spielberg was back with *Raiders of the Lost Ark*, which seemed a lot like a kick-ass version of one of Sam Katzman's serials. That same year John Carpenter paid tribute to the movie that made him want to be a director in the first place by remaking *The Thing from Another World*.

Look at some of the highest grossing films of 2014—*Transformers: Age of Extinction*, *The Amazing Spider-Man 2*, and *Captain America: The Winter Soldier*. I never thought I'd see the day when films like these would dominate the market.

Of course, once the major studios hijacked the B-movie market, it was harder for the exploitation filmmakers to make a buck. Katzman and Nicholson weren't alive to see this revolution take place but Corman was and he's been scrambling ever since. In the 1980s, when the cost of advertising drove low budget films out of the theatres, Corman shifted gears and made direct-to-video movies, taking advantage of the booming home video market. And when that market dried up he found a new home in cable television, making tongue-in-cheek campy nonsense for the Sci-fi channel. In a way he has become like one of the characters in *The Crab Monsters*, jumping from place to place as the ground beneath him is being whittled away. "I used to spend a hundred thousand to make a million," Corman lamented. "Now I spend a million and make a hundred thousand."

Since no one knows what the next delivery system is going to be, or how the films are going to be marketed, Hollywood is on shaky grounds these days, but make no mistake about it, Corman is still in the game. He'll probably die at his desk, in the middle of negotiating a deal. No. Scratch that. He'll die at his desk *after* he's closed the deal.

I never met Katzman but I did meet Nicholson, briefly, when he showed up on the set of *The Comedy of Terrors*. I was there with a friend who got us past the guard at the gate by claiming we were doing a piece on the film for

Famous Monsters magazine, which we weren't. Nicholson looked like a glass of milk, all dressed in white. He had a big smile on his face the whole time. I was in awe of him, of course. I introduced myself and shook his hand and told him *Circus of Horrors* was one of my favorite films. He told me to drop by the office and pick up a few stills, which I did. I walked off with about eighty of them as I recall.

Corman I met while I was writing a book about him. He has become a legend in Hollywood, the elder statesman of shlock cinema and in no danger of slipping through the cracks of Hollywood history. Not so Jim Nicholson who has been more or less eclipsed by his partner Sam Arkoff. Reading Arkoff's book you'd think the only thing Nicholson contributed to their partnership was a couple of money-making titles. As for Sam Katzman, it is doubtful that anyone but a rabid movie buff remembers him at all. This book is an attempt to give these three devils their due. If it hadn't been for them, we might never have seen the likes of *Jaws*, *Stars Wars* or *Raiders of the Lost Ark*. Hollywood owes these guys. Their influence can't be denied, nor should it be.

Before we get started I want to thank all of the people who made this book possible. First on the list is Boyd Magers who was kind enough to let me use all of the information he's uncovered about Sam Katzman over the years. All of the quotes from Kirk Alyn, Joan Barclay, Gregg Barton, Billy Benedict, John Hart, Ralph Hodges, Linda Johnson, Pierce Lyden, Gloria Marlen and Joan Woodbury come from Boyd's wonderful *Western Clippings* website. You should check it out. You'll have a great time.

Tom Weaver has probably interviewed more people than anyone on the planet and he was kind enough to send me his interview with cinematographer Richard Kline, who worked for Katzman for years. His interview with actor Michael Fox was also very helpful. Check out Tom on Amazon. His books are as entertaining as they are vital to people like me. Without Tom and Boyd, the Katzman section of this book would have been about two pages long.

Susan Hart and Luree Nicholson are responsible for most of the Jim

Nicholson story. I haven't spoken to Susan for decades but I still remember how helpful she was with my book on American International Pictures. She put me in touch with a lot of people who would have been inaccessible to me otherwise. She was also kind enough to invite my wife, Wendy, and me to a Beach Party reunion at the Beverly Garland Holiday Inn. Sam Arkoff, John Ashley, Frankie Avalon, Dick Dale, Fabian, Annette Funicello, Dwayne Hickman, Bobbi Shaw, Burt Topper and Deborah Walley were among the celebrities there that evening. It was bitchin'.

Luree Nicholson, another sweet lady, was so angry after she read Sam Arkoff's biography that she was ready to write her own book. I wish she had. Hopefully, with her help, I have been able to set the record straight on her behalf.

A lot of people contributed to the section on Roger Corman. My appreciation goes to Bob Burns, Gene and Roger Corman, Beach Dickerson, Miller Drake, Mark Frank, Richard Harrison, Jackie Joseph, Marty Kearns, David Kramarksy, Dick Miller, Kevin O'Neal, Gary Smith, Jim Wynorski and Mickey Zide. I also want to thank the people who are no longer with us: Forrest J. Ackerman, Samuel Z. Arkoff, William Asher, John Ashley, Paul Blaisdell, Herman Cohen, Beverly Garland, Alex Gordon, Chuck Griffith, Ib Melchior, Wyott Ordung, Ronald Stein, Herbert L. Strock, Les Tremayne, Yvette Vickers, and Mel Welles.

And a special thanks to Bob Villard, my friend for over forty years, who gave me free access to his fabulous still collection.

PART ONE

SAM KATZMAN

"There may have been twelve disciples in The Bible but there's only ten in my budget."

Before everyone was loving Lucy on television, Lucille Ball had a popular radio show called *My Favorite Husband*, and one night a producer-director named S. Sylvan Simon was listening to her program and decided it was time to bring Lucy back to the big screen. His boss, Columbia Pictures mogul Harry Cohn, thought Simon was out of his head. RKO and MGM hadn't known what to do with Lucy and now she was past her prime. Anyway, Cohn already had one redhead on the payroll (Rita Hayworth) and she was a royal pain in the ass. Besides all of that, Cohn *didn't* love Lucy. He didn't even like her. But Simon was certain that he could make money with Lucy so he kept nagging his boss until he wore him down. Reluctantly, Cohn signed Lucy to a three picture contract at $85,000 per picture. Her first two pictures, *Miss Grant Takes Richmond* (1949) and *The Fuller Brush Girl* (1950) were big money-makers for the studio. But Simon died before he could get a third picture going, leaving Cohn saddled with a star he never wanted and Lucy without an ally. It didn't matter to Cohn that her pictures had made money. He still didn't like her. And the more he thought about paying her another $85,000 the less he liked it. A call from Cecil B. DeMille started his devious mind spinning. DeMille wanted to borrow Lucy for his all-star extravaganza *The Greatest Show on Earth* (1952). Studios always made a nice chunk of change when they loaned their stars to other studios, as much as three or four times their salaries, but Cohn didn't care. He told DeMille he couldn't have her, knowing that when Lucy found out about it, and he'd make sure that she would, she'd be good and mad. And while she was good and mad he sent her a script for a movie that Sam Katzman was about to make with Shirley Temple's ex-husband, John Agar, a silly SuperCinecolor costume epic called *The Magic Carpet* (1951). He attached a note to the script, informing Lucy that he wanted her to play the villain of the piece.

A cheeseball Sam Katzman movie! What could possibly be more insulting than that? Cohn was sure she'd refuse to do it, which would violate the terms of her contract, and that would be the end of that.

Outside of Hollywood circles nobody knew who Sam Katzman was. Inside he was a notorious figure, a schlockmeister, a joke, a guy who made cheap exploitation pictures and was proud of it.

Lucille Ball and John Agar can't seem to find the magic in *The Magic Carpet.*

"Artistic triumphs, like fires without insurance, can lead to bankruptcy—and ulcers," Katzman told the *L.A. Daily News.* Sam was obsessed with ulcers. He was always talking about them.

"I don't get ulcers with the type of picture I make."

"None of my pictures have won Oscars. If you x-rayed those Oscars you'd find an ulcer in each one."

"Let the arty guys get the ulcers."

In its brief and condescending article about Sam in the early 1950s, *Life* magazine reported that he'd earned a reputation as Hollywood's only independent producer whose awful movies never lost a buck. "Lord knows I'll never make an Academy Award movie," Sam told them, "but then I am just as happy to get my achievement plaques from the bank every year." At the time the article was written, Sam's reputation as a junk man had been well established.

Actor Turhan Bey had just returned from Europe, having taken a three year vacation from the movies, and was looking forward to working with Gloria Grahame on a picture called *Prisoners of the Casbah* (1953) until his agent informed him that the producer of the movie was Sam Katzman. Bey didn't make another movie for 40 years.

Actress Charlotte Austin said she knew *The Petrified Man* (released as *The Man Who Turned to Stone* in 1957) would be terrible because Sam Katzman was (to use her words) "kind of a joke."

Harry Cohn was willing to bet his life that Lucy would rather eat ground glass than star in a Sam Katzman movie. It was beneath her standing as an actress. So he sat back and waited for Lucy to march into his office and throw the script in his face.

He couldn't help it. He felt a little smug.

But Lucy was no fool. She knew what Cohn was up to. He didn't want her to be in *The Magic Carpet* any more than she wanted to be in it. He wanted to get rid of her. That was plain enough. And if she refused to do the picture the son of a bitch would probably spread the word that she was difficult to work with. Well, she thought, two can play that game. She telephoned the studio, got Cohn on the line, and in a voice as sweet as maple syrup said: "I've just read the Sam Katzman script. I think it's *marvelous!* I'd be delighted to do it."

There was a long pause at the other end of the line before Lucy heard Cohn say, "You would?!"

Of course she would! She'd make $85,000 for five days work and wash her hands of Cohn and his studio. Best of all, there was the added benefit of knowing that she'd beat Cohn at his own game.

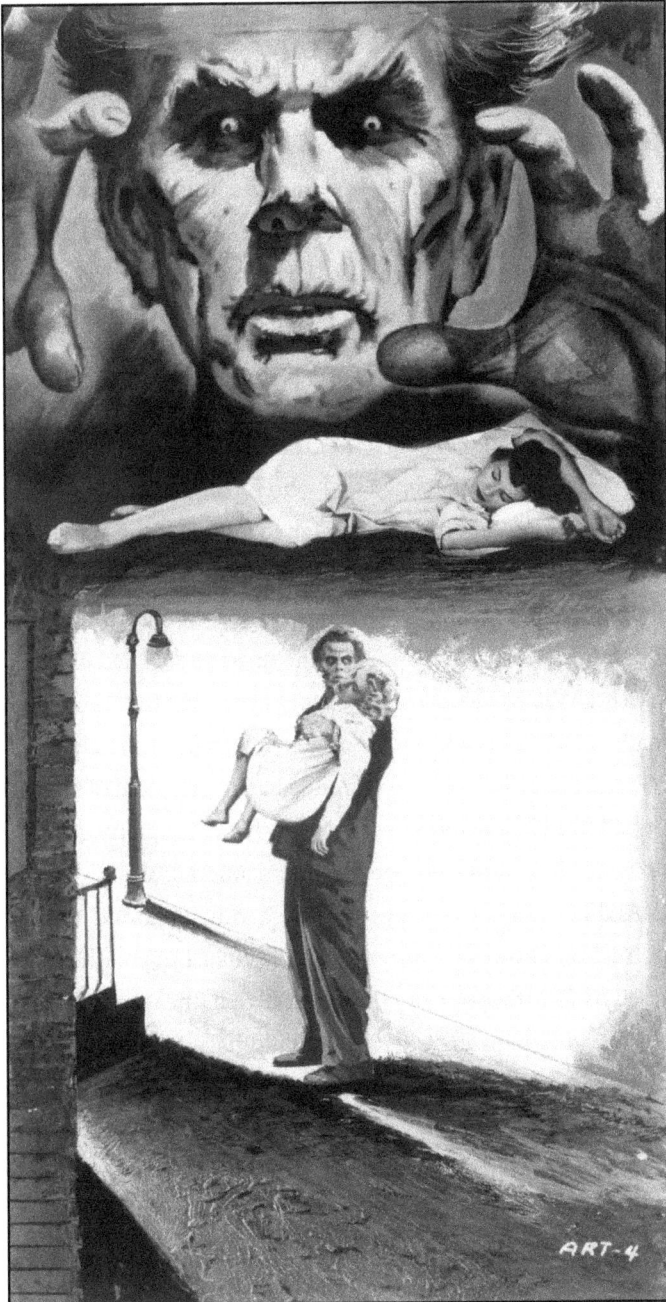

"Rock like dullness" was the way one critic accurately described
The Man Who Turned to the Stone.

Not having all of the background information at his disposal, the screenwriter felt sorry for Lucy. Someone like her in a stinky little picture like this. It wasn't right. He offered to expand her role. Lucy told him she wouldn't hear of it. She liked it just the way it was.

Harry Cohn's little scheme blew a king-size hole in Sam Katzman's budget. Normally the villain would have cost him $7,500 or less. He had to do a lot of juggling to keep the budget in line, but it was a point of honor with him. His films never went over budget. Never! With so little time before the film went into production it must have been quite a task to make ends meet but he did it, more than likely without breaking a sweat. Nobody knew how to pinch pennies and cut corners better than Sam Katzman.

"I nearly got killed on that one," said John Agar. "They had constructed this carpet with a motor on it, powerful enough to lift it into the air with a dummy riding it. But the trouble was it looked like a dummy. So the director said, 'Put the other dummy on it.' That was me. But the motor wasn't strong enough to lift a man into the air, so at a certain point in the suspension, I had to help push the carpet forward. Well, you could see the snag, so we took the scene several times until I finally said, 'This is going to be a take,' and really pushed hard. I sent myself off balance, the carpet went falling, and I had to grab hold of the piano wires to save myself from falling thirty feet. I cut my hands up pretty good."

Agar looks incredibly out of place and uncomfortable in this shortchanged Arabian Nights fantasy, wearing a ridiculous red (almost pink) costume. Yet somehow he's more believable than Lucy with her awful red wig. She seems so detached from the material that one wouldn't be surprised to see her chewing gum. However, she could have been in top form and it wouldn't have helped. Her dialogue would have torpedoed Meryl Streep. In its own way, *The Magic Carpet* is sheer perfection, another masterpiece in the Katzman library. And make no mistake about it, the Katzman library is full of such masterpieces.

Sam Katzman was a bulb-shaped, soft-spoken man with no chin. He wore loud sports shirts, sported a Bud Abbott moustache and smoked cigars the size of baseball bats.

"He looks just like you would think a Sam Katzman *would* look like," said cinematographer Richard Kline. Kline worked on dozens of Katzman's films, including *The Magic Carpet*. "He was the *perfect* Sam Katzman."

He was 'The Bossman' to his crew. To everyone else he was 'The Sultan of Sleaze,' 'The King of Crap,' or simply 'Jungle Sam.'

In Richard Thompson's piece on Katzman, written in 1969, there's much ado about how Sam coined the term 'beatnik.' In one account Sam was playing scrabble with some producer for big money, and used the word to win the game. When he was challenged by his opponent, Sam assured him that the word was real, that in fact it was in the title of his latest movie. The next morning Sam changed the covers on all of the scripts.

According to an unnamed ex-production executive, Sam was overseeing a dubbing session for one of his musicals when he heard the drummer explain to the engineer why the bass player was off his game. "He's just beat, Nick," the drummer said, and Sam walked away with a new word, not realizing that the engineer's name was Nick.

In yet another account Thompson quotes "a studio flack" who said: "You really hadda be there. All the creative people on the picture were in conference, and they wanted to know what Sam was going to call the weird kids. Somebody said hippies, Sam said no; somebody said freaks, Sam said no. Then he leaned back for a minute, quiet, then said: 'It's gotta be something special. A word like the old country, a word with a beat. That's it! We'll call them... *beatniks!*'"

Thompson quotes another anonymous source who said: "Invent it? Sure he invented it. How? Who knows how he gets his stuff? It's enough to know that it was the right time, the right place, all the forces were in line for the word, circumstances cried out for it. So Sam, almost acting as interpreter for all these aligned forces, with quiet greats like Gary Cooper saying 'Draw,' Sam says, 'Here it is: *beatnik.*'" Someone else said he got it from the extras on the set. The less flattering story has Sam buying the term from Allen Ginsberg. "I don't really understand what it's all about," Sam remarked, "but it's bound to be good business." And good business was what Sam was all about.

Sam loved lobster dinners, dirty jokes and gambling every bit as much as he loved making movies. The Santa Anita Race Track was his second home. And though he had no medical reason to carry a walking stick he always did. If things weren't going well he'd bang the floor with it. One of his walking sticks had a handle in the shape of a fist with the forefinger extended. He called it "The Fickle Finger of Fate." Everyone was on their guard when they saw that one because he liked to goose people with it. It didn't matter who you were.

"He was quite a card!" said actress Gloria Marlen. She'd been in a couple of Sam's lightweight comedies when she auditioned for a role in *Sweet Genevieve* (1947), and was taken aback when Sam said, "I'm never working with you again!" She didn't know why until he reminded her about the time he'd told her a dirty joke a few years back, after she'd asked him not to. Her husband came to the set the next morning and told Sam, in front of everyone, that he'd better not do it again. Mortified, Sam yelled as the man turned to walk away, "And *you'd* better not come to my set again!"

How he could still be sore about that was a mystery to Miss Marlen but she was resigned to it and was about to walk out of Sam's office when director Arthur Dreifuss intervened. He told Sam he was being childish and at his insistence, Sam agreed to let her be in the picture, but not for the price she was asking, which couldn't have been much or she wouldn't have been there in the first place. "Sam, you're not going to do this," Dreifuss said flatly. "I want Gloria and you're not going to pull that stuff on her. Now go ahead and sign the contract." To his credit, Sam finally caved, however reluctantly.

"I don't have anything nice to say about Sam," said Linda Johnson, the leading lady of *Brick Bradford* (1947). "He was lecherous. Very. Not so much to me because, fortunately, somebody told me when I first started in the business, if you want to be treated like a lady, act like a lady. So I, frankly, really never had any problems. I never invited any problems. With Sam Katzman, right off, no way. Anyway, there was a young girl, Helene Stanley, she was just darling and she was fairly young, and Sam was just after her all the time. I felt sorry for her because she didn't know how to cope with it. I don't mean anything serious happened but he was just… crude."

Evelyn Ankers and Julie Bishop in *Last of the Redmen.*

Angela Stevens, the star of *Savage Mutiny* (1953) and *Creature with the Atom Brain* (1955) told Michael Barman, "He was a bit 'hands on,' if you know what I mean. I had to watch out for him."

Richard Denning, who made a lot of pictures for Sam, blamed him for driving his wife out of the business, although in her case it wasn't due to his lecherous behavior. Denning was married to Evelyn Ankers, who was in just about every horror film Universal made in the 1940s. She starred in *Last of the Redmen* (1947). The way Denning told the story it had been a long, hot and dusty day on location and "Evie" was wearing a bulky, uncomfortable dress. The director had fallen behind schedule and everyone was being run ragged trying to catch up. Into this hotbed of cranky tempers came Sam, his wife, and his nephew. They plopped into their chairs, cool and refreshed, and watched the commotion as they ate their ice cream sundaes. Evie couldn't take her eyes off of them. The more she looked, the angrier she got. At the end of the day, when Sam told everybody to go home, she laid into him. She called him a tight, inconsiderate bastard. She called him this and she called him that. Denning assumed that Sam spread the word that his wife was difficult to work with. Maybe he did and maybe he didn't. Either way she continued to appear in movies and television for another 13 years, so why Denning would say Sam drove her out of the business is rather puzzling.

As irritating as those ice cream sundaes may have been to Evie, her experience on *Last of the Redmen* couldn't hold a candle to what actor John Hart went through. Hart was doubling the film's leading man, Jon Hall, and there was a sequence where Hall's character was supposed to swim across a lake, and take cover behind a tree, dodging bullets all the way. *Real* bullets.

"Usually, if you have water in a battle, they have little air things they can pull triggers on and they puff up and look like shots hitting the water," Hart said. "But, instead of going to all that trouble and hiring all that stuff, [Sam] got the idea to have a guy really shoot."

Hart wanted to see a display of the marksman's abilities before tackling what sounded to him like a risky proposition. Once he was satisfied that the guy knew what he was doing, Hart dove into the water and swam across the lake. His heart skipped a beat each time he heard the plunk of the bullets.

"When I got through with that, they wanted to do another [scene] around a tree. They usually put squibs in there and bow it out. But it was cheaper for him to shoot. So I ducked behind a tree, he'd shoot, then I'd stick my head out, duck back, he'd shoot—later I thought that's the dumbest damn thing I ever did!"

In his book, *Those Saturday Serials*, actor Pierce Lynden wrote about his experiences working for Sam:

> Like once on *Pirates of the High Seas* [1950], with Buster Crabbe, they threw five or six of us baddies overboard from the ship we were trying to capture. We were supposed to swim ashore, the camera would cut and a motorboat would come out and pick us up—only the guy couldn't get the boat started.

Sam didn't exactly bend over backwards for his actors except when he had 'a star,' someone like Rhonda Fleming or Ricardo Montalban. Harry Sauber took care of those people. Sauber was a gentleman, the class side of Sam's operation.

"Sam's appreciation was for the below-the-line crew," said Richard Kline. "Actors… well, he was kind to them and all, but he really believed in crew and he put them first and he treated them extremely well. As a camera operator in the Katzman unit, I had to have been making 180 or 200 dollars a week, which was very good money. We worked six days a week in that period of the industry, and on a football weekend when SC was playing somebody, Sam would show up in the morning and say, 'Guys, if you finish at noon, there'll be a bus outside, lunch will be served on the bus, and I've got tickets for you on the 40-yard line.' Well, sure enough, we'd finish, and that afternoon we'd be at the Coliseum. And after almost every quickie show, there was always a wrap party on the set, with hors d'oeuvres and drinks. Sam threw all kinds of 'appreciation parties,' he was very good about that. At these parties, his wife Hortense would show up. Sam called her Hortie. She was a flaming redhead—dyed, of course, and she wore mink coats so long, it was just unbelievable. A very nice lady. When people talk about Sam today, they often talk about how cheap he was, but Sam was actually a very generous person."

House Peters didn't think so. The actor was sitting in Sam's waiting room one afternoon while his agent tried to negotiate a twenty-five dollar raise. The door to Sam's office was wide open and Peters could hear everything that was said. Sam cried poor, of course. There wasn't a dime to spare. (There never is.) He and the agent dickered for quite some time before Sam put the conversation on hold long enough for him to place a two thousand dollar bet with his bookie.

Charles Quigley had a similar experience, only he was actually *in* Sam's office while his agent negotiated his salary. When Quigley first started working for Sam he was making $800. Then it was $600. Now he was told he'd be making $400. He stepped forward, looked Sam in the eye and said: "What the hell is it? I've worked hard for you. I am always here on time, I always know my dialogue, and I don't have a drinking problem. You've told me you're happy with my work, but every time we negotiate, you drop my salary. Well, now I've had it. This is the last job I'll do for you!"

Ralph Hodges saw the other side of Sam. They were on location at Catalina, and on weekends Hodges liked to go sailing in a little rowboat with a sail he'd made from a bath curtain. He was three or four miles from the beach one afternoon when he realized that someone had taken his oars and he was heading out to sea. "Somebody on the pier saw I was in trouble and they called Sam Katzman. He charted a seaplane and came out looking for 'his kid.' From then on I had the nickname of Mile-Away."

In its December 1964—January 1965 review of American producers, *Cashiers du Cinéma* observed that Sam was "the most prolific of all producers. His films (science-fiction, crime thrillers, Westerns) beat all records for speed of shooting, modesty of budget, and artistic nullity. Socio-musicologists are excited by his study of the evolution of modern dance, from *Rock Around the Clock* to *Hootenanny Hoot*, including *Calypso Heat Wave* and *Don't Knock the Twist*, not to mention the deafening *Mambo Boom*. We await, with impatience but without much hope, *Don't Knock the Shake-It-Out-Baby*."

Sam Katzman was born on July 7, 1901, the son of Abraham and Rebecca Katzman, a poor Jewish couple living in New York City. His father played the violin and hoped that one day Sam would follow in his musical footsteps. But Sam had other ideas. He went to work for William Fox at the Fox Film Corporation in Fort Lee, New Jersey where one and two reelers were coming off the assembly line with breath-taking regularity. Sam made $9 a week carrying mail and props, making lab runs, and doing just about anything else he was asked to do. He learned everything about the business of making movies and by 1917 he was an assistant director on the original *Cleopatra* with Theda Bara. When Fox merged with 20th Century Films, Sam and a lot of other people found themselves out of a job, after which he could often be found at the corner of Gower Street and Sunset Boulevard, a hangout for Hollywood's cowhands, in the heart of Hollywood's Poverty Row.

When he got wind of some job that was open at some two-bit company, he'd race off to apply for it. During this period he worked as a production manager for First National, Cosmopolitan and every other small-time outfit in town. He was involved in a series of Bob Steele westerns when he started dating a Pathé bit player named Hortense Petra. (Her real name was Petrimoulx.) He fell in love with her and asked her to marry him. "I didn't leave Mississippi to get hitched to an assistant, I came to marry a producer," she told him.[1] So Sam wrote a script, scraped together $13,000 and became a producer. He rented space at the old Beachwood Studios (which later became part of the Columbia lot) and made a film called *His Private Secretary* (1937). Everyone involved worked on a promise-to-pay pay basis.

"There are no outstanding names with which to decorate the marquee," wrote the critic for the *Motion Picture Herald*, "the two leading players being

Sam Katzman's first feature was *His Private Secretary*,
made for a modest $13,000.

Evelyn Knapp and John Wayne, familiar names but that's about all." Wayne's biographer, Scott Eyman, said it was the first time that Wayne turned in a credible performance.

Now that Sam was a producer, he and Hortie got hitched. He took a lease on the old Bryan Foy studio and started his own company, Victory Pictures, and produced over thirty forgettable features, most of them westerns and crime dramas. Victory also had a couple of serials on its roster. Actress Lucille Lund played a supporting role in one of those serials, *Blake of Scotland Yard* (1937). She told Mike Fitzgerald:

> It was shot as both a serial and a feature, but the whole thing didn't make any sense. There is a scene in the serial where I'm to go over a cliff into the water. Sam wanted me to wear my own dress, but I refused! Sam was very funny, but a bit chintzy. He'd want you to work in your own clothes to cut down on wardrobe expenses. He also brought furniture from his own house to dress a set. You'd see notes in the script, 'Mr. Katzman's own radio to be used here.' The budgets were shoestring!

Sam closed Victory Pictures in 1940 and went to work for Monogram, another Poverty Row outfit, where he formed a partnership with Jack Dietz, once the owner of Harlem's famous Cotton Club and the former president of Mutual Pictures. Mutual had a mobster named Johnny Rosselli on its payroll and it was common knowledge that Dietz had mob ties but nobody ever proved it. As Banner Productions, Dietz and Katzman created two franchises—the East Side Kids comedies and the Bela Lugosi thrillers.

Sam Goldwyn, who was the polar opposite of Sam Katzman when it came to spending money on a movie, made a picture called *Dead End* (1937), based on a successful Broadway play about crime in big city slums. Many of the young actors who'd played the juvenile delinquents in the play, Leo Gorcey and Huntz Hall among them, were cast in the movie. Collectively, these young actors came to be known as The Dead End Kids. Warner

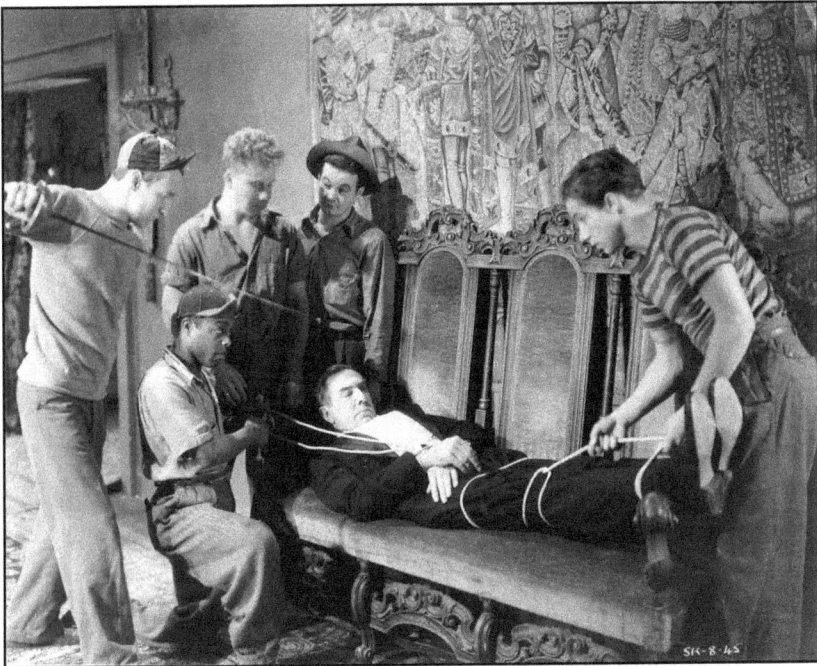

Bela Lugosi has been exhausted by the East Side Kids
in this scene from *Spooks Run Wild*.

Bros. cleaned them up a little and put them in six movies. They weren't delinquents any longer, just a little rough around the edges. When Sam Katzman
got a hold of them he shaved off the edges and turned them into a pack of
illiterate comic do-gooders called The East Side Kids. From 1940 to 1945
Banner produced 22 East Side Kids features, directed by such fast-schedule
experts as Joseph H. Lewis, Wallace Fox, William Nigh and William Beau-
dine. Actor Billy Benedict said the movies "were on a strict budget and got
by just as cheap as they could, and didn't worry about a lot of things they
should have. Katzman would hang around with his cane and beat the floor
when things weren't going well."

One afternoon, hoping to save himself a couple of bucks on a stuntman,
Sam asked Leo Gorcey to take a tumble down a flight of stairs. Gorcey told
him to go fly a kite. "Come on, Leo, be a sport," Sam told him. "The stairs

are padded. There's nothing to it." "Then *you* do it," Gorcey said and went back to his dressing room. A few minutes later Huntz Hall was knocking at his door. "Hurry up," he said. "You gotta see this." Hall and Gorcey hurried back to the set in time to see Sam standing at the top of the stairs, wearing Gorcey's outfit. "Okay. Roll 'em," the director yelled. Sam braced himself and did a tuck and roll down the stairs.

I've heard several versions of this story. One version has Sam doubling for Huntz Hall, which is funnier still, since Hall's quite a bit taller and thinner than Sam. His outfit would have made Sam look like a scarecrow. In any event, it's probably a fairy tale, concocted to illustrate what a tight-fisted producer Sam was. I don't believe it for a minute but it's a funny story and like the man said, print the legend.

The East Side Kids series came to an end when Gorcey, who'd become the leader of the gang, wanted a pay hike. Naturally Sam wasn't having any of that so Gorcey quit and with the help of his agent created his own, even more successful series—The Bowery Boys.

When I was around six or seven years old one of the local stations showed an East Side Kids movie every Sunday at five in the evening and my older brother and I would be parked in front of the TV. I know that we both enjoyed them at the time but they're pretty tough going for anyone but children.

Bela Lugosi had been a major horror star at Universal in the early 1930s but he was picking up crumbs on Poverty Row long before the decade was up. He played a villain in one of Sam's Victory serials, *Shadows of Chinatown* (1936), and his situation hadn't improved, making him a ripe candidate for Sam and Dietz. They put him in two of their East Side Kids comedies and made him the star of seven horror movies. The most interesting thing about these wretched potboilers is they appear to have been written by people who were under the influence of some heavy duty drugs. All of these movies take place in a wacky, alternate universe. For instance, in *Bowery at Midnight* (1942) Lugosi leads a double life. By day he's a college professor. At night he's the mastermind of a criminal gang working out of the bowery. It's never made clear whether he works two jobs to make ends meet or if he's a split personality or what. Essentially, it's a crime film. And yet there's a bunch of zombies in Lugosi's bowery basement. They don't serve any purpose. They're just there.

In *Invisible Ghost* (1941), the first of the Katzman-Dietz-Lugosi thrillers, Lugosi plays a mild-mannered doctor named Kessler, the kindest man you'd ever want to meet but a little unhinged. Every night he pretends to have dinner with his wife, who ran off with his best friend. The servants have been instructed to set a place for her and they politely ignore the conversation that Kessler has with her chair. Kessler doesn't know that his wife and her lover ran their car into a tree on their way out of town. The lover was killed and his wife suffered brain damage. Kessler's gardener found them and she's been secretly living in his basement ever since. You might wonder why the gardener didn't take her to the hospital and why he never told anyone about the accident, but see, in the wacky world of Sam Katzman, characters live outside of the laws of rhyme and reason. This is just one of many eccentricities the audience is asked to swallow. Every night Kessler's wife wanders away from the basement so she can stand in front of Kessler's window. Somehow, no matter what he's doing, he will sense her presence and go to the window. Each time she tells him that she's afraid to come home. "You'd kill me," she says. "You'd kill anybody." Kessler goes into a trance, becomes psychotic and kills someone, usually one of his servants. Each time he has no memory of his crime. We're never told why he becomes so ill-tempered each time he sees the woman he supposedly loves. The fact that he never questions these blackouts remains a mystery as well. One can only speculate why his wife would think that he wanted to kill her. She must know something that we don't. Perhaps he had these psychotic spells when they were together. Maybe that's why she left him. Or maybe she's just nuts. You might also ask why the Devil anyone would stay in a house where the body count continues to rise. The answer, my friend, is blowin' in the wind.

There's a wonderful moment in *Voodoo Man* (1944) that's reminiscent of one of the Marx Brothers routines. The local sheriff comes calling on Lugosi to ask him if he's seen a detour sign on the highway. (Lugosi knows all about

Bela Lugosi attempts to transfer the life out of Louise Currie into his zombie wife played by Evelyn Marlowe in the zany *Voodoo Man*.

the sign but for the sake of brevity we won't go into that.) To what would seem like a simple "yes" or "no" question Lugosi replies, "I don't know, are they repairing the road?" The sheriff shakes his head. "No, that's just it. The road's okay." Lugosi looks puzzled. "Then why should there be any sign?" he asks. "There shouldn't," the sheriff tells him. "This is all very confusing to me, sheriff," Lugosi muses. "You're telling me," says the sheriff.

Once the Lugosi and The East Side Kids movies ran their course, Dietz and Katzman dissolved their partnership. It took Dietz five years to make another movie. It took Sam five minutes. He was still working at Monogram when he hooked up with director Arthur Dreifuss and made a series of squeaky clean teenage comedies for Columbia. For two years Sam divided his energy between the two studios until he allied himself with Columbia exclusively. Columbia was a bigger outfit and Harry Cohn gave him a sweet deal. In exchange for taking over the serial division of the studio, Sam could pick his own projects. All he had to do was throw a title at Cohn and if it sounded like something they could sell, Cohn would greenlight it. In addition to his salary, Sam was entitled to 25% of the profits.

Sam worked out of Columbia's dingy, five-stage subsidiary studio on Lyman Place, once the Tiffany-Stahl studio and before that the Fine Arts studio where *The Birth of a Nation* (1915) was shot. According to *Time* magazine the place was usually "buzzing with assorted pygmies, giants, animals (wild and tame), half-dressed women (wild and wild-eyed!), cowboys and papier-mâché interplanetary vehicles. With these props Sam can roll into a picture at the drop of a dollar."

Hortie would often play a small part in Sam's movies. He called her his good luck charm. "Somebody called her a bitch on wheels," said Joan Barclay. "She had red hair and an awful temper, but she was nice to me."

When Harry Cohn spread the word that he didn't want Hortie in any more pictures, good luck charm or not, she blew into his office one afternoon and in a voice loud enough to be heard in the next zip code asked him: "Do you want me to tell your wife Joan about all the women you've been with, and tell the wives of the other Columbia execs who they've been cheating with?"[2]

No, he did not.

According to actress Noel Neill, Hortie liked playing the horses as much as Sam did. "I had a lot of friends that would go to the track and we'd always see Hortense… with her red hair, usually a fuchsia, or a lime dress and a silver mink, so we could all spot Hortense."

Every head in a Las Vegas casino turned to watch Hortie (who was in her late sixties at the time) as she came down a long flight of stairs with her bright red hair, wearing a full length mink that was a patchwork of one-foot crimson and white squares. She was quite a spectacle. And when she saw that everyone was looking at her she turned to her companion and in a masterpiece of self-deception remarked: "You see darling, I've still got it!"

In his article for *Collier's*, "The Happiest Man in Hollywood," Willard L.

Wiener reported that Sam would give his serial scripts to his son Jerry and his friends. "If the kids outguess the writer, then we change the gimmick," Sam told Wiener. As an example Sam pointed to a sequence in *Cody of the Pony Express* (1950) where the unconscious hero, played by Jock Mahoney, has been left to die in a flaming tent. Jerry assumed he'd regain consciousness and cut his way out of the tent, which is exactly what the writers had planned. Sam told them to come up with something better. So instead of cutting his way out, Mahoney stumbles onto a secret underground passage, one of the oldest gags in the book.

Frankly, this whole business with Jerry and his friends trying to second-guess the writers sounds like a load of crapola. Any kid who's seen two or three serials knows what's going to happen 90 per cent of the time. If you see the good guy in his car and the car goes over a cliff, he'll jump out first at the beginning of the next chapter. If he's in a building and the building explodes, he'll jump out a window or (as Mahoney did) leave by way of a secret passage. Leaving out a key scene at the end of a chapter was a standard cheat. All of the serials did it all of the time. Jerry and his buddies would have been wise to that old wheeze. But the smartest person in the world can't second guess a writer who won't play by his own rules. Counting on the short-term memories of their audiences, writers thought nothing of having the hero crushed by a boulder at the end of one chapter, only to have him dive out of the way in the next.

That's right, kid, we pulled a fast one on you. What are you gonna do about it? Go ahead. Try to get your money back. See where that gets ya. What are you so sore about anyway? You shoulda known better.

In *The Lost Planet* (1953), the ever-stiff and dull Judd Holdren is propelled into the air like a guy fired out of a cannon at some carnival. He's facing a two-mile drop at the end of the chapter and it's important to note that he's *not* a super hero. If the writers had had a sense of humor, Holden might have fallen on a stack of mattresses at the Acme Mattress Factory. Instead, he simply hits the ground, gets up and walks off with nary a scratch. Jerry Katzman couldn't have guessed that one in a million years.

Joan Woodbury was in Sam's first Columbia serial, *Brenda Starr, Reporter* (1945). Her husband had gone off to war and with a little girl to support she took any part that came along. "The only reason they gave me the role was the fact I could learn dialogue fast enough to do everything in one take." On the last night of the shoot, everyone was waiting for her to finish 19 pages of dialogue so they could party. The back of the set was one solid bar with not an inch of space between one bottle and the next. Joan didn't dare disappoint them. She did everything in one take "because they were going to kill me if I didn't, with all that booze waiting."

Sam made three, sometimes four serials a year, cranking them out with less care than he gave his features, if such a thing is possible. Serials were bottom of the barrel stuff aimed at 10-year-olds. How good did they need to be? Any director who entertained thoughts about a second take was asked: "Will it get by with a serial audience?"

Sam assumed that his young audience, numbed by his rampant penny-pinching and shameless disregard of rhyme and reason, would eventually fall in line and accept anything that he threw at them. When Batman reaches beneath his cape and pulls a blowtorch out of his utility belt, nobody thinks twice about it. In the viewer's mind Batman has, for the moment, become Harpo Marx.

"How is it possible to have cosmic cannons and mind psychometers and death ray guns?" a reporter once asked Sam. Taking a pull on his Corona-Corona, Sam replied, "You just gotta have faith. You just gotta have faith."

"To me, the greatest all time producer of serials was Sam Katzman," said Pierce Lyden (although most serial fans would give that honor to Republic Pictures). "He had 15 years or so tenure at Columbia and I was with him off and on the whole time. He may not have paid the biggest salaries in town, but it was five to six weeks steady work on each one. The 'Bossman', as Sam was known to his friends, was the most prolific serial producer around. He kept the wolf from my door many years. He was loyal and easy to work for. He always remembered the supporting actors, his stock company."

Some of the actors in his "stock company" included Jack Ingram, Charlie King, Terry Frost, Eddie Parker, I. Stanford Jolley, Rick Vallin, Gene Roth, Robert Barron, Pierce Lyden, William Fawcett, Pierre Watkin, Nelson Leigh, and John Hart.

"He had a coterie of actors and stunt guys who were very loyal to him," said Hart. "He *hated* drinking—anybody who was a boozer didn't work for him. I was always there on time and I always knew all my lines, and Sam knew that. I could just walk in there, if I couldn't make a car payment or something, and say, 'Hey, Sam, can you use me in something?' He never let me down, I'd always get to do something big or little or... whatever! Ol' Sam was always a friend."[3]

Michael Fox was another actor who worked a lot for Sam; four serials and ten features altogether. "I always did the heavy," he recalled. "Every serial had a brains heavy and a physical heavy. The physical heavy was always a stuntman, Davey Sharpe or somebody like that, who did all the dirty work and all the fighting. I was the brains heavy, the boss; the one that did all the dialogue. I did the heavy in *Blackhawk*, and it was an interesting role because I played three different people: At first I was posing as a good guy, a fellow named Mr. Case who wore a hearing aid; then Mr. Case disguised himself as a Spaniard, and I played that with a dialect; and then at the end I also turned out to be the brains heavy, the leader of all the bad guys...When we were doing *Blackhawk*, I wasn't yet very familiar with film. It was a Saturday, and we were going to shoot at Signal Hill in Long Beach, at the oil fields. I woke up and it was pouring rain, and I thought, 'Oh, Christ, we're not gonna go down there!' But there was no phone call, so I got in my car and drove over to the Lyman Place lot, and there was the limo and everything else. They said, 'Sure we'll shoot,' and I said, 'My God, how can you shoot in this rain?' This was second unit, and Freddie Sears was directing. Fred said, 'If we don't back-light it, you won't see the rain'—which was true!"[4]

With everyone working twelve-hour days, six days a week, Sam could knock out a serial in seventeen days, which is the equivalent in length to five feature films.

"A serial script is as thick as a phone book," Tommy Farrell told Mike

Fitzgerald. "You shoot out of sequence so you never know who you're looking at, what you're seeing, or what you're reacting to. You have no idea who the hell you're talking about!"

The gentle and humorless Spencer Gordon Bennett directed most of the serials Sam made at Columbia. He was a family man who never used profanity and kept physically fit. His entry into the business was as a stunt man at Thomas Edison's Studio, and his first assignment was to dive off a 60ft cliff for which he received $62.50. By 1920 he was working second unit on a serial for Pathé and ultimately became typed as an action director. As well he should have been for he was always more interested in staging action sequences than he was in working with the actors.

"He was big… about six foot two… quiet, gentle man who got what he wanted by just being nice," Gregg Barton recalled. "You couldn't possibly let him down, because he was so quiet and gentle and knew what he wanted. So long as you knew what *you* were doing, knew your part, knew your words, he was just as gentle as a lamb. His pace was even. He wasn't hysterical at all and he was very affable after hours when we went in to have a couple of drinks before dinner. He would mingle with people. He was just one of 'em. When he worked, he'd bring you up to where he wanted you to be without you even knowing it. He planned things out. He knew where he was going. I never heard the man raise his voice."

"If he got ahead on a shooting schedule, he got really excited… pushing like hell, you know," said John Hart. "But if he was behind or just going along, he took it in stride. Really a nice guy. Very friendly… and competent."

Tommy Farrell recalled an incident on *Roar of the Iron Horse* (1951) that gives a pretty good picture of Bennett's ability to take things in stride. At one point in the story, Jock Mahoney was tied to a stake by a bunch of Indians who intended to set fire to him after they'd done a little war dance. Sam had hired members of the Ute tribe to do the dance.

"It's been too long," a young interpreter told Bennett. "They don't remember the war dance."

"What dance *do* they remember?"

"How about the corn dance?"

"Great!" Bennett said. "Do the corn dance, whatever."

The boy went back to the elders and told them to do the corn dance. All of the women lined up on one side, the men lined up on the other, and they started bobbing up and down.

"That's the corn dance?" Bennett asked.

"Yeah," the young man replied.

"What else you got?"

"How about the rain dance?"

"Fine, do the rain dance."

That wasn't so hot either. So Bennett put war bonnets on some of the actors and had them dance around Mahoney while the real Indians sat in the background watching.

"The minute I would finish a scene, I knew exactly what the next setup was going to be," Bennett remarked. "I would have it all mapped out. I kept the crew busy. I don't know any other director who cut in the camera as I did. I said to Katzman, 'You aren't paying me anything on these pictures. I'm saving you my salary on the lab bill.' And I did."

Ultimately, Bennett felt he'd done himself a disservice by bringing all of his films on time and on budget. As the years went by he was saddled with even lower budgets and shorter schedules because people knew he could handle it.

George H. Plympton (working with writers such as Lewis Clay, Royal Cole, Harry Fraser and Joe Poland) wrote most of the serials that Spencer Bennett directed for Sam. As a matter of fact it seemed like Plympton co-wrote every serial ever made. Born in Brooklyn in 1889, Plympton has over 300 titles on his resume, most of them serials. Michael Fox said Plympton derived a lot of pleasure from writing tongue-twisting dialog.

"It got to be a game between us," Fox said. "In *The Lost Planet* I played the evil Dr. Grood and I was in my mountain laboratory, looking into a periscope, and I had a line: 'It worked! The atom repulse set up a radiation wall which cut off the neutron detonator impulse!' Now that's a tongue-twister, and of course, George had written it accordingly. So we rehearsed it once, as you always did with Spencer, and then I went for a take."[5]

Bennett called for action and Fox dashed to his periscope. He looked into the eyepiece and was ready to say his line when the photograph of a naked woman, sitting in a chair with her legs spread, placed in the eyepiece as a gag, caught him off guard. It took all of his willpower not to laugh as he said: "It worked! The atomic propulse set up a radiation wall which cut off the neutron detonator impulse!" To which his assistant replied: "For every weapon, there is a *counter*-weapon." That line proved to be more than Fox could take. He burst out laughing and ruined the take. It took him nine more times to get it right.

Bennett directed *The Adventures of Sir Galahad* (1949) starring George Reeves who became the hero of children everywhere as Superman on the popular television series a few years later. As young Jerry Katzman watched Reeves engaged in sword fights and fisticuffs he shook his head. "You've got them fighting with their fists," he told his dad. "That's too modern. They didn't fight like that in the time of King Arthur. What's more, you can tell the armor they're wearing is phony. They're supposed to be wearing that heavy stuff and yet they get on and off their horses as if they didn't have any armor on at all."[6]

Sam probably had a long talk with the boy about ulcers.

Superman (1948), based on the comic book character created by Jerry Siegel and Joe Schuster, was the most anticipated serial Sam ever produced. The superhero had been on the radio and in cartoons, but he'd never been in a live-action feature before. Republic wanted to bring the character to the big screen a few years before. They even had a script ready but they couldn't come to terms with the people at DC Comics.

Having recently appeared in Sam Katzman's *Sweet Genevieve*, Kirk Alyn picked up the phone one afternoon and the voice at the other end of the line said, "Hi! Kirky." *Nobody* called him *Kirky*. "Who *is* this?" Alyn asked. "Sam." "Sam who?" "Katzman, you dope. Your producer. You want to do *Superman*?" Alyn wasn't sure. He'd never heard of Superman. "What is it," he asked, "a picture or a publicity stunt?" Sam told him to come to the studio to meet a couple of guys from DC comics. They gave Alyn the once-over and agreed that he could pass for Clark Kent but they weren't sure if he was built for Superman. They asked Alyn to take off his shirt. And then they wanted to see him without his pants. "Now wait a minute," Alyn balked. They reminded him that he'd be wearing tights. They needed to see what his legs looked like. Fifteen minutes later his name was on a contract.

Alyn recalled how exciting it was to sit in the screening room, watching Superman fly, scenes that were accomplished by suspending the actor on wires in front of a process screen. "It was wonderful to see the Man of Steel nose-diving and banking around with the greatest of ease," Alyn said, "but there were the wires, plain to see! When the lights came on, a lot of faces were bright red. Sam Katzman's voice was loud and clear. The whole special effects crew was fired summarily for not having done their homework by pre-testing the invisible wiring."

Now unless Sam had had a bad day at the track, it's hard to believe that the man who shrugged his shoulders when he saw *The Giant Claw* for the first time would let a few wires upset the balance of his nature. However, if he did fire the "entire" special effects crew, how many people could that have been? One guy? Maybe two?

Box office-wise, *Superman* proved to be the most successful serial Sam ever made, taking in well over a million bucks. He brought Alyn back for a sequel, *Atom Man vs. Superman* (1950) and talked about the film with a writer from *Collier's* magazine:

"There's never been anything like this on film," he modestly declares, and he might be righter than he thinks. The Supermantic feats accomplished in this film by Sam's hero... include steadying the Tacoma Bridge; crashing through a wall of rock; allowing bullets to bounce off his chest; catching a lovely lady in mid-air after she has fallen from a high building; hurling a huge boulder into the stratosphere thus creating a synthetic meteor; transmut-

Kirk Alyn as *Superman.*

ing ordinary nails into Plutonium; stopping an onrushing train single-handed; using his super sight to decipher impressions on paper; catching a rocket in mid-air and riding it, and battling a spaceship in mid-air, forcing it to collide with an asteroid. Katzman discarded the original working title, *The Return of Superman,* as too flat and unimaginative. He felt *Atom Man vs. Superman* was more to the point, although at one time, in an effort to keep pace with tomorrow's headlines, he toyed with the idea of calling his masterpiece *H-Man vs. Superman.*

Blazing the Overland Trail (1956), written by Plympton and directed by Bennett, was the last of the Katzman serials, pieced together with massive amounts of action footage from two of his earlier serials. Appropriately, when Bennett passed away in 1987, they carved "His Final Chapter" on his tombstone.

Between 1947 and 1954 Sam Katzman produced over fifty features. These were the same sort of assembly line programmers that he'd always made, designed to appeal to the widest possible audience. "In my opinion, action pictures, Westerns, costume pictures and serials have never failed to entertain and that's what movies are for—to entertain," he told *The Sunday Herald.*

In a conversation with historian Wheeler Dixon, Jerry Katzman said: "My father was always making movies at an incredible pace. There were the serials, which ended in the mid-1950s, and there were the twenty two features he did on an annual basis. It was insane. The production schedule was just stunning. My father was way ahead of the curve when it came to popular culture. Today many feature films are based on comic book heroes or heroines, but my dad pioneered this trend."

It would have been impossible for Sam to make as many movies as he did without writers and directors who could move as fast as he could. And there was no writer who could move any faster than Robert E. Kent.

"As fast as he could type, that's how the script came out," Richard Kline recalled. "I'd walk by his little office, the door would be open, and he'd say,

Lee Roberts and Dennis Moore are *Blazing the Overland Trail*.

'Oh, hi, Richard!' and we'd talk about (say) a ballgame from the night before, and he'd still keep typing while we were talkin' the ballgame! A lovely man and, even though I never really read one of his scripts, I know he was a very competent writer; he really knew the technique of writing. Sam would throw him an idea or show him a newspaper item and say, 'Here, make a story out of this,' and Kent would knock out a completed script in no time at all. I can't imagine there were many screenwriters who wrote more scripts than he did!"

Kent, who once said there was no difference between making sausages and making movies, finally burned out as a writer and became a producer, first at Columbia and later at United Artists.

Sam also had a group of directors he worked with and the three he seemed to favor were Lew Landers, William Castle, and Fred F. Sears.

Born Louis Friedlander in 1901, Lew Landers changed his name shortly after directing *The Raven* at Universal back in 1935. He made short schedule movies for most of the major studios and was none too happy about it. "They gave me these small pictures to do and want them finished by Thursday," he complained. "They don't want them good, they just want to get it out."

"Lew Landers was really a no-talent guy," Budd Boetticher told Wheeler Dixon. "They called him the 'D' director there at Columbia; he just wasn't any good. Whenever they had a picture they really didn't care about, they'd give it to Landers."

Landers directed *The Magic Carpet.*

Between takes one afternoon, Landers was feeling sorry for himself and said to no one in particular, "Damn it! Everybody else gets thirty, forty, fifty days to do a picture, and I only get six, eight, ten days." One curious technician wanted to know what he'd do if they gave him thirty days to make a picture. Landers thought for a moment. "I'd probably shoot it twice."

William Castle (real name Schloss) learned everything about making movies from Harry Cohn. When Castle was still wet behind the ears, he would finish a scene and then turn to his crew and ask what they thought. Behind his back they'd agreed to wait until the fourth take before they'd nod their heads in approval. His first assignment for Sam Katzman was *Fort Ti* (1953), a 3-D western written by Bob Kent. The critic for the *New York Times* complained that the film kept "well in a two-dimensional rut." Castle eventually left Columbia, teamed with writer Robb White and made two successful horror films for Allied Artists. Harry Cohn asked him to come back with the promise that Castle could call the shots, providing he kept his budgets low. He made a series of gimmicky horror movies that established him as the P. T. Barnum of cinema shock. Castle believed in barnstorming. And it paid off.

Frederick Francis Sears was Sam's favorite director. Born in Boston in 1913, Sears had been a dancer, stage actor and director. His first screen job was in Columbia's *The Jolson Story* (1946) as an uncredited extra. He appeared in so many of the studio's Durango Kid series that the producer let him direct a few. His ability to work both sides of the camera, his way with actors, and his endless energy caught Sam's eye.

"Fred was from New England," Richard Kline said. "He had a New England accent, and he was a very bright, intelligent man. He developed into a very good craftsman, but I don't think he really cared to do better pictures, I really don't."

Between 1953 and 1957 Sears directed twenty-nine features and nineteen television dramas, sometimes working on three episodes of three different series simultaneously. He was, perhaps, the only director in Katzman's entourage who could run as fast as his boss. Together they produced a body of work that tackled just about every current event, from H-bombs to organized crime, from rock 'n' roll to juvenile delinquency, with the emphasis on action. Always action.

"I make movies in which something is happening every minute," Sam boasted. "The man in the cinema looking at them can forget his mother-in-law or that job unfinished at the office or factory, as he hangs from a cliff or shoots it out with the villain of the piece."[7]

"He really understood pop culture, why it mattered, and where the trends were going," said his son Jerry.

"I got a kind of feeling, a knack," Sam said. "Knock on wood—I've never been wrong yet."

Sam believed if a picture made money it was a good picture. And his pictures always made money. But knacks and feelings had very little to do with it. His films cost so little they were guaranteed a profit. That's why they were called bread and butter pictures. They didn't build studio prestige, and they weren't likely to be nominated for Academy Awards, but these were the pictures that paid the studio's overhead.

Never loyal to any one genre, Sam went anywhere he thought the audience would follow. He got his ideas from other people's movies, comic books and newspaper headlines. "We don't get stories," Sam told *Time* magazine. "We get titles and then write stories around them or to fit them. For instance, we had this title *Flame of Calcutta* [1953]. Naturally, we had that area of India around Bombay in mind, and naturally we worked in those old Arab tribes."

A few days after war broke out in Korea, Sam walked into Harry Cohn's office and told him he wanted to make a movie about it. Six weeks and two days later *A Yank in Korea* (1951) was in the can.

Sam could move faster than just about anyone in the business, giving Columbia an edge on exploiting a subject before the public had a chance to lose interest in it. Sometimes Sam would lift the plot of an old film and bring it up to date, as he did with *A Yank in Korea* which was a remake of *A Yank in the R.A.F.* (1941). "They were good in the old days. They're good now," Sam said. "We got a new generation, but they got the same old glands."

Supposedly *A Yank in Korea* was inspired by a letter written by a PFC to his wife and kids shortly before he was killed in action. The movie is dedicated to him.

"It has as much suspense as any of my cliff-hangers," Sam told *Collier's*. "We went into the trenches in Burbank every night for a week. We fired real bazookas, blew up an ammunition dump, crossed 'enemy' lines and rescued

Lon McCallister and Sunny Vickers (the only woman) in *A Yank in Korea*.

a stalled train carrying wounded GIs. Finished our job well ahead of two other producers trying to beat us to the punch with a Korea story."

Sam's ability to beat people to the punch was matched by his capacity for keeping a cool head during a crisis. He was making a film in Columbia, California when he was told, after everyone was packed and ready to leave, that they'd have to stay. The running lights on one of the airplanes were out and the regulations said you couldn't take off without them. With the threat of overtime closing in on him, Sam raced to the tower and went through the regulations book. He discovered that a plane *was* allowed to take off with *one* running light. So Sam had them juggle the lights so that each plane had one good one.

On the fifth day of a six day picture called *Sky Commando* (1953), the word rippled through the stage that two days of shooting had been sabotaged

William Lundigan and Rhonda Fleming star in *Serpent of the Nile*. One Colorado exhibitor thought this modestly budgeted film did a better job of "supplying an air of reality" than Fox did with its multi-million dollar epic *The Robe*.

by a faulty camera. Sam would have to pay time and a half to shoot them again. Dan Duryea told Mike Connors they were going to finally make some money from old Sam. On the sixth day Sam came to the set and said, "Thanks very much, fellas, that's a wrap." When asked about the two days of ruined footage he replied: "Aw, don't worry about it, fellas, we'll put in more stock footage."

Is that all the stock footage you got?

Sam would often stroll around the lot, looking for standing sets. One afternoon he happened upon the sets for the studio's Biblical epic *Salome* (1953). He had Bob Kent whip up a script and before you could say 'Cleopatra' William Castle was directing *Serpent of the Nile* (1953) with beautiful Rhonda Fleming (in a black wig for Crissakes) as the Queen of the Nile. Raymond Burr was her Marc Antony. And lovely Julie Newmar made her screen debut as one of a dozen dancing, gold-painted virgins.

Newmar was going through her gyrations when the phony jewel in her belly button popped out. "Cut! Cut!" Castle shouted. An exposed belly button was a "no-no" in the uptight, sexually repressed 1950s. A little scotch tape put everything back in order. Newmar made $250 that day, more than her father made in a week. She danced her way through another one of Sam's costume pictures, *Slaves of Babylon* (1953) with film noir favorite Richard Conte and Linda Christian, the woman who was famous for being famous. Sam was very excited about this one. He told *Time* magazine, "We got underwater stuff and we got overwater stuff, and we got three characters in the fiery furnace and on top of that we got Linda Christian doing her first screen dance."

Sam told the press that he was going to Italy to make his next costume epic, *The Saracen Blade* (1954), based on the novel by Frank Yerby, but he never got any further than Columbia's backlot. Most of the film's budget went to its star, Ricardo Montalban, who had just been dropped by MGM. Sam had to pay him $40,000, which was an outrageous sum for Sam, but he obviously thought Montalban's name would sell tickets.

Rick Jason (well-known to fans of the *Combat* TV series) played the villain of the piece. He thought his career would skyrocket after landing his first role in a Technicolor MGM movie called *Sombrero* as Cyd Charise's

Julie Newmar wants to cut Terrence Kilbourne's throat but Richard Conte intervenes. *Slaves of Babylon.*

lover, but the movie (which starred Montalban) tanked and Jason found himself scrambling for work in television. When his agent Harry Friedman told him they had an appointment with Sam Katzman, Jason was anything but pleased. On the way to the studio he was sullen. "I guess it's secondary at this point, but do you mind if I ask how much this nine-day picture is going to pay?" "*Fourteen!*" the agent peevishly snapped. He told his client he'd be making $750 a week. "I got a thousand a week at MGM," Jason sulked. "I need some film on you, Rick," Friedman sighed. "At this point that's the most important consideration."

Jason and his agent were ushered into Sam's office and Jason was quickly won over. Sam told him how much he'd enjoyed *Sombrero* and how happy he was to have him in the picture. In his autobiography, *Scrapbooks of My Mind,* Jason wrote:

He was about as tall as Harry and about seventy pounds heavier, little mustache, no pretensions, pleasant and often smiling around a big cigar that almost never left his mouth. He could have been in the junk car business, there was really no difference to him; he just happened to be making movies. How could you not like a man like that?

"Even when swords are crossed in anger with the Saracens or the evil Italian nobles, all one gets is a loud clang with no zing," wrote the critic for the *New York Times* in his review of *The Saracen Blade*. Sam wasn't about to get an ulcer over that. He never cared what the critics thought.

After making more than a dozen costume pictures, Sam put the brakes on *Ten Nights in a Harem* and told the press, "No more costume films, the market's

Patricia Medina and Paul Henreid from *Pirates of Tripoli*, one of the last of Katzman's sorry costume melodramas. Most of the action scenes were cribbed from an earlier Katzman epic, *The Golden Hawk*.

flooded with 'em!" (He forgot to mention that he'd done most of the flooding.) Of course once Sam exhausted one genre, he simply moved on to another.

In 1950, a Senate investigation into organized crime was televised and for the first time the public was introduced to a collection of unsavory characters, the likes of which they'd only seen in the movies. Frank Costello. Mickey Cohen. Jake 'Greasy Thumb' Kuzic. Meyer Lansky. Louis 'Little New York' Campagna. These guys were the real deal. People were glued to their sets. How Sam could have let an obvious exploitation gold mine like this slip through his fingers for four whole years boggles the mind, but that's how long it took him to produce *The Miami Story* (1954), written by Robert Kent and directed by Fred Sears. "Puts the big heat on the mob," promised the advertisements. It took Sam another year to produce *New Orleans Uncensored* (1955) but once he got into gear he hopped from city to city, searching

Beverly Garland and Barry Sullivan from *The Miami Story*, one of Sam Katzman's crime dramas.

for sin and corruption. *Chicago Syndicate* (1955) exposed 'the gun-and-girl empire.' It was followed by *Inside Detroit* (1956) which had gangster Pat O'Brien trying to take over the United Auto Workers union. The *New York Times* critic found the film "low on gas." Sam produced two more mob movies that year, *Miami Expose*—"the mob's battle for billions along Florida's pleasure coast"—and *The Houston Story*—"the Hi-jack Mob moves in on the Lone Star state!" Robert Kent wrote most of these crime dramas. William Castle directed two of them.

Castle claimed that the film's star, Lee J. Cobb, suffered a heart attack when they were on location making *The Houston Story*. Three days into production Castle found Cobb on the floor of his hotel room, clutching his chest. The director rushed to the phone, called for a doctor, then placed a frantic call to Sam. "What should I do?" he asked his boss. "You look kind of like Cobb from behind, don't you?" Sam said. "Keep on shooting."

Once they were back in Hollywood, Castle assumed they'd have to wait for Cobb to recover before they could finish the picture. He was surprised when Sam hired Gene Barry to take over the role. Barry didn't look anything like Cobb. Or Castle for that matter. It was the editor's problem to make it work.

Good story, huh? And that's all it is. A good story, probably cooked up by Castle, who besides being known as 'The Earl of Deferral' was even better-known for being a little reckless with the truth. I watched *The Houston Story* recently and you couldn't prove it by me that anyone but a second unit crew ever went to Houston. Like Sam's *Last Train from Bombay* (1952), *Target Hong Kong* (1953), and *Drums of Tahiti* (1954), the cast probably never left California. Cobb did star in *Miami Expose* that year so maybe he was supposed to be in *The Houston Story*, but my guess is if he did have a heart attack it was *before* a single frame of film was shot.

Sam spent the better part of the day in his chartreuse-and-red draped office with a white leather couch. There was a refrigerator, an intercom system, and a midget 24-key piano to give the joint a little class. When he wasn't there he was either in the screening room or on the set. And if he wasn't in either of those places you could probably find him at the track.

Two scenes from *The Houston Story*. Above: Barbara Hale, Paul Richards and Gene Barry. Below: Edward Arnold, Gene Barry and John Zaremba.

"[He] didn't spend a lot of time on the sets, he'd spend it in his office on the lot, prepping his *next* pictures," Richard Kline said. "If we got a little bit ahead and finished a movie early, we'd start the next one that same day. He didn't waste a moment. He could zig and zag like nobody's business."

At the urging of Sam's publicist, *Life* magazine sent a writer to spend the day with Sam. Sam drove up in his cream-colored Jaguar and ushered the writer into his office. Sam sat behind his desk and the first thing he did was order a big sign that said: "Movies are better than ever." From that point on he was on the phone or the intercom, ordering this and ordering that, approving construction of some Spanish galleons for one of his costume pictures (he called them 'bosom and sandal' pictures), making casting decisions, examining props, and when he was done with all of that the reporter followed him to one of the screening rooms to watch the rushes from three different movies.

The title of the article was "Meet Jungle Sam." Why 'Jungle Sam'? That was the nickname he'd picked up after he'd made a series of Jungle Jim movies with Olympic swimming champ Johnny Weissmuller.

Weissmuller had won five Olympic gold medals, fifty-two US National Championships and set sixty-seven world records. His fame led to his being cast as Tarzan, a character he played from 1932 to 1948 at MGM and RKO for a total of twelve feature films. And when he became a little too old and a little too beefy to carry on as Tarzan, Sam was right there with a deal that Weissmuller couldn't resist. Each year he'd make two movies back to back. He'd make $50,000 on each one. He also had a say in the productions, a percentage of the take, plus residuals. There was only one hitch. If the first two pictures flopped, the deal was off. The fact that Weissmuller could wear clothes and speak like everyone else for a change was almost reason enough to take the deal. He went on a crash diet and lost 39 pounds. He had no illusions. The films were crap but they paid the bills and he didn't have to work hard. It was like having a part-time job that paid more than most full-time jobs.

"Maybe it's too much dialogue that causes our old friend to sag," wrote Bosley Crowther in his review of *Jungle Jim* (1948). "He has to speak words

Jungle Jim ad art.

of two syllables and some sentences as much as ten words long. And maybe he needs more inspiration than he gets from Lita Baron and Virginia Grey. In any event, it's a tired gent that we see in this life-sized comic strip."

But as *Time Magazine* pointed out in their March 28 issue that year:

Hollywood may shout about a movie and New York critics rave about it—but Main Street can still give it a cold shoulder. Theatre owners generally listen to Main Street, where most of their paying customers live. Before booking a movie, many a cautious exhibitor scans the pages of BOXOFFICE... for the thumbnail reviews by exhibitors who have already shown the picture.

Exhibitors weren't the only ones who were interested in those 'thumbnail reviews.' After advising his fellow exhibitors to play *Jungle Jim* in the September 24 edition of *Boxoffice*, Harlan Rankin, the owner of four theatres in Ontario, was surprised to get a letter from Sam. "Needless to say," Sam wrote, "we appreciate your enthusiasm, and such comment as yours is indeed a source of pleasure to us."

"Johnny Weissmuller will never learn to act," wrote Texas exhibitor L. D. Montgomery, "but the customers like him so naturally I do too." Montgomery thought *The Lost Tribe* (1949), the second entry in the series, was much better than the first, if for no other reason than it did better business. Likewise *Captive Girl* (1950) drew a favorable response from Colorado exhibi-

Johnny Weissmuller, Peggy the chimp and champion swimmer Anita Lhoest as the *Captive Girl.*

tor Bob Walker: "This series is better than Tarzan ever was and this one got out a crowd... If you aren't using these you're missing a bet." West Virginia exhibitor Ralph Raspa thought the Jungle Jim movies were easily the best family-action series on the market. And while J. D. Shepherd, an exhibitor in Arkansas, thought the series was "mill-run junk," he had to admit they filled his theatre. "Money in the bank" was the way Oregon exhibitor Elaine George put it.

Peggy taking a much needed break between scenes.

"On one of the Jungle Jims that we did we were on the back lot at Columbia with Peggy the chimpanzee, who was really wonderful, and certainly much brighter than Sam," said Michael Fox. "Peggy sat next to Sam and Johnny Weissmuller said, 'Look! They're carrying on a conversation!'"[8]

Sam was poised to make *Cannibal Attack* (1954), which would have been the 14th entry in the series, when he was informed that Harry Cohn, believing the series had played itself out, sold the character to Columbia's television subsidiary Screen Gems. A similar thing had happened to Sam when he was making a serial called *The Phantom*, only in that instance he was already several days into production before the legal department told him the studio didn't own the rights to the character anymore. John Hart, who played the Phantom, recalled:

> ...they cut a bunch of junk from other serials [Sam] owned and they called me back and they put me in a different suit, a god-awful-lookin' thing with a leather aviator's helmet! And I did my whole part over again in seven days. They changed the script around and I just talked and talked all day long. And it was released as *Adventures of Captain Africa* [1955] when it was intended to be The Phantom. I actually saw some of it—it's just terrible... and it didn't hardly make any sense.[9]

The Jungle Jim problem was a much easier fix for Sam. He simply changed the name of the character to Jungle Johnny. Weissmuller could wear the same outfit and he'd be in the same jungle. Who the devil cared whether he was Jungle Jim or Jungle Johnny? It was still the same old stuff.

Will it get by with a serial audience?

But Cohn was right. The series had played itself out. The returns were dwindling and the exhibitors were starting to complain that even the kids were getting restless. Reporting on the final entry in the series, *Devil Goddess* (1955), exhibitor Michael Chiaventone wrote: "Take the monkey out of the picture and you don't have anything in it."

No more Jungle Jim!

Jungle Jim is dead.

Jungle Johnny too!

About the time Sam was making *Killer Ape* (1953), one of the producers in his unit wanted to make a movie about a giant octopus. Charles H. Schneer had been in charge of editing, casting and finding stories for Sam. Now he wanted to produce his own picture and Harry Cohn was willing to let him so long as Sam kept an eye on things. Sam was more than happy to oblige. Warner Bros. had just made a ton on dough with a picture called *The Beast From 20,000 Fathoms* (1953) in which a prehistoric animal stomped its way through the streets of New York. Schneer wanted to do the same thing to San Francisco with an octopus. It sounded like a good bet to Sam.

The stop-motion special effects had been the trump card that sold *The Beast* and Schneer knew it. He had a meeting with the man responsible for those effects, Ray Harryhausen, and the two men entered into a partnership that lasted 19 years.

The December 1, 1953 edition of *Variety* reported: "Sam Katzman plans to film his upcoming science-fiction yarn, *Monster of the Deep*, in 3-D, dependent on outcome of underwater tests which will be conducted during the next 30 to 60 days. More than half of the picture is to be lensed underwater, and if Columbia producer decides to make use of the depth medium it will make the first use of 3-D for below-the-surface photography."

Two weeks later *Variety* confirmed Sam's intentions to shoot the film in 3D *and* Technicolor! But it was nothing more than hype. Ray Harryhausen confirmed that "no experiments were made with 3D. We didn't have the budget for that type of thing. It would have taken three times as long with the animation."[10]

When Harryhausen showed Sam his designs for the octopus, Sam told him it wasn't realistic and drew what *he* thought the thing should look like. His sketch resembled a character out of a Popeye cartoon. Sam had probably never seen a real octopus. His skewed concept of reality would later play an important role in the design of the laugh-provoking bird-monster in one of Sam's most notorious films, *The Giant Claw*. (More about that later.)

Poster art for *It Came from Beneath the Sea.*

Variety reported that Sam signed Steve Fisher (known for his gritty crime dramas) to script Schneer's film. Except Schneer was the one who hired the writers, not Sam, and Fisher wasn't one of them. He would have been a good choice, much better than George Worthing Yates, the son of Herbert J. Yates, the founder of Consolidated Film Industries and Republic Pictures. According to historian Bill Warren, G. W. Yates wrote a very good script for *Them!* (1954), another Warner Bros. movie that made a lot of dough. Although his script wasn't used he does receive story credit, a credit that netted him a number of sci-fi assignments. Unfortunately, for whatever reason, none of his sci-fi scripts are very good and *It Came From Beneath the Sea* (1955, the new title for Schneer's film) was no exception. Hal Smith rewrote it.

There is some confusion about which Hal Smith we're talking about. There was an actor named Hal Smith who played the town drunk on *The Andy Griffith Show*. He was a writer. But Harold Jacob Smith, an Academy Award winning writer, used Hal Smith as a pseudonym after he found himself on the Hollywood blacklist. Schneer and Katzman often hired blacklisted writers because they worked cheap. It was probably him.

According to Schneer the script was submitted for approval to the fellow in charge of public works in San Francisco. By a remarkable coincidence he was the same guy who'd built the Golden Gate Bridge, targeted for destruction by the giant octopus. "Nobody is gonna destroy my bridge," Mister Public Works told Schneer. Schneer claimed they had to use a bakery truck with a little window in the back to surreptitiously shoot the footage of the bridge that Harryhausen needed for his back projection. For three days the truck went back and forth across the bridge, racking up $300 in toll charges.

Hooey!

What really happened was a guy posing as a reporter shot the locked off background plates that Harryhausen needed.

For the male lead in his picture, Schneer chose Ken Tobey, the star of *The Thing from Another World* and a supporting player in *The Beast From 20,000 Fathoms*. "I thought *It Came from Beneath the Sea* [1955] was a better picture," he told me. He probably thought so because he had more screen time.

Kenneth Tobey, Faith Domergue and Donald Curtis
watch the giant octopus destroy the Golden Gate Bridge.

His co-star was one-time Howard Hughes starlet Faith Domergue. She was having marital problems at the time and was looking for any excuse to get out of the house. She begged her agent to find her a job fast. He asked her if she'd mind working on a Katzman picture at three or four times what everybody else would be getting. She jumped at it.

Sam's nephew, Leonard, was the assistant director on the film. Taking a cue from his uncle, he paid the dock workers and other locals $10 to be in the picture, a figure way below the Screen Actors Guild minimum.

"On the last day of the movie Sam showed up," Tobey recalled. "He asked the director how many pages he had left to shoot. 'Just these three pages,' the director said and handed him the script. Katzman ripped them out. 'How many now?' he asked. That was a helluva way to end a picture."

The film opened in Los Angeles on June 22. It wasn't in 3-D and it wasn't in color but it made quite an impression on some other studio executives by becoming one of the top money-makers that year.

"The whole thing is done in a spirit of diverting extravagance, and if you don't mind stretching your credulity a bit you should heartily enjoy it," wrote the critic for the *Los Angeles Examiner*. *Variety* agreed. "Most of the time the script, Robert Gordon's direction and the trouping keeps the thrills playing convincingly and horror fans should find it to their liking." The critic for the *Los Angeles Times*, however, found it boring, "with a lot of footage given to technical matters and many scientific conferences." *Hollywood Citizen News* felt the same way. Too much talk and "and hobble-gobble" for their taste. Perhaps *The Motion Picture Herald* summed it up best. "Although not unusually original it's continuously exciting and the special effects are quite fascinating."

Again under Sam's watchful eye, Schneer produced *Earth vs. the Flying Saucers* (1956), supposedly suggested by the book *Flying Saucers from Outer*

It Came from Beneath the Sea surprised everyone by being one of the top money-makers of 1955.

Richard Denning solves the mystery of the *Creature with the Atom Brain*, a science-fiction horror thriller packaged with *It Came from Beneath the Sea*.

Space by Donald E. Keyhoe, a former rocket scientist and a respected authority on UFOs. Sam hired Curt Siodmak to develop the story but Siodmak and Schneer rubbed each other wrong so Schneer got rid of him and gave the assignment to George Yates. Once again Schneer was dissatisfied with Yates' work and let Bernard Gordon rewrite his script. Schneer chose Gordon because he had a reputation for working fast and since he was on the blacklist he also worked cheap. Schneer was one of the many producers who ignored the blacklist.

"You can either give Charlie credit for being courageous enough to do it, or you can say he was smart enough to get a writer cheap," Bernard Gordon told Ted Newsome. "Both were true."

Gordon felt he should have been given solo credit since he threw out everything that Yates had written, but writers who hid behind aliases and needed to keep a low profile generally didn't squawk. He was paid $1,500 for his work.

Hugh Marlowe and Joan Taylor. *Earth vs. the Flying Saucers.*

Hugh Marlowe and Joan Taylor were in the lead roles. Taylor recalled that Marlowe was very involved with the union.

"We got along wonderfully," she said, "but once in a while he would get stern with me when I'd go another five or so minutes on a scene. Hugh would step in and say 'Oh no you won't!' This led up to me learning about what you do and don't do regarding unions. He had a theatrical background and was such a professional, and we both took our jobs quite seriously. This was a great experience for me in learning my trade, because there was little time to do these pictures and only professional people were able to get the job done on time and in order, especially in only 12 days."[11]

Earth vs. the Flying Saucers really delivered the goods. Before the credits had a chance to roll the audience was treated to a couple of shots of the saucers in action. And when Harryhausen turned his saucers loose on Washington in the film's exciting finale, the audience really got its money's worth. And yet the critic for the *Los Angeles Times* thought the whole thing was a bust. He thought the flying saucers looked like "art department concoctions," whatever that means, and that the devastation they caused looked "rather like a tempest in a thimble." Well, even an idiot is entitled to his opinion. *Variety* thought the effects were excellent and thought the film achieved "a neat measure of suspense and thrills." The critic for the *New York Times* said, "This is surely high-frequency science-fiction stuff—this sabotaging of scientist Hugh Marlowe's artificial satellites, this creation of meteorological convulsions, this destruction of the Capitol and invasion of the earth." Did he like it or dislike it? Your guess is as good as mine.

Frankly, this was a film that Sam should have made back in 1952 when the flying saucer scare was up and running. But once again he was asleep at the wheel. Shame on him for letting an underling get the best of him, although he was happy to treat Schneer's film as if it were his own.

Sam supplied the co-feature to Schneer's film, and a pretty good one at that. *The Werewolf* (1956) is one of Sam's best films. Fred Sears seemed to be trying a little harder on this one and location photography in the California Big Bear mountains helped take the low-budget sting out of the thing. The script has some decent dialogue and characterizations and the performances were generally on-target, especially Steven Ritch in the title role. Canadian exhibitor W. L. Parrent said his customers "loved it."

In the early 1950s juvenile delinquency was on the rise in America. Figures on the number of court cases involving juveniles had almost doubled

---

Above: Joan Taylor and the aliens. Below: Joan Taylor, Grandon Rhodes and Tom Brown Henry think Hugh Marlowe looks ridiculous. *Earth vs. the Flying Saucers.*

in the years between 1948 and 1954. The causes behind the statistics were vigorously debated but one thing was clear: the problem was growing at an alarming rate. By 1953 teenagers were responsible for 54 percent of car thefts, 49 percent of burglaries, 18 percent of robberies, and 16 percent of rapes. MGM's *Blackboard Jungle* and Warner's *Rebel Without a Cause* took the lead in exploiting the subject of juvenile delinquency, but Sam wasn't far behind. His *Teenage Crime Wave* (1955) was in theatres three weeks after *Rebel* premiered.

Written by Ray Buffum and Harry Essex, *Teenage Crime Wave* told the tale of two young losers on the lam—Tommy Cook and his hard-as-nails girlfriend Molly McCart. They take refuge in the house of an elderly, religious couple. Cook vents a lot of his pent-up anger on the old gummers while they try to bring the gun-toting youth to his senses. The woman asks Molly if she's ever read *The Bible*. Molly shakes her head. "Na, I read comic books. I need laughs." The cops close in and Molly is killed in a shootout. Tommy is taken away in cuffs, bawling like a baby.

Teenage Crime Wave half sheet.

The exhibitors were beginning to notice the change in the demograph-ics of their audience. It was a real eye opener to learn that the teenagers were spending nine billion dollars a year on clothes, hamburgers and movies. Six billion came from their allowances and three billion came from part-time jobs. They had their own magazines, their own hair styles, clothes, and mu-sic. Sam thought it was time they had their own movies. The next film on his roster would turn out to be his greatest success, a film that was tailor-made for the teenagers—the first rock 'n' roll musical.

Bill Haley had the number one record in the nation, 'Rock Around the Clock,' when Sam signed him for his fictionalized biography of the singer's rise to fame with the Comets.

"We started out as a country-western group then added a touch of rhythm and blues," said Haley. "It wasn't something we planned, it just evolved. We got to where we weren't accepted as country-western or rhythm and blues. It was hard to get bookings for a while. We were something dif-ferent, something new. We didn't call it that at the time, but we were playing rock 'n' roll."

The song 'Rock Around the Clock' was originally recorded by Sonny Dae (real name Pascal Vennitti) and His Knights and may well have been the only

Bill Haley and the Comets

record he ever cut. He didn't have much luck with it and neither did Haley until the song was used (at the suggestion of Glenn Ford's son) during the main titles of MGM's *Blackboard Jungle*. That's when it caught fire. By July it was the best-selling record in the nation, the national anthem for the teenagers.

In *Rock Around the Clock*, Haley is discovered by a down on his luck promoter named Steve Hollis. Hollis takes Haley and his band to New York where, with a little help from real-life disc jockey Alan Freed, Haley becomes a star.

The plot was never too far away from a song and Haley sings nine of them. As a bonus The Platters, the most popular singing group in the nation at the time, sang two of their biggest hits—'Only You' and 'The Great Pretender.'

As *Rock Around the Clock* went into production, Sam's good luck charm filed for divorce. Hortie charged Sam with extreme cruelty, a vague but popular accusation at the time. She wanted $3,160 a month in alimony and support for their 18-year-old son, Jerry. Sam was earning roughly $9,000 a month at the time. Once the judge factored in his stock in five film companies, a uranium company, insurance policies, and the couple's $200,000 Beverly Hills home he figured Sam was worth something in excess of a million bucks.

The events that led to this unfortunate episode would no doubt make for interesting reading, and if I knew what they were I'd be happy to share them with you. All I can tell you is Hortie changed her mind and the couple lived under the same roof for the rest of their lives, in separate beds, in separate rooms.

Rock Around the Clock raked in the money, topping all Columbia grosses in Holland, Norway, Ireland, Indonesia, India, Australia and the Philippines. One exhibitor played the picture so many times he thought Columbia should let him keep the print to save the shipping costs. Within the first few weeks of its release the movie had recouped most of its modest budget and within six months it had taken in over $4 million dollars, making it one of Columbia's biggest hits.

As impossible as it may seem now there were a lot of people in the 1950s

The Platters were the most popular vocal group of the 1950s. Here they sing one of their biggest hits, 'Only You,' in Sam Katzman's *Rock Around the Clock*.

who believed that rock 'n' roll music *caused* juvenile delinquency. Dimitri Tiomkin was one of them. The Academy Award winning composer thought the music was a sure sign that the country was reverting to savagery. And he pointed to the number of rock 'n' roll concerts that had erupted in violence as proof. Frank Sinatra was another one who hated rock music. He called it "the most brutal, ugly, vicious form of expression" he'd ever heard and shared Tiomkin's belief that the music provoked violence. Apparently Ol' Blue Eyes had forgotten about the afternoon when he was playing the Paramount Theatre in New York and 10,000 of his fans tore the box office apart. Traffic was blocked, bystanders were trampled and store windows were broken. It took 700 riot police and 200 patrolmen to restore order.

One of the biggest problems that white people had with rock music, besides the fact that it didn't sound like the music they'd grown up with, was that it was black music, or race music as it was called at the time. There was a conspiracy to keep black singers off the radio. Their songs were routinely re-recorded by white singers. These sanitized and bland 'cover versions' weren't what the kids wanted to hear. Listen to Pat Boone's cover versions of Fats Domino's 'Ain't That a Shame' and Little Richard's 'Tutti Frutti' and you'll know why.

The government, acting on behalf of the American Society of Composers, Authors and Publishers (ASCAP), went about the business of killing rock and roll music in a battle that came to be known as the 'payola scandal'.[12]

Apparently having too much time on his hands, Senator Owen Harris formed a subcommittee to go after disc jockeys who accepted bribes to play rock records. Disc jockeys (like politicians) routinely accepted bribes to play all kinds of music. Harris and his committee drew their bead on Alan Freed, the disc jockey who led the pack when it came to promoting rock music. For his refusal to sign an affidavit denying that he'd accepted bribes, Freed was fired and thrown into the slammer, charged with income tax evasion. He died of alcoholism at the age of 43 and served as a warning to D.J.s across the nation that playing rock 'n' roll could be hazardous to their health.

The new clean cut pop singers that emerged in the aftermath of the Payola Scandal had a lot more in common with Dean Martin and Perry Como than they did with Elvis Presley or Jerry Lee Lewis. In 1959 the top-selling song in the nation was Bobby Darin's 'Mack the Knife,' a song that could easily have been recorded by Frank Sinatra.

Sam's response to Sinatra and Tiomkin and all of the other narrow-minded nitwits was *Don't Knock the Rock* (1956), which opened at New York's Paramount Theatre. The teenagers started lining up at 6:30 in the morning and filled the block from Seventh to Eighth Avenue for three days straight. 135 cops were on hand to keep the peace. The manager of the theatre wouldn't allow anyone to sit in the first four rows of the balcony, fearing that all of the foot-stomping might cause the balcony to collapse. I only wish I could have been there to enjoy Bosley Crowther's discomfort as the movie-hating critic for the *New York Times* sat amongst the enthusiastic crowd, probably wishing he were dead. "What is rock 'n' roll?" he wrote in his review. "Well, to one comparatively middle-aged man who made the awful mistake of grabbing a seat down front, it goes thump, thump, thump, thump." Crowther not only hated the music, he hated the movie and the audience. "The picture ended with the view of a slogan, 'Dig It Soon.' Your own grave, no doubt, and fair enough."

Had Crowther seen the movie at any theatre other than the Paramount, he would have had the opportunity to pan another one of Sam's films, *Rumble on the Docks* (1956), which was packaged with *Don't Knock the Rock*. But it was not part of the program at the Paramount that afternoon. Instead, the audience was treated to one of Alan Freed's live stage shows. And what a show! The Platters. Ruth Brown. Jimmy Bowen. Frankie Lymon and the Teenagers. The Cadillacs. "I didn't know you old folks went in for this stuff," one pig-tailed girl in dungarees said to Crowther as she attempted to pry him out of his seat to dance with her in the aisle. Do I need to add that he declined her offer?

Don't Knock the Rock made money, but nowhere near what its predecessor had made. Now if you're Sam Katzman, there's only one possible explanation.

Rock 'n' roll is dead!

No more rock 'n' roll!

Any time a picture didn't perform as well as Sam thought it should, or had expected it would, then that was it, brother, he'd never make another one.

"No more mobsters!" he said after one of his crime films came in short.

"No more stabbings!"

"No more shootings!"

"I've got kids," Sam told Dick Williams at the *Los Angeles Mirror* in 1957. "One goes to college. I'm trying to bring him up right and I don't think these pictures of messed up youngsters are doing our youth any good."

If Sam had been as savvy as people credit him (as savvy as *he* thought he was), he might have done a little homework before he gave up on rock 'n' roll. He would have discovered that the reason *Don't Knock the Rock* didn't do as well as *Rock Around the Clock* wasn't because the music was dead. Bill

Haley was dead. In the few short months between the two films, Haley had been eclipsed by younger, sexier and more energetic singing idols. The teenagers didn't want to see a pudgy, thirty-eight year old guy with a little spit curl playing country swing when they could get real rock music from guys like Elvis Presley, Chuck Berry and Little Richard. How Sam could have thought that rock 'n' roll was dead, with the big beat throbbing from every radio and jukebox in the nation, boggles the mind.

True to his word, however foolishly given, Sam's next musical was *Cha-Cha-Cha Boom* (1956), "the sensational story of the hottest dance craze that ever set the world ablaze." Even though rock 'n' roll music was absent from this tepid entry, I'm sure it was on every teenager's must see list. What bobbysoxer could resist the fever-pitch frenzy of Perez Prado and Helen Grayco? Apparently quite a few.

No more cha-cha-cha!

The cha-cha-cha is dead!

In 1957 Harry Belafonte's hit record "Day-O" turned Calypso into a

Calypso Heat Wave.

popular music fad and Sam was Johnny-on-the-spot with *Calypso Heat Wave* (1957). But this time even Sam wasn't fast enough to capitalize on the new fad. It was dead before the ink was dry on his one sheet.

No more calypso!

At this point I would like to add that although it takes someone with the patience of a saint to sit through these miserable musicals, they are often the only visual record we have of some of these legendary performers in their prime. For that reason alone they are worth preserving.

With no new music trend in sight, Sam returned to a genre he could always count on—horror! He had Bernard Gordon whip up a pair of scripts for a double feature package—*The Zombies of Mora Tau* and *The Man Who Turned to Stone* (1957). The TV spots warned the parents of children under 12 that these two features might prove to be too horrifying for the little ones.

"There's just about as much horror in them as in a tranquilizing pill," wrote the critic for the *Herald Examiner* and he was right on the money. However, having read the script for the zombie picture I can assure you that even

The walking dead guard a box full of diamonds in *Zombies of Mora Tau* (1957)

though it didn't always make sense, it was creepy, scary and exciting. But an unambitious director like Edward L. Cahn can drain the life out of anything.

In Gordon's scenario treasure hunters come to Africa in search of the diamonds believed to have been on The Susan B when it went down in a typhoon in 1894. The diamonds are there all right but they're guarded by the crew of the Susan B, who have become a bunch of zombies.

"There was a scene where the zombies get out of their coffins and they looked ridiculously awkward trying to climb out," Bernard Gordon told writer Ted Newsome. "I said to the director, 'Why didn't you change it? Why not shoot it over, put the coffins upright so they can get out from a standing position instead of looking like goofs?' This exasperated director, Eddie Cahn, said, 'Look, I got six days to make a 90 minute movie. You think I got time for retakes?'"

It was a 70 minute movie and he *did* have time for retakes. He simply didn't give a damn. The film is so static it looks like it was directed by a zombie.

The Man Who Turned to Stone was even worse. "Rock like dullness," was the way one exhausted critic described this throwback to the sort of movies Sam had made with Bela Lugosi in the 1940s. Victor Jory (in the role that Lugosi should have played) is the head of a detention home for unruly young ladies. Jory and his staff are over 200 years old and they use their prisoners to keep themselves alive by draining the life out of them while simultaneously draining the life out of the audience. Friedrich Ledebur was in the role that would have probably gone to John Carradine. For the scenes of Ledebur turning to stone, Sam achieved the old trick with colored filters. By slowly changing the colors, invisible on black and white film, it looks as if Ledebur is developing sunken eyes and gaunt cheeks before our very eyes.

"When I was watching the movie and he began to change, I fell on the floor laughing," leading lady Charlotte Austin told Tom Weaver. "I cannot believe how awful that was. And another thing that struck me about that movie was the lighting. When it was nighttime, we were *squinting*, we couldn't see, because they had bright reflectors in our eyes. And when it was daytime, it was pitch black! Everything was opposite! I'll never forget the scene where poor William Hudson was sitting outside at 'night,' using a flashlight to try to read a book, and yet you could that it was bright sunlight!"

Ann Doran, Victor Jory and George Lynn try to keep Fredrick Ledebur
from becoming *The Man Who Turned to Stone*. The critic for
The Motion Picture Herald said the movie was "somewhat
long for the little it has to say," which was being generous.

The profits from this package must have been weak because Sam never
made another horror picture.

No more horror!

Horror is dead!

Not so. In fact horror was hotter than it had been for a decade, revived
by the release of Hammer's *The Curse of Frankenstein* (1957) a few months
after Sam's films had passed through town like shit through a goose. Hammer's Frankenstein film was in color and handsomely mounted. The acting was first-rate. The dialog was literate. It was everything that Sam's two
movies weren't. But the issue of quality never raised its ugly head with Sam.
To him one movie was pretty much like another. If something didn't fly it
was because the audience wasn't interested in the subject, *never* because the
movie was a flimsy piece of junk. It was a convenient, self-serving point of
view that Sam chose to exercise throughout his career.

Fred Sears directed and narrated Sam's next package—*The Night the World Exploded* and *The Giant Claw* (both 1957). Horror may have been dead in Sam's mind but so far as he knew science-fiction was still alive and well.

"Those who lived to tell the tale remember that the day began with fragile, breathtaking beauty. The temperature was cool. Air Mountain pure. A day unreal enough to serve as the setting for the birth of the world or the death of it."

This was Fred Sears' opening narration for *The Night the World Exploded*, "the most explosive science fiction movie ever made!" What followed certainly seemed like death. There were no special effects to speak of in this listless effort, save the one or two shots that were lifted from some old Republic serials. Scratchy newsreel footage of floods, fires and earthquakes is edited together in a collection of montages, between which we find William Leslie trying to neutralize the explosive new element that threatens to tear the world apart. Leslie has invented a machine that can predict earthquakes. Much is made of this new device, yet for all the good it does it might just as well have been an electric can opener. It saves no one from being caught in an earthquake and plays no part in solving the crisis. The only thing it does is get in the way of the narrative.

The companion feature, however, was a horse of a different color. *The Giant Claw* was loaded with special effects, all of them terrible. The monster looked like some goofy Howdy Doody puppet, as alive as a pile of poop. Adding to the hilarity are the actors who are dead earnest about it all. The harder they try to pump life into this thing the bigger the laughs. Like *The Magic Carpet*, the film is perfect in its own way.

Again the package failed to perform to Sam's satisfaction, which could only mean one thing…

Science-fiction is dead!

No more science-fiction!

And, sadly, no more Fred Sears.

On November 30, 1957, back from a location shoot in Hawaii, Fred Sears was working late at the studio, researching another 'topical' project for

William Leslie, Kathryn Grant and Fred Sears take a break
from *The Night the World Exploded.*

Here it is, in all its glory, *The Giant Claw.*

Sam, when his heart gave out. Albert Wingerter, the chief of studio security, found him dead on the floor of the bathroom the next morning. He'd been worked to death.

Sears had attempted suicide at one point in his life, after a bitter argument with his wife Judith. As the years rolled by his marriage became more strained and Sears took refuge in his work. When Judith finally left him, taking their two children with her, Sears moved in with his sister, who lived in a small house near the Columbia lot. He practically lived at the studio.

Sam took out a full page in *Variety* and wrote: "Those of us at Clover Productions are saddened over the passing of our good friend, fellow workman and artist, Fred F. Sears.

"A painstaking director, Fred demanded and got the most from his actors, actresses and co-workers—and they loved him—not alone for his ability as a craftsman, but for his inherent goodness, humbleness and humanitarianism.

"We here at Clover Productions are still stunned from the blow. It came at a time when Fred's greatness in his field was soon to be heralded by one and all.

"We all miss you, Fred Sears, but at least God granted us the privilege of knowing you and working with and for you."

With Sears gone, Sam's output dramatically fell. Where he'd once averaged thirteen or fourteen pictures a year he was down to four in 1958, three the following year, and two after that. It must have hit him pretty hard.

The lightning and thunder didn't disturb Sam's or Hortie's sleep. They were out cold, he in his bedroom and she in hers. They didn't hear the burglars cut the screen on the back door of their Beverly Hills home. The thieves crept into Hortie's room and pressed a gun against her ribs. When she opened her eyes and saw two phantom shapes behind the blinding glare of a flashlight her heart skipped a beat. "Turn over, lady," one of them said in a hushed and raspy voice. "Face down."

They tied her hands and feet with a rope, then crept into Sam's room and did the same to him.

"The thunder was crashing and the lightning flashed in the darkness outside the house," Sam told reporters, "while inside my wife and I were tied up in our beds and threatened by the robbers. They used flashlights to prowl around the house. It was just like you would make a horror movie with the storm raging outside and the men talking in whispers."

"Where's the safe?" one of them asked.

"I don't have one," Sam told them.

They didn't believe him. They pounded on every wall in the house before they were convinced. Once that was settled they began a systematic search of the house, looking for anything of value. More than an hour passed before Sam was able to work his hands free. He assumed, as he untied his feet, that the thieves had gone because he hadn't heard them puttering around for a while. He was about to set Hortie free when he felt the barrel of a gun in his back. He was marched back to his room and tied up again, a little tighter this time, but he got loose again anyway, just about the time he heard the bandits drive off. He untied Hortie and called the police. There wasn't much the police could do. Sam and Hortie couldn't identify the thieves. They'd never seen their faces. They sounded young. Young or old, they made off with quite a haul—$780 in cash, a $25,000 mink stole and thousands of dollars in jewelry, all stuffed into three stolen pillow cases.[13]

No more robberies!

Four months later Sam was sitting in his chair on one of Columbia's stages, pounding his cane on the studio floor, yelling: "Time's a-wastin', folks! Time's a-wastin'." He was saying it for the sake of saying it. No one was listening. Everyone was too busy doing their jobs.

Right on schedule director Oscar Rudolph had the cameras rolling on Dee Dee Sharp singing 'Mashed Potato Time,' for Sam's new musical *Don't Knock the Twist* (1962). When Sam said he wouldn't be making another rock movie he didn't know a guy named Chubby Checker was going to start a new dance craze with a rock 'n' roll record called 'The Twist.' Sam never could resist a new dance craze, rock 'n' roll or not.

Chubby Checker from *Don't Knock the Twist* (1962).

'The Twist' was originally recorded by Hank Ballard. American Bandstand host Dick Clark thought the song had potential but he was afraid that Ballard was too old for his audience. Chubby Checker's cover version sounded so much like Ballard's that when Ballard heard it on the radio, he thought it *was* his.

Suddenly everybody, youngsters and oldsters alike, were twisting. Three years later the song was reissued and it was a hit all over again. It was all too much for Sam to ignore. He flew to New York and signed Chubby to star in *Twist Around the Clock* (1961), a remake of *Rock Around the Clock*. And like *Rock Around the Clock*, it made a lot of money.

Sam wasn't with Columbia anymore. He'd given them his resignation in 1960. He had a new deal with the studio now, a fifty/fifty split. *Twist Around the Clock* grossed $6 million in six months. Sam hoped *Don't Knock the Twist* would do even better. He had two weeks to rehearse the dancers, write new songs, record the songs, build the sets, and get the wardrobe together. On the first picture he'd had two days.

Rowland Barber wrote a piece about Sam for *Show* magazine, in which he described what it was like to spend seven days watching this movie come together.

"We're shooting the big ones the first three days—dance numbers, scenes with lots of people," Sam told Barber. "Then we kill the musicians and most of the dancers and extras. Fourth day we shoot the exteriors at the ranch, then we're down to shooting the story, the dramatic stuff. After the fifth day we kill Chubby Checker, and the last two days we only need three principals, three character people, three bit players, and six extras, tops. We shoot the finale on the third day and the opening scene on the last day, and nobody gets paid for just sitting."

Hortie's in the movie. She's sitting at one of the tables when The Dovells sing 'The Bristol Stomp.' She surprised everyone when she decided to join the dancers on the floor instead of just sitting there like she was supposed to do.

"That's my girl!" Sam said.

Sam Katzman and his wife Hortie.

Bob Kent wrote one of the songs for the picture, 'The Salome Twist.' It was sung by the Carroll Brothers while Georgine Darcy performed the provocative Dance of the Seven Veils. The first take was ruined when the sixth veil wouldn't come loose. Sam was okay with that but when Georgine missed her swipe at the fourth veil on the second take he started tapping the floor with his cane. "Kill the bit people Oscar!" he ordered. "Only keep the ones we have to carry! Let's go!"

Rudolph called for action. This time Georgina ripped her costume. Rudolph buried his face in his hands. It took three ladies from wardrobe seven minutes to get her back in front of the camera. Three minutes later the sequence was in the can. Two months later the movie was in theatres. It was Sam's last film for Columbia. His next stop was Metro-Goldwyn-Mayer.

Once the crown jewel of the Hollywood studios, MGM had fallen on hard times after a five year run of epic flops. A couple of new guys had taken over the studio and put an end to the practice of relying on blockbusters to keep the place afloat. They needed to make smaller budgeted movies. They needed movies they could rely on to turn a profit. They needed Sam Katzman.

MGM's reputation for making the biggest and the best musicals of all time probably wasn't enhanced by *Hootenanny Hoot* (1963) or *Get Yourself a College Girl* (1964), but the pictures made money. The studio was so happy with Sam they signed him to a three-year, ten picture contract.

"No picture being made today should cost over $2 million," Sam told Phillip Scheuer from the *Los Angeles Times*. "Anything over that is wasted. And I'm including *Mutiny on the Bounty* [1962] and *Cleopatra* [1963]. If you can convince an artist that the budget will stay at $2 million—90% of 'em will take a percentage. It's when they know the figure's going to climb into many more millions that they feel they are entitled to their share."

Sam told Bill Ornstein from the *Hollywood Reporter* that none of the writers he would be working with on these new projects would be over 25. "We're going strong on youth, but they will have older writers, more experienced men, working with them. All films will be aimed at the kids of today, the newer generation. The films will be made by youth for youth."

A quick glance at the films Sam made during this period says otherwise. Robert Kent was 56 when he wrote *Hot Rods to Hell* (1967) and the director, John Brahm, was 74. Orville Hampton was 50 when he scripted *Riot on the Sunset Strip* (1967) and Hal Collins was 57 when he wrote *The Love-Ins* (1967) and both of those films were directed by 59-year old Arthur Dreifuss. Sam probably didn't trust anyone under 50.

Most of these movies had the over lit, half-baked quality of any given television show at the time. Sam started to think that perhaps that was the market he should be in. *Hot Rods to Hell* was produced for ABC's Sunday Night Movie but the studio executives thought it was good enough for a theatrical release. Sam set up a TV unit to produce two half hour shows: *Honey*, created by Larry Brody for Sammy Jackson, and *Robin Hood, American Style*, created by Charles Marion. Supposedly all three networks were interested in these two hot properties but apparently not enough. They bit the dust along with every other project Sam told Ornstein he was going to make, except for the pretentious and silly *Angel, Angel, Down We Go* (1969) which Sam ended up making for American-International. And the only reason he made that picture was to establish his son Jerry as a producer. Jerry told *Variety* his next picture was going to be a hard-hitting drama called *Jeremy Rabbit, the Secret Avenger*. "Here again I want to say something about society. It deals with a court reporter who concentrates on tax evasion to get the Mafia." He made two more pictures before retiring from the business but *Jeremy Rabbit* wasn't one of them. Instead he hooked up with Bert I. Gordon to make *How to Succeed with Sex* (1970) which has to be one of the worst pictures in anybody's arsenal.

"One must congratulate Messrs. Katzman and Gordon for allowing not one iota of either intelligence or wit to interfere with their plodding exposition," wrote critic Judith Crist, "They sledge-hammer home their feeble attempts at humor and doggedly telegraph every punch line long before it arrives to fizzle."

The Loners (1972) was Sam's swansong. He died the following year at the age of 72, and was buried at Hillside Memorial Park. A few years earlier he'd talked about retiring but after taking some time off to tour Europe with Hortie he realized, like so many people who enjoy their jobs, that he wasn't happy unless he was working. Maybe that's why he died so soon after he retired.

"Sam Katzman was a B picture maker, and probably the best," said Richard Kline. "I mean that sincerely; I'm very high on him. Sam was a sensational person, really, just a marvelous man. I wish we had more production people like him. If today's executives had his moxie, we wouldn't be in the trouble we are now. I don't think pictures would cost that much, there'd be no playing around, and there'd be no actors or directors who could ever use the word *organic*!"

Selected Filmography

SUPERMAN (1948) with Kirk Alyn, Noel Neill, Carol Forman, Tommy Bond and Forrest Taylor. Written by Lewis Clay, Royal K. Cole, Arthur Hoerl, George H. Plympton and Joseph F. Poland. Produced by Sam Katzman. Directed by Spencer G. Bennett and Thomas Carr. A Columbia Serial.

Republic's Howard and Theodore Lydecker had used a papier-mâché dummy attached to wires and pulleys to get *Captain Marvel* (1941) into the air but apparently their method wasn't good enough for Sam. He sent a special effects crew to Mt. Wilson and had them make a contraption that resembled a double ski lift. Kirk Alyn was placed in a harness that was attached to a cable while the camera was placed on a parallel cable. It worked about as well as you would think it would. So Sam came up with what he thought was an even better idea.

"Not a cartoon," boasted the ads for *Superman*. "It's an all new serial in 15 thrill-packed chapters." But, in fact, it *was* a cartoon. Howard Swift, an animator who had worked for Walt Disney, was called in at the last minute to help stage the flying scenes so they'd have a 'backplate' for Superman to fly over. Whenever Superman took to the air, Kirk Alyn was replaced (in the middle of the scene mind you) by a cartoon figure, at a cost of thirty-two dollars a foot. Sam may have thought he'd bested the Lydeckers but he would have been the only one.

Swift was the fastest animator around and Sam was so pleased with him he brought him back for *Atom Man vs. Superman, Bruce Gentry* (1949), *Captain Video* (1951) and *The Lost Planet*.

The Exhibitors. "This isn't as big as we had hoped, but we feel we do extra business with it."—Harland Rankin, Ontario; "This is terrible—no business and we paid extra coin for this but it keeps patrons from my theatre. It is the worst serial I ever have seen in the past 12 years. Don't play it."—Ray S. Hanson, MN; "Columbia sure sold me a bill of goods on this serial. It is the poorest serial that we have played to date and at extra cost, too."—L. A. Knott, WA.

Pierre Watkin as Perry White, Kirk Alyn as Clark Kent,
Noel Neill as Lois Lane and Tommy Bond as Jimmy Olson.

JUNGLE JIM (1948) with Johnny Weissmuller, Virginia Grey, George Reeves, Lita Baron and Rick Vallin. Written by Carroll Young. Produced by Sam Katzman. Directed by William Berke. Black and White 71 minutes. An Esskay Pictures Corporation Production for Columbia Pictures.

The Jungle Jim movies were strictly by-the-number according to Richard Kline. "They took six or seven days to shoot, and the direction was always the same when it came to Johnny Weissmuller. As he walked through the jungle, the direction was, 'Okay, roll 'em. Speed. Action. Come ahead, Johnny. You see something. You stop. You react. And now you go.' That was all the direction! He'd be walking along, and then all of a sudden he'd stop, a blank stare when he'd see something, and then he'd react with a puzzled look, and then on he would go. Somebody once said that Johnny could go on a one-man theatre tour, and call it An Evening of Blank Stares and Double-Takes."

The Critics: "…Weissmuller is impressive as Jungle Jim. If the youngsters take to him in this role, as I think they will, Johnny is set for a number of years to come."—

Johnny Weissmuller as *Jungle Jim* (1948).

Los Angeles Examiner; "...it's not quite the same old Johnny... A heavy accretion of boredom is in his attitude as he guides a scientific party to the jungle temple of Zimbalu, hiding place of untold treasure and source of a magical cure for polio. Even a hand-to-paw battle with a lion doesn't seem to pep him up."—*New York Times*; "... the jungle and wild animal shots, excellent though they are, seem to be incorporated in a haphazard fashion instead of bearing a direct relationship to the plot."—*Hollywood Reporter*; "...the type of film which usually occupies the lower half of a double bill, and presumably only the fact that it is the introductory offering in a scheduled series accounts for its present billing as a stellar attraction."—*Citizen News*; "...is pretty much formula stuff, but most kids and some grownups will like it."—*Los Angeles Times*.

The Exhibitors. "... has all that should please Tarzan lovers, despite a few technical story and acting flaws. It is a good start for the series."—William J. Harris, AR; "The picture has everything any jungle picture needs, but the theatre was short one item—people! I have seen this theatre have standing room only on every jungle picture I ever showed here on a Saturday—yet this time I was left holding the bag. The trailer is good and so is the paper on this. Some tell me they like Tarzan better."—Kenneth

George Reeves has the advantage over Lita Baron, Virginia Gray and Johnny Weissmuller. But not for long.

Clem, MD; "My patrons liked this one. It seemed odd to see Tarzan act and talk like a regular guy but it was good jungle entertainment."—Bill Leonard, KS; "For a good weekend business, fellow exhibitors, don't pass this up. Your patrons will love it."—Harland Rankin, Ontario; "You can't fail with this kind of picture in a small town. Business was very, very good and I showed a profit."—E. M. Freiburger, OK; "We lost money on this picture—in fact, we are unable to show a profit on any low bracket jungle picture or any of the new Tarzans. No more for us."—E. A. London, MI; "This is a very good action picture filmed in that easy-on-the-eyes sepia tone photography. Business fell, however, due to the circus in town."—Wayne Stebbins, MI.

SLAVES OF BABYLON (1953) with Richard Conte, Linda Christian, Maurice Schwartz, Terrance Kilburn and Michael Ansara. Written by DeVallon Scott. Produced by Sam Katzman. Directed by William Castle. Technicolor 81 minutes. A Clover Production for Columbia Pictures.

After Warner Bros. announced that they would be making *Daniel and the Woman of Babylon*, Sam beat them to the punch with this movie, using the sets and costumes left over from *Salome*.

The *Hollywood Reporter* called it "a pretentiously dull, slow moving affair" that fashioned its story with a complete disregard for Biblical history. The film's writer, DeVallon Scott, took issue with the critic. He claimed that most Biblical scholars agreed that the Book of Daniel, on which the film was based, is full of errors. Darius did not, as the critic maintained, overthrow Babylon. Cyrus did. DeVallon did admit to taking "small dramatic license" by placing the story of Daniel in the Lion's Den in the reign of Nebuchadnezzar instead of Darius but (according to DeVallon) Rabbi Nussbaum of the Temple Israel not only had no objection to this liberty but had "complimented the screenplay on its adherence to the important historical and spiritual truths inherent in the subject." In all probability this shift in chronology was due to Sam's desire to have a happy ending (Cyrus's defeat of the Babylonians) and still include the story of Daniel in the Lion's Den. Bottom line: don't expect historical accuracy from the movies. Or anywhere else for that matter. As Gore Vidal once said: "History is the ultimate fiction."

The Critics: "William Castle's direction is rather tame, the action being listless, particularly the battle scenes, which are handled lethargically."—*Boxoffice*; "...a plodding programmer for routine playdates."—*Variety*; "...because the script tried to cover too much, the film grows tedious."—*Hollywood Reporter*.

The Exhibitors. "Mr. Skouras can have his Scope so long as I've got Mr. Katzman making this kind of material for my little old screen and I think I'll still be a competitor. This has more realism in the set department than one of the 'so-called' all-time greats in the religious field … we enjoyed excellent business opening night and would really have hit the peak Saturday night except for power trouble just before show time."—Bob Walker, CO; "… business was better than average. Richard Conte was good as always and Linda Christian got plenty of wolf calls as the sexy princess. Usually these costume dramas are a flop but this was a happy exception."—Norman Merkel, IA; "An excellent Biblical picture in beautiful color. Better than average draw here."—L. Brazil Jr., AR.

JACK McCALL, DESPERADRO (1953) with George Montgomery, Angela Stevens, Douglas Kennedy, James Seay and Eugene Iglesias. Written by John O'Dea. Produced by Sam Katzman. Directed by Sidney Salkow. Technicolor 76 minutes. Columbia Pictures.

Angela Stevens told Michael Barman in his *Classic Images* interview that this was her first big leading role. "I'd never been on [a horse] before in my life. Growing up we couldn't afford to have horses or go riding and we didn't even live near any

Richard Conte and Linda Christian.

horses that I know of, so this was all new to me at the time I made this picture. But it all went just fine." The film premiered at the Western Theatre in Hollywood. "We pretty much crept in and crept out of the theatre," she said.

The history books tell us that Jack McCall staggered into the Nuttal and Mann Saloon in Deadwood, South Dakota and shot Wild Bill Hickok in the back of the head, putting a damper on his poker game. McCall spent three months in jail before he was hanged on March 1, 1877. In this film screenwriter John O'Dea turns McCall into a hero. He shoots Hickok in a fair fight after Hickok framed him for treason, killed his family and stole his home. As a piece of entertainment it isn't nearly as interesting as its star, George Montgomery. Wendy and I saw a display of his art work at the Palm Springs museum many years ago and we were impressed to say the least. He was a fabulous painter and sculptor and if that wasn't enough he made beautiful furniture. His statue of Dinah Shore stands at the 18th hole at the Mission Hills Country Club in Rancho Mirage and there's a gallery named after him at the Autry Museum. If ever anyone had call to brag, it's this guy.

The Critics: "Thesping is along routine lines, as is Sidney Salkow's direction."—*Variety*; "There's enough shooting and fighting… to satisfy the most avid of action fans, plus a fine performance by George Montgomery…"—*Hollywood Reporter*; "…never a dull moment…"—*Boxoffice*.

The Exhibitors. "Color in this outdoor, action, soldier, Indian thing was good."—Frank Sabin, MT; "Picture really brought them in. Appeals to adventure fans. Excellent western that pleased the particular audience of my theatre here in Robstown."—T.J. Stout Jackson, TX. "…pleased the Friday-Saturday customers and made me a little money."—E. M. Freiburger, OK; "Very poor feature. Poor business. Bad comments."—Richard Barr, TX; "I didn't see it myself but the comments were good and business was—very good."—Lloyd Hutchins, AR' "Doubled with Columbia's *49th Man* to reasonably good business."—R. B. Tuttle, MI; "Another western that didn't click…this is the type that is good for TV but theatregoers want something better."—Walt and Ida Breitling, MN.

CREATURE WITH THE ATOM BRAIN (1955) with Richard Denning, Angela Stevens, S. John Launer, Michael Granger and Gregory Gaye. Written by Curt Siodmak. Produced by Sam Katzman. Directed by Edward L. Cahn.

"In a sense, this film's title sums up the appeal of the science fiction/monster movies of the 1950s," wrote Bill Warren in his fabulous book *Keep Watching the Skies!* "It's lurid, it's to the point, and it deals with (a) monsters, (b) atomic radiation and (c) intelligence, all within a single exploitable phrase. *Creature with the Atom Brain.* Run that around on your tongue for a while, and imagine yourself 12 years old and realizing the film exists—but it will be weeks, if ever, before you get to see it."

Packaged with *It Came from Beneath the Sea*, this gruesome sci-fi thriller has the look and feel of one of Sam's serials. For its time it was quite shocking. Backs are broken, necks are snapped, people are stabbed, and it was one of the first movies to use squibs for bullet hits. Writer Curt Siodmak must have been ashamed of it because he never talked about it. It was silly to be sure but a helluva lot more entertaining than some of the films he *would* talk about, such as *Bride of the Gorilla* (1951), *Curucu, Beast of the Amazon* (1956) or *Love-Slaves of the Amazons* (1957). In the hands of a good director, in spite of its shortcomings, this could have been a really good picture.

The Critics: "Curt Siodmak concocted the horror plot...and until he has the mad master of the atomic zombies turning them loose on the whole city will keep his audience with him, even if things get rather distastefully violent."—*Variety*; "Curt Siodmak has written some excellent screenplays but this mismatched marriage of horror story and science-fiction isn't one of them."—*Hollywood Reporter.*

The Exhibitors. "A fantastic science fiction picture of walking dead men. Played with *It Came from Beneath the Sea* for a good double bill..."—Robert Klinge, MO; "This fantastic thing was just what the little guys had been begging me to show, and they were tickled pink when they could brag it wasn't scary enough...more business than we've had in many weeks. Thank heaven!"—Bob Walker, CO.

TEEN-AGE CRIME WAVE (1955) with Tommy Cook, Molly McCart, Sue England, Frank Griffin and James Bell. Written by Ray Buffum and Harry Essex. Produced by Sam Katzman. Directed by Fred F. Sears. Black and white, 77 minutes. A Clover Production for Columbia Pictures.

The Critics: "Performers are good, while the direction of Fred Sears not only maintains the suspense throughout, but builds to a thrill-packed climax."—*Showman's Trade Review*; "Under the direction of Fred F. Sears, these youngsters have delivered what the trade likes to call a 'sleeper.' The film pulls no punches..."—*Citizen News*; "...a fairly good suspense drama...even though it contains too much dragged-in

Bible reading and forced dialogue."—*Hollywood Reporter*; "...a meager effort and lacking in entertainment values."—*Variety*; "...the tenor of this one is so brutal, the youthful gangster so depraved and its conclusion so depressing that the only message it seemed to carry was—crime almost pays."—*Los Angeles Times*.

The Exhibitors. "I can't get many in, but the kids between 12 and 18 went for this in a big way. The plot really lives up to its title."—Ralph Raspa, WV. "Below average business. Good entertainment, and one that you wish every teenager would see."—Ben Spainhour, KS; "A good crime picture which carries a lesson in it about how a person can become involved innocently in a brutal crime."—B. Berglund, ND; "If you can tie your local police department in with this against the same thing happening in your town, by all means, it's a good opportunity."—Lew Bray, TX; "No kicks. Business lots better than average. Small town folk pass up glorified musicals and historicals and come in droves to see hash."—C.J. Otts, TX; "It did all right in fine style for a few extra bucks."—I. Roche, FL; "Too much rental for a programmer. This is the trend: pictures for the teens, but why always in the brutal vein? Why not about good or normal American teenagers? This picture, for its kind, is one of the best-as good as *Rebel*. Mollie McCart! Let's have more of her."—Ken Christianson, ND.

ROCK AROUND THE CLOCK (1956) with Bill Haley, Lisa Gaye, John Archer, Alix Talton and Alan Freed. Written by Robert E. Kent and James B. Gordon. Produced by Sam Katzman. Directed by Fred F. Sears. Black and white, 76 minutes. A Clover Production for Columbia Pictures.

The owner of a Texas drive-in parked a pickup truck in the middle of town with posters from this movie plastered all over it and a sign that read: "All you cats who want to rock, free bop session at the Crescent Drive-In, Thursday, Friday, and Saturday nights." The bop session, coupled with a screening of *Rock Around the Clock*, took in more money than the Crescent had seen in years.

In London, the kids were swaying and rocking outside of the theatre playing Katzman's musical, blocking traffic and throwing beer bottles. The police were called in to restore order. At another London screening the crowd got so rowdy the police were forced to turn a hose on them. Queen Elizabeth II wanted to know what all of the fuss was about and canceled a showing of *The Caine Mutiny* (1954) to watch this film instead.

After seeing the movie, overzealous Norwegians swarmed through the downtown section of the city shouting: "More rock. More rock. More rock!" The military

Fred Sears and Molly McCart.

John Archer, Alix Talton, Johnny Johnston, Lisa Gaye and Henry Slate (I think).

arrived and demanded: "More order. More order. More order!" The manager of the theatre could shed little light on the cause of the disruption, except to say that he didn't think the picture was to blame. *Variety* was afraid that rock 'n' roll was getting too hot to handle. "While its money-making potential has made it all but irresistible, its Svengali grip on the teenagers has produced staggering juvenile violence and mayhem." A number of exhibitors kept the volume low, hoping to curb some of the excitement. Others were afraid to play the picture unless they had some assurance they'd survive it.

The Critics: "Speaking as an admittedly middle-aged square, I still have to say that I found this off-beat, low budget, black and white musical thoroughly entertaining. In theatres catering to bobbysoxers and hep-cats, it should have the joint really jumping."—*Hollywood Reporter*; "It contrasts heady rhythms of rock and roll with the musty atmosphere of booking agency intrigue, and in this instance the rhythm comes out on top. Some clever lines and fast paced plot that doesn't intrude too much on the music."—*Los Angeles Times*; "[It] will not only draw hep-cats, but people of all ages who love good rock and roll rhythm."—*Los Angeles Examiner*; "...speaks the teenager idiom and will prove a handy entry for exhibitors picking a show aimed at the sweater-levi trade. It takes off to a bouncy title beat and never lets up for 76 minutes of foot-patting entertainment."—*Variety*; "...a rapid-fire story compressed between 17 musical numbers in 77 minutes...could easily turn into a boxoffice bonanza..."—*Boxoffice*; "...is a cut above many of the items [Sam Katzman] turns out for the B-picture market under the Clover label and Fred F. Sears has handled the directorial assignment competently."—*Film Daily*.

The Exhibitors. "Every teenager in town will be on hand to see this one when you play it... A well-made rock show that will rock the aisles of your theatre and make you feel good when the show is over."—Robert Kling, MT; "This show sure did have the kids dancing in the aisles and it did happen on a Thursday night, which really caused a panic, but was enjoyed by all."—L.J. Bennett, IL; "We are bringing this one back, due to do many requests."—Mickey and Penny, LA.; "Good solid box-office all three days...the teenagers were there to see it in spite of the fact that the local indoor played it twice before we got it."—Robert B. Tuttle, MI; "Best Sunday and Monday for several weeks. The kids will pour in, no matter if they have seen it before."—Joe and Mildred Faith, MO; "The teenagers ate it up and the older people who saw it liked it also."—Audrey Thompson, AR; "Best business in a long time."—L. Brazil, TX; "Now this picture was good. I was surprised...The trouble was that only myself and the staff saw it!"—Fred L. Murray, Canada; "A good show, but we overmatched it a little by giving it our best time. Did an average Sunday, but we got mostly teenagers and missed a lot of our regular family trade. Monday and Tuesday didn't hold up so well. Would have done better on Friday-Saturday. Was well liked by the young people."—Paul Ricketts, KS; "We played [it] once, then played it twice (only a month apart), and likely will play it once again, if the youngsters keep pleading! Frankly, the teenagers were so enthusiastic they got the personnel in the snack bar sort of swaying and rocking, too. The Platters' two numbers in the movie are worth the price of the show. Anyway, our patrons were satisfied and so were we with a favorable gross."—C.J. Otts; "... has plenty of life and brings the teenagers out. The teens seem to have been the lost audience. Let's get more like this and get back in show business again."—D. W. Trisko, TX; "Boy, howdy! Here is one...that young and old liked. Had repeat business. May bring it back. Give us some more rock and roll."—Mel Danner, OK.

THE GIANT CLAW (1957) with Jeff Morrow, Mara Corday, Morris Ankrum, Louis D. Merrill and Edgar Barrier. Written by Samuel Newman and Paul Gangelin. Produced by Sam Katzman. Directed by Fred F. Sears. Black and white,

Lisa Gaye and Bill Hayley.

75 minutes. A Clover Production for Columbia Pictures.

"Winged monster from 17,000,000 B.C! Big as a battleship! Atomic Weapons Can't Hurt It! Flies 4 Times Faster Than the Speed of Sound!" Good Lord! At that speed the audience couldn't see it. Which would spoil the fun. The long-necked "mange-stricken swan" with "the face of a worried worrybird" as one reviewer described it, was an absolute delight and in a class by itself. The Saturday matinee audience I saw this film with back in 1957 exploded with laughter when the monster made its first appearance and they didn't stop laughing until the film was over. Sam wanted Ray Harryhausen to do the effects but he was involved with another project at the time. (Good thing, too. He would have spoiled the fun.) Sam gave the task to Ralph Hammeras, George Teague and Larry Butler. To save money, these three created their "magic" in a little studio in Mexico where Willis O'Brien and Pete Peterson were working on *The Black Scorpion* (1957). These guys can be blamed for everything that's wrong with the special effects except for the design of the bird. Sam was responsible for that.

"I think *The Giant Claw* is right up there with Ed Wood's movies," said leading lady Mara Corday. When she first met with Sam Katzman he was raving on and on about the wonderful special effects people he'd hired. He told her he was spending most of the budget on the special effects. "The film was near completion when Katzman finally had the chance to see the incredibly comical *flying battleship*. Well, Katzman was shocked, but he opted to accept the thing as a joke, because it was not economical to create a more realistic monster. I saw the film in a theatre where it played to roars of laughter from the audience."[14] She wondered if her husband, Richard Long (who did everything he could to sabotage her career) had been right. Maybe it *was* time for her to retire.

The film went into production as *The Mark of the Claw*. Fred Sears and his crew went to Griffith Park for a scene where Mara Corday and Jeff Morrow have to hit the ground to avoid the flying debris from an exploding airplane. Out of fear that it would keep her from getting the part, Miss Corday didn't tell anyone she that she was pregnant. "Are you pregnant?" Lenny Katzman asked her when the scene was finished. "Why are you saying that?" she asked defensively. "Do I look pregnant?" "No," he said, "but you favor your stomach a lot."

She'd had very little sleep the night before because her husband threw an all-night party, knowing she had to be up in the morning. It was one of the many ways he tried to sabotage her career. She was getting a cup of coffee when Sam walked up to her and said, "You look like hell." *If you think she looks like hell, wait until you see the bird!*

Jeff Morrow told me when he read the script he imagined something like a hawk, diving past the camera, almost faster than the eye could see. When he saw the film for the first time with his family at a theatre near his home, he was so embarrassed he snuck out of the theatre before the film was over. He would routinely see his movies at the local bijou and hang around in the lobby afterwards, shaking hands, talking with his friends. "And we were all so serious," he said, which is part of the fun.

The Critics: "…often more laugh-provoking than frightening…"—*Boxoffice*; "Ideally suited to a steady ingestion of popcorn."—*Mirror News*; "…cliché-ridden script is a powerful aid in reducing the picture to near-complete ludicrousness."—*Los Angeles Times*; "…the corny dialog…caused the audience with this reviewer to break out laughing. Some even jeered."—*Citizen News*; "…the bird itself is somewhat clumsily executed."—*Variety*; "These plots are easy to kid but the fact remains that they form the basis for pictures that have a definite programming value."—*Hollywood Reporter*.

The Exhibitors. "…it's not only the teenagers who like this type of movie, some of the older people get a kick out of them, too."—Stan Farnsworth, NE; "Doubled with *Night the World Exploded* to the best Tuesday-Wednesday we've ever had."—O. M. Shannon, TX; "Business was off and the people were not too happy with the program. The bird in *Giant Claw* was so phony it made people laugh."—Victor Webber, AR; "Did above average but even some youngsters were disappointed. Some walked out. The big bird looked so artificial and when it picked up a whole train there was ridiculing laughter."—Leonard J. Leise, NE; "These horror pictures seem to jar them loose, although I believe *The Giant Claw* and two Three Stooges comedies would have done just as well. *The Night the World Exploded* is the better of the two, but I don't believe in double bills, so I think *The Claw* is the one that drew them in."—B. Berglund, ND; "…was disappointing to all who saw it."—Harold Muir, MI.

TWIST AROUND THE CLOCK (1961) with Chubby Checker, Dion DiMucci, Vicki Spencer, Cornelius Harp and Clay Cole. Written by Robert E. Kent. Produced by Sam Katzman. Directed by Oscar Rudolph. Black and white, 86 minutes. A Four Leaf Production for Columbia Pictures.

Sam must have been on speed when he made this picture. A call to some big-wig in Columbia's New York office got things rolling on a Friday morning in November, after which Sam flew to New York that night and spent the weekend lining up a bunch of singers he'd never heard of—Chubby Checker, Dion, Clay Cole,

The beautiful and talented Mara Corday.

Morris Ankrum, Mara Corday, Edgar Barrier and Jeff Morrow wonder if they're being paid enough to be humiliated by *The Giant Claw*.

Vicki Spender and The Marcels. He flew back to Hollywood and told James B. Gordon he had five days to write the script, during which time Sam cast the rest of the picture with more people he'd never heard of. By Friday he had a script and the assistant director started working on a shooting schedule. The following Monday the dancers were rehearsing while Chubby was recording. The next day when the cameras started rolling, Sam realized he needed three songs. During lunch, Fred Karger (Sam's musical director) and a member of his staff wrote three songs on the back of a lunch check and some note paper. The film editor was working day and night, putting the film together as it was being shot. According to Dick Williams, the entertainment editor for the *L.A. Mirror News* who was invited to come to the set, the principal requirements for performing The Twist seemed to be "skin-tight clothes and a total lack of inhibitions." Williams thought one young lady in a pair of blue Capri pants was especially provocative as she writhed opposite her partner "like she had a cold goldfish dropped down her blouse." He noticed that she caught Sam's fancy too, as well as bunch of other producers, directors and writers of the more refined pictures being shot at the studio who just happened to find the time to drop by. After seven days the picture was done. Five days later the editor had a rough cut and the picture was scored. On December 8 the executives in New York had a print and it was in theatres in time for Christmas. Sam was sure it would make millions. And he was right.

The Critics: "[An] obnoxious blend: Hillbilly music done to an Afro beat."—*Los Angeles Times*; "It is cliché-riddled and threadbare in story content, and so 'corny' in spots, I thought for a moment I was back in Iowa. But in spite of it all (or perhaps I should say, in spite of itself), the picture is really kind of cute."—*Hollywood Citizen News*; "The astute and timely showmanship of producer Sam Katzman...again leaps to the fore with this made-overnight exploitation offer built around the current Twist craze."—*Boxoffice*; "...is at least attractively and resourcefully mounted and endowed with a reasonable sense of dramatic content and concern for characterization..."—*Variety*; "To the uninitiated, all twisting rhythms sound pretty much alike, and the dance itself does not seem to lend itself to much variation."—*Hollywood Reporter*.

The Exhibitors. "This drew better than lots of the big pictures."—Bill Roth, TN; "Since I played it, the Twist has died a miserable death, so I suggest you leave it alone."—Don Statt, MD; "Business was wonderful, we drew from towns all around."—Harry Hawkinson, MN; "This put the lid on the coffin—we pronounce the Twist officially dead—and are we happy."—Roy Boriski, TX; "Wish we could play one like this every week."—P. B. Friedman, KY; "The boxoffice was above average, the teens enjoyed it and the adults were curious."—Ken Christianson, ND; "You'll feel like Twisting all the way to the bank."—Ray Kendrick, OK; "This is the type of stuff that will bring them in."—Larry Thomas, WV; "The teenagers here went wild and the older folk were right there with them."—Roy Kendrick, OH; "Now here is a company that is really on the beam. They make a twist picture and they sell it to us while it is hot. The results—the theatre does a terrific business and is happy."—Harry Hawkinson, MN; "Wish we could play one like this every week. People came out who hadn't found their way to this theatre in years."—P. B. Friedman, KY; "It did very well on Sunday night and everyone was pleased."—James Hardy, IN; "This drew better than a lot of big pictures. Play it."—Bill Roth, TN.

HOOTENANNY HOOT (1963) with Peter Breck, Ruta Lee, Joby Baker, Pamela Austin and Bobo Lewis. Written by Robert E. Kent. Produced by

Sam Katzman. Directed by Gene Nelson. Black and white, 91 minutes. A Four Leaf Production for Metro-Goldwyn-Mayer.

Sam promised MGM executives that he'd deliver this film in 9 days. "We finished 35 minutes late, with 1,200 feet of extra footage," Sam told Philip Scheuer from *The Los Angeles Times*. "I sent a note upstairs and apologized. When the executives saw the first cut they applauded. No kidding. The choreography compares favorably with *Seven Brides for Seven Brothers*."

The Critics: "...a zesty film full of youth, music, dancing and romance...It is fast paced and entertaining from start to finish."—*Citizen News*; "...television material, trying to pass as cinema."—*Films and Filming*; "...well-timed to cash in on the current folk-singing craze."—*Hollywood Reporter*; "...it should do well enough to justify one of Katzman's sequels, say something along the order of *Don't Refute the Hoot*."—*Variety*; "...its plot involving a double romance wouldn't stand steady in a light breeze, but producer Sam Katzman and director Gene Nelson have assembled a lively group of youthful hootenanny experts—and that's probably enough to insure success."—*Los Angeles Times*; "Unfortunately, the only thing to give a hoot about is the music."—*Los Angeles Examiner*.

The Exhibitors. "...broke all records for all times for the four days...This is a wonderful example of what the people really want, regardless of low budget."—Art Richards, SC; "...they came, they saw, they liked. Let's have more comedy musicals like this."—Harold J. Smith, TN; "Struck the right chord with this one. Just plain corny and how they did like it."—Carl W. Veseth, MT; "Same old Katzman formula, but they satisfy."—Jim Fraser, MN; "They liked this one real well. Had an above average house."—Paul Fournier, NB; "The teenagers came and they were happy."—John Baily, KS; "A hootenanny troop was in the area at the time we played this. We capitalized on their appearance and did very well at the boxoffice."—Ken Christianson, ND; "Good business and good entertainment. Good all the way around. For us folks around Comfrey we do not need any million dollar productions...We can live on this type. Come again."—W.A. Windschilt, MN.

GET YOURSELF A COLLEGE GIRL (1964) with Mary Ann Mobley, Joan O'Brien, Nancy Sinatra, Chris Noel and Chad Everett. Written by Robert E. Kent. Produced by Sam Katzman. Directed by Sidney Miller. Metrocolor 87 minutes. A Four Leaf Production for Metro-Goldwyn-Mayer.

Sam originally wanted to call this picture *Watusi A-Go-Go* but producer Al Zimbalist had already registered that title. It went into production as *The Swingin' Set* with a script that clumsily touches on issues of sex, feminism and the generation gap. Like all of the Sam's musicals, the audience can have a good time with the musical numbers without having to pay attention to the rest of the picture.

The Critics: "Sam Katzman seldom stubs his toe when he turns out one of his music fad-exploitation pictures, but he does with this one ... a poorly developed script and the specialty acts are below par."—*Hollywood Reporter*; "... a series of swinging performers tied together in the loosest style possible by a flimsy story."—*Los Angeles Herald Examiner*; "... proceeds like a Watusi-dance fling along a wild and spirited course."—*Film Daily*; "... the actors perform at the level of the script, alternating between archness and toothy smiles."—*Motion Picture Herald*; "... the story is in extremely bad taste more than once and the efforts to bring the suggestive situations into the plot so awkward and contrived they leave the viewer squirming."—*Boxoffice*; "Picture has an academic storyline and lackluster appeal."—*Variety*; "... strives to be witty. The best that can be said is that it succeeds in being inoffensively silly."—*Los Angeles Times*.

The Exhibitors. "We did very well with this one and here is a picture your teenage patrons will really enjoy."—Harry Hawkinson, MN; "Did okay and pleased."—C. A. Swiercinsky, KS; "Just what the younger set likes. Full of fun and songs, plus beautiful color."—I. Roche, FL; "This did better than average business, but not as much as expected. Teenagers liked it. Not too good for older patrons—but they don't come anyway."—S. T. Jackson, AL; "A lot of nonsense with popular singing groups of teenagers that will get their business."—Terry Axley, AR; "... a natural for teenage trade and that means good business..."—George C. Clayton, VA; "The teens will love it."—Arthur K. Dame, NH; "Dandy picture for anytime your teenagers are looking for a movie to go to."—Lew Bray, Jr., TX.

KISSIN' COUSINS (1964) with Elvis Presley, Arthur O'Connell, Glenda Farrell, Jack Albertson and Pamela Austin. Written by Gerald Drayson Adams and Gene Nelson. Produced by Sam Katzman. Directed by Gene Nelson. Metrocolor, 96 minutes. A Four Leaf Production for Metro-Goldwyn-Mayer.

Complying with Colonel Tom Parker's request to cut costs, MGM put Elvis Presley in his first low-budget feature. Presley had made some pretty stinky films in the past but they were respectable stinky films. Now, thanks to Parker's greed and

Presley's mindless obedience to him, the singer had sunk about as low as he could get.

Sam hated to pay Presley's million dollar salary. According to his son, he was able to justify it because Presley played two parts.

Actor/dancer Gene Nelson had only directed one film (*Hand of Death*) and he was a little intimated. "I'd get uptight—and this upset Elvis," Nelson said in Peter Gurainick's *Careless Love: The Unmaking of Elvis Presley.* "He came to me the last week and said he didn't like to work this way, it wasn't worth it. He said he knew what kind of pressure I was under, and he volunteered to get sick or show up late if it would help. I thanked him and said to hang in; it was *my* problem."

When asked about Sam Katzman, Nelson told Gurainick: "The man knew how to make pictures. The fact that he had lousy taste has nothing to do with it. He knew every angle, every possible way to 'cheat'; he could have done a good picture the same way and he would have been even more of a hero. He just had lousy taste in writers, and he wouldn't know a story if it hit him in the face."

"I've been asked many times, many times as to how I got the part of PFC Midge Reilly in *Kissin' Cousins*," said Cynthia Pepper, "and the answer is quite interesting and something I will always remember. It was a Friday and I received a call from my agent telling me that Elvis Presley saw me on some TV show. He watched a lot of TV back then and he happened to see me and thought I was right for a co-starring role in his upcoming film. My agent told me, 'Get over to MGM studios, go to wardrobe, try on the uniform you'll be wearing and see if it fits. If it fits, you're in!' Of course, I flew to the studio. Thank heavens, the uniform fit and, as they say, the rest is history. I never auditioned! On Monday morning, Yvonne Craig, Pamela Austin and I were driven to a Cedar Lake location in a limousine and before you know it I was on a film set standing next to Elvis Presley!"[16]

The Critics: "Producer Sam Katzman, who specialized in low-budget, lower intelligence cinema product, turns his attention here to hillbilly humor, and with Elvis Presley playing dual roles, comes up with some pretty awful stuff."—*Cue;* "...a broad, meandering rehash of 'Li'l Abner.' For Pete's sake, El!"—*New York Times;* "This new Elvis Presley concoction is a pretty dreary effort, one that certainly won't replenish the popularity of Sir Swivel. Presley needs—and merits—more substantial material than this if his career is to continue to flourish as in the past. A few more like this and Cuhnel Parker may have to press the panic button."—*Variety;* "...even with its neglect for characterization...it is more entertaining that the last three Presley films and fleetingly catches some bouncy enthusiasm."—*Films and Filming;* "...gives the reliable singing star a fine showcase in an amusing dual role..."—*Hollywood Re-*

Elvis Presley plays twins in *Kissin' Cousins*, one of his worst pictures. And that's saying something.

porter; "It's a gay romp, sure to please Elvis fans for he has many song opportunities as well as getting romantic with two cuties."—*Los Angeles Herald Examiner*; "…isn't the greatest entertainment ever conceived, but it does offer slight more than an hour and a half of light escapist fun."—*Citizen News*; "You get your money's worth before monotony sets in as it does in nearly all the Presley pics."—*Los Angeles Times*.

The Exhibitors. "This show is what teenagers go for."—Slim Lasater, NM; "More country-type pictures will bring more grosses than the 'classy, high-falutin.'"—A. A. Richard, SC; "A good bet in a small town."—C.D. Simmons, ID; "Played it for second time and did more business than the first time."—Terry Axley, AR.

HARUM SCARUM (1965) with Elvis Presley, Mary Ann Mobley, Fran Jeffries, Michael Ansara and Jay Novello. Written by Gerald Drayson Adams. Produced by Sam Katzman. Directed by Gene Nelson. Metrocolor, 95 minutes. A Four Leaf Production for Metro-Goldwyn-Mayer.

Once again, Sam couldn't seem to decide what to call this thing. It was first announced as *In My Harum*. A month later it was *Harum Holiday*. A week after that it was *Harum Scarum* and back again to *Harum Holiday* a week after that. Finally, Sam settled on *Harum Scarum*. It smells just as bad under any title. If Elvis was hoping that this picture would be better than *Kissin' Cousins*, the first day on the set cured him of that. Dressed in a costume left over from *Kismet*, Presley was painfully aware that the picture was a joke and that the joke was on him. He said to his co-star, Mary Ann Mobley: "This isn't going to change history, is it?" On a photograph that he gave to the director at the end of the shoot Presley wrote: "Someday we'll do it right."

Sam asked Presley's co-star, Mary Ann Mobley, if she knew how to ride a horse. She said she did. "Good," he said, "we don't have to hire a stunt double." As she approached the horse, the old wrangler sitting beside it, whittlin' and chewin', looked at her and asked, "You ridin' this horse?" She said that she was. "Just remember one thing," he said, "it ain't my idea." She climbed on the horse and it took off like its tail was on fire.[17]

After seeing the film, Col. Tom Parker told MGM it would take "a 55th cousin to P.T. Barnum" to sell it. He suggested they add a talking camel to narrate it. Surprisingly, Sam didn't like the idea.

The Critics: "The film, which avoids placing a strain on Presley as actor and singer, makes no attempt at taking itself seriously"—*Film Daily*; "...seems to have all the usual ingredients that make his films a success..."—*Hollywood Reporter*; "With anybody but Elvis Presley to gun possibilities this would be a pretty dreary affair..."—*Variety*; "Mr. Presley wanders through the improbable whimsies of *Harum Scarum* with all the animation of a man under deep sedation..."—*New York Times*; "...a slow-paced, labored spoof on the Arabian Nights..."—*Citizen News*; "....could be called a spoof in the sense that the story doesn't stand up to even the most cursory examination."—*Films and Filming*; "...enough action, romance and humor to keep audiences, particularly the younger members, in a happy frame of mind."—*Motion Picture Herald*.

The Exhibitors. "Hope Elvis doesn't make too many more like this, because after a while even the name won't draw."—Harold Bell, Quebec; "No complaints, but I hope they keep him out of this type picture."—S.T. Jackson, AL; "Elvis is really slipping. This is his worst picture to date and the kids must have known that as business was below that of a usual Elvis picture."—Donald E. Bohatka, IL; "It's a fine picture. Don't miss it. Play it!"—Herman Powell, AR; "Not up to his others, but don't pass it up."—Harold E. Thompson, OH; "The word got around before we opened that it was no good. Can't figure how he was talked into this one."—Leon Kidwell, OK;

What's that sound, Elvis? Could it be your career circling the toilet?

"Heard comments that this was Presley's worst movie yet. It failed to bring out many 'faithful' Presley fans."—Wes Stuckwish, OK; "We can forgive one like this, but no more."—Arthur K. Dane, NH; "Absolutely no draw. I heard folks telling others not to go see it the minute I started advertising it."—M.W. Long, IA.

WHEN THE BOYS MEET THE GIRLS (1965) with Connie Francis, Harve Presnell, Peter Noone, Louis Armstrong and Liberace. Written by Robert E. Kent from the play by Guy Colton and Jack McGowan. Produced by Sam Katzman. Directed by Alvin Ganzer. Metrocolor 102 minutes. A Four Leaf Production for Metro-Goldwyn-Mayer.

Sam rounded up the most eclectic musical cast ever assembled for this reworking of the George and Ira Gershwin musical *Girl Crazy*, filmed once in 1932 and again 1942. Where else but in a Katzman film could you find Herman's Hermits *and* Liberace! As he listened to Liberace singing "Aruba Liberace," the Hermits' Peter Noone told the director he didn't think the song was in the Gershwin Brothers repertoire. The director informed him that Liberace had insisted on singing one of his own songs. "Then we'd like to do one of *our* songs," Noone told him. And they did. Paul Anka wisely bowed out of this miserable thing and was replaced by Joby Baker.

The Critics: "If the music of the Gershwin brothers can survive a terrible little musical such as [this], chances are it could outlast atomic annihilation."—*New York Times*; "Perhaps to insure teen-age interest in the movie, showbiz personalities are paraded before the camera to do a spot. They don't help. Even King Kong on roller skates couldn't."—*New York Herald Tribune*; "The picture is an odd combining of the old-fashioned *Girl Crazy* story and the new-fangled youth-for-youth's-sake format that succeeds so well when the mixtures right and dies so hard when it isn't."—*Motion Picture Herald*; "The brains behind *The Boys* undoubtedly believe that their movie reflects changing tastes, but they seem to confuse updating with downgrading."—*Time*; "As entertainment, it never gets going."—*Los Angeles Times*; "...a spotty comedy films loaded with often extraneous tunes, also limited to some okay performances and gags."—*Variety*; "The staging of the musical numbers, the acting, the editing, the script—all combine in a ghastly plot to perpetuate the great square myth that pop music is a load of fertilizer."—*Films and Filming*.

The Exhibitors. "The adults walked out but the teenagers loved it."—Donald E. Bohafsla, IL; "A very good musical which pleased the few who came. Should have done much better. Weather was against us on this one."—Harold Bell, Quebec; "Give us more like this."—Arthur K. Dane, NH; "Fairly good at the boxoffice and pleased the young folks."—C.A. Swiercinsky, KS.

HOLD ON! (1966) with Shelley Fabres, Sue Ann Langdon, Bernard Fox, Herbert Anderson and Peter Blair Noone. Written by Robert E. Kent. Produced by Sam Katzman. Directed by Arthur Lubin. Metrocolor, 85 min. A Four Leaf Production for Metro-Goldwyn-Mayer.

The working title of this *Hard Day's Night* inspired romp was *There's No Place Like Space*. Someone who was either a halfwit or had a sense of humor changed the title to *A Must to Avoid*, a fitting title for most of Sam's movies. Saner minds prevailed and the title was changed again to *Hold On!*

In an interview for *Popdose*, Peter Noone said director Arthur Lubin was amazing. "And he was a real gentleman. He gave us all kinds of good advice. I was already an actor—I'd gone through acting school and stuff like that—but none of the others had. They were just thrown into the deep end. And he gave them time to be…themselves, basically."

The Critics: "…an occasionally amusing but nonsensical pastiche…"—*New York*

Peter Noone.

Times; "…the group's high spirits have been cut down to fit producer Sam Katzman's trite formula for teen-age entertainment."—*Los Angeles Times*; "The story is one of general audience appeal and easy to follow as it proceeds along a routine narrative trail."—*Film Daily*; "…for swingers who are really with it."—*Boy's Life*; "…an exception to the usual idea that teenage musicals are designed to give youngsters a chance to exercise their screams, and adults the opportunity to reaffirm their belief that the world has gone mad."—*Los Angeles Herald Examiner*; "A diverting script, good direction, acting and pace are supported by fine Sam Katzman production values."—*Variety*; "Even with the shaggy hairdo and eccentric dress, Noone makes a nice impression…"—*Hollywood Reporter*.

The Exhibitors. "Terrific business."—Paul Gamache, VT; "Did better-than-average business." S. T. Jackson, AR; "Okay if you can buy right."—Terry Axley, AR; "These boys are good enough to deserve better material to work with."—Arthur K. Dame, NH; "Strictly for the teens and they turned out in mass to see it."—I Roche, FL; "Did okay, with the young folks turning out in good numbers."—C. A. Swierensky, KS; "Just fair. However, the Hermits brought in most of the teens in town, so can't complain."—Paul Fournier, NB; "Thanks, MGM, for giving me a chance to keep out of the red."—Carl Lankford, VA; "Teenagers sure liked this. Let's have another Hermit feature."—S. T. Jackson, AL.

HOT RODS TO HELL (1967) with Dana Andrews, Jeanne Crain, Mimsy Farmer, Laurie Mock and Paul Bertoya. Written by Robert E. Kent. Produced by Sam Katzman. Directed by John Brahm. Metrocolor, 92 minutes. A Four Leaf Production for Metro-Goldwyn-Mayer.

In the early 50s, MGM had planned to follow *Blackboard Jungle* with a movie about a family terrorized by a gang of hot-rodding teenagers called *52 Miles to Terror*, based on a short story by Alex Gaby that appeared in a 1956 issue of the *Saturday Evening Post*. Rod Serling was going to script it and Richard Thorpe was going to direct it. Casting problems shelved it. More than a decade later the studio resurrected the property and gave it to Sam. The movie was made for ABC's *Sunday Night Movie* but the studio decided it was too intense for television. They changed the title and released it theatrically. Apparently it was less intense two years later when it finally aired on television.

The Critics: "…will make a vivid impression on the minds of those who see it."—

Film Daily; "A first rate shocker for the teens ..."—*Los Angeles Herald Examiner*; "... is aimed at the kids, but not all of them are going to like what it had to say."—*Los Angeles Times*; "... has some interesting second unit auto sequences, some misused good names in the cast and little else."—*Hollywood Reporter*; "Many scenes are tedious due to repetition; others are overly embellished dramatically and lose strength rather than gain it."—*Citizen News*; "Over-acted, poorly-directed and cliché-ridden..."—*Variety*; "It is unfortunate that the screenplay leans so heavily on preachy dialogue, as when a policeman scolds a loud-mouthed older man for speeding, in a speech that sounds too-well-memorized, and when Andrew mumbles something about 'you crazy punks,' and then forgives them after giving another lecture."—*Motion Picture Herald*.

The Exhibitors. "... all but laughed off the screen."—Larry Thomas, WV; "All I can say is that's where the week's business went with this one."—Bernard Van Tipton, AZ; "The title sure doesn't help describe the picture. Many were fooled. They expect much more in the line of hot rods racing, but as it turned out, this was pretty good."—Peter A. Silloway, VT; "We had a fair crowd for this and it was well liked, but played too soon after the drive-in, which doesn't help."-Leonard Wahl, WS; "There have been lots of 'hot rod' pictures, but if you can sell them that this is different it'll do business in small towns."—Leon Kidwell, OK; "They said it was a 'snafu' that put *Welcome to Hard Times* on TV so soon. Now *Hot Rods to Hell* is being advertised for next week on ABC-TV. So what's the excuse this time? G-r-r-r-r."—Charles Burton, MO; "This is a good feature for your drive-in patrons. Lots of action and that's what our people like."—J. McKinnon, B.C.

RIOT ON THE SUNSET STRIP (1967) with Aldo ray, Mimsy Farmer, Michael Evans, Laurie Mock and Tim Rooney. Written by Orville H. Hampton. Produced by Sam Katzman. Directed by Arthur Dreifuss. Color, 83 minutes. A Four Leaf Production for Metro-Goldwyn-Mayer. Released by American International Pictures.

In the mid-to-late sixties the Sunset Strip was a place where thousands of teenagers congregated every weekend. A misguided attempt to disperse the crowds and return the strip to some order resulted in one horrible weekend of violence and police brutality in 1967. And before you could say "Starts Wednesday at a theatre or drive-in near you" Sam Katzman made a film about it. Sort of.

"For *Riot on the Sunset Strip*, it took just a day and a half to write the script, and the picture was out within ten days after the actual riots" recalled Jerome Katzman.

"But that was unusually fast. The average for a complete script was a couple of weeks. Then preproduction would take a week to ten days. For the editing, my dad liked to have the editor on the set, to make sure he had all the coverage he needed. Then, he'd go back into the editing room, he knew exactly what he had. It would take about a week to cut it, and then my dad would look at it, and the director would look at it. But they would build a rough-cut while they were shooting, so it moved that much faster. And if there was a continuity problem, he would use stock footage from something to make up for whatever was missing."[18]

MGM's distribution set-up couldn't move fast enough to get the picture into theatres while the incident was still topical so the studio sold the picture to American International.

The Critics: "Sam Katzman, as alert to film marketing potential as anybody in the business, has a sure winner here."—*Variety*; "Orville H. Hampton contributed a tepid screenplay, one that never explores the underlying issues."—*Citizen News*; "The film embellishes a worthwhile comment on adult delinquents and their offspring with some ridiculous dialogue and romanticizes hallucinatory drugs."—*Los Angeles Herald Examiner*.

The Exhibitors. "Not for weak-minded youngsters."—Harold Bell, Quebec; "Top price, did monstrous ad and waited for the dough to roll in. Nothing. I knew the show was terrible, so naturally expected great business. Sure enough, show was terrible, but business was worse. Keep away."—Don Stott, MD; "Oh boy, it will do business. There was one bad scene in it, but can pass it by changing reels just before it gets into it. It's doing business in small towns."—Leon Kidwell, OK; "Didn't do as well as expected on this, but picture okay."—Terry Axley, AR.

THE LOVE-INS (1967) with Richard Todd, James MacArthur, Susan Oliver, Mark Goddard and Carol Booth. Written by Hal Collins and Arthur Dreifuss. Produced by Sam Katzman. Directed by Arthur Dreifuss. Eastmancolor, 86 minutes. A Four Leaf Production for Columbia Pictures.

Susan Oliver didn't want to do this film. She felt it trivialized the whole Timothy Leary, flower-child, hippie scene. She was promised that the topic would be handled with "taste and empathy." In her autobiography, *Odyssey: A Daring Transatlantic Journey*, the actress wrote: "Besides, I'd played Hank Williams's wife in *Your Cheatin' Heart*, which I was proud of, for these same producers, so I felt some loyalty...so I'm an actress and I have to act. But I went through a sort of hell during filming when I began to realize it really was just 'exploitation time' after all. Richard Todd...was sensitive to what I was going through since he'd gone through much the same thing with his own career, but he'd told me, 'Look, you can't just run away, you have to work somewhere, even if it's crap and not Shakespeare.' Yet the night of our wrap party at MGM I went alone to an empty sound stage and sat there in the dark and wept over lost dreams and compromised principles and dishonest romances and my helplessness in it all." In his own autobiography, *In Camera*, Todd said he thought the movie "was quite the most extraordinary and disturbing film" he'd ever made. Most critics agreed with critic Judith Crist who thought it was "mawkish, old hat and un-hip."

The Critics: "...for the most part this lurid melodrama is a gaudy, gleeful glorification of the fun that hippies have at their jolly outdoor love-ins and on their phantasmagorical trips...Evidently Sam Katzman wanted his picture to be both psychedelic and socially indignant. It is neither. It's a very weak trip."—*New York Times*; "...they have substituted topical melodrama for a compelling in-depth study."—*Boxoffice*; "...a solid, if standard story, fringed in fine style with love-ins and hippie happenings..."—*Variety*; "If the film does not fully accomplish its intentions with an important dramatic result, it is still a very good, possibly even valuable film."—*Hollywood Reporter*; "...skims the surface in a moderately interesting fashion calculated to arouse curiosity, if nothing else."—*Motion Picture Exhibitor*; "One banana-peel orgy we witness is about as titillating—and only a little less wholesome—as the June Allyson sorority dance in *Good News*. In fact, the only favorable comment on this superficial and phony look at hippie-LSD society I can summon up is that it is not one tenth as vulgar as its newspaper advertising."—*Cue*.

The Exhibitors. "Lots of walkouts."—Terry Axley, AR; "...draws the teenagers."—B. Berglund, ND; "If your customers go for long hair and whiskers this is as good as any of them."—Harold Bell, Quebec.

ANGEL, ANGEL, DOWN WE GO (1969) with Jennifer Jones, Jordan Christopher, Holly Near, Roddy McDowell and Lou Rawls. Written by Robert Thom. Executive Producer Sam Katzman. Produced by Jerome Katzman. Directed by Robert Thom. Color, 103 minutes. A Four Leaf Production for American International Pictures.

At this point in his career, Sam Katzman announced that he was going to turn over a new leaf and produce more artistic and meaningful movies and this was touted as Sam's first non-exploitation movie, "The day of the exploitation picture is gone," Jerry Katzman told *Variety*. "We learned that with *Riot on the Sunset Strip*. We learned that people are no longer interested in headlines. There is so much sensationalism on TV it doesn't work anymore." Sam was acting as an executive producer on this one. His son was producing it. "AIP is trying to go much more highbrow," Jerry said. "They have made a fortune, but this is a business of money as well as art. This will be one of the first pictures in an effort to change their image."

In spite of Jerry's claim, this mish-mash of currently fashionable clichés and cinematic devices was more interested in exploiting its subject than understanding it. It played exclusively at one of the more prestigious Hollywood theatres and proved to be such a disaster that it was withdrawn and shelved for over a year. When it returned it had been recut and given a new title, *Cult of the Damned*, hoping to capitalize on the then recent disclosures about Charles Manson and his hippie murder cult. And *still* nobody wanted to see it. Years later, when Jennifer Jones's personal trainer, a young lady in her twenties, told the actress that she'd seen the film, Jones replied: "I'm sorry to hear that. I'm afraid I might owe you an apology."

The Critics: "The under-30s may go for this hodge-podge of ideas dressed up with multi-collages ... and psychedelic trappings ... but what a waste of time and talent."—Ann Giarino; "Miss Jones, apparently uncertain as to what her role is supposed to be, wavers between sensuality and matronliness."—*Variety*; "Miss Jones' once mannered twitch has become an unpleasant snarl, in no way softened by the lines she is forced to mouth."—*Hollywood Reporter*; "It's a disjointed fare, despite a plethora of anti-establishment remarks that leave little impact even on a willing viewer."—*New York Times*; "Once in a great while ... a critic meets a film so suited to a dramatically opposed taste that it produces an acute sensation of disgust."—*New York Post*.

Notes

1. George Christy, "The Great Life," *Hollywood Reporter*, March 19, 1992, page 27.

2. Ibid.

3. Tom Weaver, *Eye on Science Fiction*, McFarland & Company, North Carolina, 2003, pages 141-142.

4. Tom Weaver, *It Came from Weaver Five*, McFarland & Company, Inc., North Carolina, 1995, pages 103-104.

5. Ibid, page 104-105.

6. Willard L. Wiener, "The Happiest Man in Hollywood," *Colliers*, December 30, 1950, page 33.

7. Howard McClay, "Sam Katzman," *Los Angeles Daily News*, Feb. 7, 1952, page 37.

Sam Katzman with Rhonda Fleming
on the set of *Serpent of the* Nile.

8. *It Came from Weaver Five,* page 107.

9. *Eye on Science Fiction,* page 150.

10. Mike Hankin, *Ray Harryhausen, Master of the Majicks,* Vol. 2, Archive Editions, 2008, page 115.

11. Paul Parla and Charles P. Mitchell, *Screen Sirens Scream,* McFarland & Company, North Carolina, 2000, page 219.

12. ASCAP had once made its money from sheet music, piano rolls, and recordings. When radio came into its own, stations battled with ASCAP over royalty payments and many stations refused to play anything that was registered with it. Broadcast Music Incorporated (BMI) was formed to pick up the slack. BMI ended up with most of the rock songs because ASCAP didn't want to sully its hands with black music and hillbilly music. When rock 'n' roll turned the music business upside down, ASCAP found itself on the outside looking in. So ASCAP convinced Senator Owen Harris to legally kill its competition. It would, after all, be a mutually beneficial act. Plenty of people hated rock 'n' roll. The only people Harris would piss off were the kids and they didn't vote so what did it matter?

13. *Los Angeles Times,* Aug 12, 1961, page 3.

14. Paul Parla, "Beauty and the Beasts," *Filmfax* No. 91, 2002, page 81.

15. Tom Lisanti, *Fantasy Femmes of the Sixties Cinema,* McFarland & Company, North Carolina, 2010, page 37.

16. Gary Brumburgh, "Cynthia Pepper, "The 'Camelot' Blonde," *Classic Images* No. 477, page 12.

17. Alanna Nash, *Mary Ann Mobley Remembers Elvis Presley.*

18. Wheeler Winston Dixon, *Lost in the Fifties,* Southern Illinois University Press, 2005, page 52.

PART TWO

JAMES HARTFORD
NICHOLSON

*"Some people come up with brilliant reasons for their success.
I wish I could say there was some strange formula such as
I don't drink water—but I don't have any. Maybe it
was just being at the right place at the right time."*

He came home tired and frustrated from another mind-numbing, soul-sucking day at the office. There'd been another meeting, about what he couldn't say because once again he heard about it after the fact. He was the president of the company and yet he was out of the loop. He had about as much say in policy as the mail clerk. Maybe less. It was Sam Arkoff's company now, not his.

He loosened his tie, unbuttoned his collar and all but collapsed into his favorite chair. He felt as empty as a football. He had to face facts. Things weren't going to get better. Every day Sam pushed the knife a little deeper into his back.

Susan came into the room and saw immediately that her husband had been squeezed dry again. Actually, she would have been surprised to find him in any other condition.

He glanced at her and in a moment of clarity said, "If Sam wants to run things, let him." The time had come to put an end to the torture.

The next morning James Hartford Nicholson told his partner Samuel Zachary Arkoff that he was leaving the company. It wasn't done in an angry fashion. That wasn't Jim's style. And if Sam Arkoff felt a sense of victory, it wasn't on display when he showed up on Al Kallis's doorstep later that night, in tears. "Why did he do it?" Sam asked.

Is it possible that Sam didn't know the answer to his own question? Hadn't he done everything he could possibly do to force his partner out of the company? The only thing surprising about what Jim did was that it took him as long as it did to do it.

In typical Hollywood fashion a phony baloney cover story was concocted for the press: Jim was leaving because he wanted to become an independent producer, when in fact he was leaving because he'd been humiliated and systematically stripped of his authority.

"Because of our close personal relationship over the many years, I naturally regret Jim's decision," Sam lamented. "Jim will still be with us in an advisory capacity, member of the board of directors as well as a large stockholder."

A friend of mine once told me that the stated reason for *anything* was *never* the real reason. Keeping that in mind, when I met Sam Arkoff ten years after the fact, I asked him why Jim left AIP. Naturally, he held fast to the party line. "Around about '68 or '69," he said, "Jim didn't have the energy he used to have. He seemed to be more tired. He wasn't as enthused. I don't know if he didn't like the fact that the company was getting bigger—I don't think he minded that—or if he didn't feel like he could cope with it. Ultimately, he decided he wanted to be an independent producer. He came to me with it and I must admit that the idea kind of floored me."

Later, when I talked with Susan Hart I asked her the same question. At the time she was in the middle of a legal battle with Sam and couldn't be as frank as she might have been and I left knowing that I still didn't have the whole story.

In September of 1972, Sam Arkoff was among the 800 people who turned out to pay tribute to Jim Nicholson at a Variety Club luncheon in the Grand Ballroom of the Beverly Wilshire Hotel. Seated at Jim's table were Dorothy Lamour, Annette Funicello, Harvey Lembeck, Fabian Forte, Les Baxter, Roger Corman, and Morey Amsterdam. Jim was given a plaque which read: "To James H. Nicholson, whose inspirational leadership in showing the way to help those less fortunate has made all our lives fuller and meaningful and who is the living embodiment of the word 'humanitarian.'"

Charity work had been a part of Jim Nicholson's life since his days as class president at Aptos Junior High when he cajoled the manager of the local bijou to have special screenings to raise money for the Red Cross. True to form, as a chief barker of the Variety Clubs, he would often show American International movies to raise money for different causes. In 1969 he produced a 50 minute documentary called *The Heart of Variety*, narrated by Greer Garson, Charlton Heston, Vincent Price, Ed Begley and Burt Topper (who wrote the script). According to the *Hollywood Reporter*, the film modestly and hauntingly showed how $165,000 had been raised by Variety to ease the suffering of afflicted and deprived children. After Jim's death, thanks to the efforts of Susan Hart, the name of the Variety Children's Heart Center at the UCLA School of Medicine was officially changed to the James H. Nicholson Variety Children's Heart Center.

Jim and Sam were in the awkward position of having to pay tribute to each other at the Variety Clubs International 45th annual convention in New York. It must have been a stretch for Jim to assure the audience that he and Sam would always be friends. He promised that AIP, "the company with a heart," would continue to support the organization. He maintained the fiction that he would be producing pictures for AIP when, in fact, that wasn't his intention at all, as evidenced by a meeting he had with Mickey Zide who worked in AIP's publicity department.

Mickey Zide's father had the AIP franchise in Detroit. In the early 1960s Mickey had been involved in a couple of advertising campaigns that Jim liked. "I got a call from him asking me if I'd like to come work for the company. I said, 'When do you want me?' When my son died I was really in bad shape. I didn't go to work for two weeks. Jim called and said he'd just bought two tickets to Hawaii. He wanted me to take two weeks off, go to Hawaii and get some rest. That's the kind of a guy he was. You've never met a nicer guy. So when he asked me to meet him for lunch, at some Beverly Hills restaurant, I went. When I walked in I asked for his table and they took me upstairs to where he was. He told me he was making a deal with Fox and wanted me to come with him. I told him the same thing I'd said ten years earlier. *When do you want me?*"

Jim walked away from AIP and signed a six picture contract with 20th Century Fox. Fox president Gordon T. Stulburg told the press that Jim's uncanny ability to anticipate trends, plus his experience in marketing and merchandising made him quite a catch. The first movie on Jim's agenda was *When the Sleeper Wakes*, based on the novel by H. G. Wells. It was a movie that had been on AIP's list of coming attractions since 1961. In 1963 *The Hollywood Reporter* announced that Jim Nicholson and Nat Cohen would be co-producing it. Cohen was the president of Anglo-Amalgamated, AIP's distributor in the U.K. He'd purchased the rights to the story from the Wells' estate. He and Jim agreed that Vincent Price would star in the picture and that Roger Corman would direct it. One year later the only sign of progress on the project was the addition of Martha Hyer to the cast. Three years later, having gone through two title changes—*2066 A.D.* and *2067 A.D.*—Nicholson and Cohen *still* didn't have a script. It struck Jim that if they continued to drag their feet, the future events described by Wells in his novel would have already transpired. Taking the bull by the horns, Jim asked producer Harry Alan Towers to get the ball rolling. The first thing Towers did was hire director Don Sharp to write a script. Once that was done, Towers negotiated a deal with two companies, Constantin Films in Germany and Avala Films in Czechoslovakia, effectively raising AIP's half of the budget. At this point the title of the picture was *2267 A.D.—When the Sleeper Wakes.* Unfortunately, the money from Avala came with a stipulation. Avala insisted on making the picture in Czechoslovakia. Ultimately, the logistics proved to be more trouble than Avala's money was worth and the deal fell through. Louis M. Heyward took over the project in 1968 and had television writer Sheldon Stark fashion a new script which was given to director Michael Reeves. When Reeves died the project was shelved, only to be revived again two years later when George Pal, well-known for his fantasy films at Paramount and MGM, came on board. Richard Matheson wrote a new script but Pal and AIP couldn't come to an agreement on the approach to the project and once again it collapsed.

So when Jim announced, for the umpteenth time, that he would be making *When the Sleeper Wakes,* there were some of us who were skeptical. With good cause it seems because the first picture he made at Fox was *The Legend of Hell House* (1973), based on the novel by his old friend Richard Matheson. The movie was still in the editing stage when Jim started pre-production on an action picture, *Dirty Mary, Crazy Larry* (1974). He didn't live long enough to see either picture in release.

Jim was having dinner with Susan Hart at the Cock 'n' Bull on the Sunset Strip, where seventeen years earlier he and Roger Corman, over a spare rib dinner, discussed the new distribution company that Jim had in mind. Now, all of a sudden, in spite of the fact that he'd eaten at the place a million times, it was as if he'd never seen it before. He might as well have been on some other planet. Susan didn't know what to do. A concerned waitress suggested she take him to the hospital, which proved to be no easy task. Jim could hardly stand, much less walk. Susan kept a firm grip on him as they negotiated their way across the floor to the exit. He kept bumping into the parking meters on the way to the car and the drive to the hospital seemed to take forever.

The doctor said that Jim had had a seizure. It wasn't the first time. A few months earlier he walked into the New York hotel suite he was sharing with Les Baxter and collapsed. Once he recovered he said to the composer, "I don't know what happened. I've never done that before."[1]

Despite the optimistic predictions by the doctors that he might live another year-and-a-half, Jim Nicholson died from a malignant brain tumor a few months later on December 10, 1972 at the UCLA Medical Center. He was 56 years old. Services were held at Manchester Chapel at Inglewood Park Cemetery. Mickey Zide, Leon Blender, Joe and Milton Moritz, David Melamed, Norman Herman, Al Simms and Salvatore Villitteri were his pall bearers. Sam Arkoff gave the eulogy. Twenty years later Sam wrote his autobiography, *Flying Through Hollywood by the Seat of My Pants* in which he seemed to be doing everything he could to push his ex-partner deeper into the ground. One month after the publication of his book Sam got a star on the Hollywood Walk of Fame.

"He sent copies of the book to my sisters and me," said Jim's daughter, Luree. "After reading it I became so livid and so angry that I wanted to picket his getting that star. He rewrote history and took credit for almost everything my father created. When he was confronted, his response was: 'He's dead. I'm alive.'"[2]

In his book Sam places himself at the center of all of the action, hijacking events that he never participated in with shameless ease. He took credit for nearly every decision that his partner made and much of what his partner said. In Sam's version of American International's history, Jim Nicholson comes off as little more than a footnote.

A decade or so before the publication of his book, I interviewed Sam at his comfortable, but not ostentatious home in Studio City. I sat on his back porch, listening to the soothing sound of the running water in his fountain as

American International Pictures toppers, James H. Nicholson (left), president, and Samuel Z. Arkoff, executive vice-president, are observing the tenth anniversary of their company with the implementation of plans to carry AIP to new plateaus of progress in the "celebration year" and for the future. The program is well under way, with a stepping up of product output, both in quantity and quality. Story on page 8.

Will Rogers Hospital Leaders Make Annual Progress Report
—Page 6

Jim Nicholson and Sam Arkoff.

he told me the story of his life and his days at AIP. His wife Hilda served us a very good fish lunch. Throughout the meal Sam never stopped talking and I didn't want him to. He talked mostly about AIP's formative years, when he and Jim nursed each and every movie along as if it were a new born baby. Whenever I attempted to ascertain who did what on any given film he became annoyed with me and finally said, "Who knows what exactly anybody does on any picture? I mean we get that shit all the time. And it bores the shit out of me because I couldn't care less. You would think when you see credits that the credits must mean something, and they do in a sense. But on the other hand, I've been on pictures where the director was a dolt and yet, somehow, the picture came out all right." As far as Sam was concerned all of this fussing about who did what was "little minds at work." As for *his* involvement, he didn't feel the need to take credit for *anything*. "It's so ridiculous," he said, "as if somehow posterity's gonna give a shit."

Sam may have been right about posterity. Over the years American International has become little more than a hiccup in motion picture history. But obviously Sam gave a shit or he wouldn't have written his book, a book that was prompted by the publication of Roger Corman's autobiography. Corman made movies for American International. Books and magazine articles had been written about him. He was even the subject of a couple of documentaries. It probably irritated the hell out of Sam that just about the only reason people came knocking on his door was to pump him for information about Corman. Why? Because Corman was a filmmaker. He'd been in the trenches. Sam was a lawyer. He sat behind a desk and negotiated contracts. He rarely came to the set unless there was a legal problem. By no stretch of the imagination was he a filmmaker, in spite of the fact that his name appears on hundreds of films.

It never suited Sam to think of films as art. To him motion pictures were merchandise. Commerce. He had nothing but contempt for anyone who thought otherwise. *Arty-farty.* That was his favorite expression, his way of dismissing quality. When some critic praised one of Corman's movies, Sam nearly fell over himself in an effort to set the critic straight. "Don't believe

Roger's arty façade. The important thing to remember about him is that he's a good, sound businessman." That remark betrays Sam's jealousy of Corman's ability as well as his fear that a good film might actually sink the company. In many ways Sam was like the kid in school who wasn't smart enough or motivated enough to get good grades and made fun of the kids who did. To be fair, most of the people working at the ass-end of the motion picture business agree with Sam's contention that it made no sense to make some arty-farty picture that might lose money and put you out of business. Who could argue with that? But what exactly did he mean by arty-farty? Was he talking about deeply personal introspective movies or simply movies that were made with skill and care by someone who was interested in making a good piece of entertainment? Because if you care enough, even with the odds against you, you can still make a good low budget movie that'll make money. Corman proved that often enough. So did Anthony Mann and Sam Fuller. The fact of the matter is Sam Arkoff never cared if a movie was good or bad so long as he could sell it. And that's giving him credit for knowing the difference, by which I do not mean to suggest that Sam was not an intelligent man.

Sam often said that he couldn't care less if people didn't like his movies and that included his wife Hilda (he called her Slim). The movies she liked never made money. When you factor in all of the elements, his lack of regard for public opinion, his indifference to quality, and the fact that he never had a dream project of his own, you have a businessman, not a filmmaker. And Sam was perfectly satisfied with being a businessman until he made his fortune. Like so many other scoundrels, once he got the money he wanted respect. But to get it, he needed to be remembered as something other than a businessman, and if that meant he had to throw his partner under the bus, so be it.

"He had no interest in making movies, only in making deals," said Susan Hart. "Sam continues to take full credit for films he made with my late husband, which distorts true history. But he has to live with himself on that issue."[3]

The one bone Sam was always willing to toss Jim was his ability to dream up money-making titles, though he finally threw water on that bit of praise by falsely claiming Jim lost his creative edge when he stopped drinking. The fact of the matter is Jim Nicholson never *started* drinking. And he *never* lost his creative edge. His parting gift to Sam and AIP was *Blacula* (1972), a title and concept that kicked off a successful cycle of black exploitation films in the early 1970s that Sam was able to milk for years after Jim was pushing up dirt.

Unfortunately, Sam's campaign to seize the lion's share of the credit for everything has succeeded. Over the years lazy journalists have printed everything that Sam told them without question. He now dominates AIP's history to the point that when you Google James H. Nicholson you get an image of Samuel Z. Arkoff. But the people who were there, who worked with them both, know the truth.

"Jim Nicholson was the brains of the outfit," said actor Michael Connors. "Arkoff was the businessman. Sam never met a man he didn't like... to screw. As far as I'm concerned, he didn't have a lot of integrity. You never knew what he was going to do. And he was always angling, maneuvering... always had that phony smile on his face and a great big cigar."[4]

"Of the two, Nicholson and Sam Arkoff, I felt that Jim was the more literate," said Louis M. Heyward, the man in charge of the company's overseas productions. "There was Arkoff, puffing his big brown cigar and pontificating on the lack of art in the business, but really not doing anything *but* business, and Jim, really being involved in film. Jim truly loved film, and he also loved horror—he was the one who came up with the idea of doing the Edgar Allan Poe films."[5]

"Jim Nicholson was the head of production, the idea man and—just as importantly—the title man and the poster man," said Roger Corman. "He had been a theater owner and ran double-bills where he had learned from experience what would work. Jim realized that if you put two low-budget black and white films on a similar theme together, more people would come. For instance, two science-fiction films, two horror films, two gangster films, or two teenage-gang films, which were very popular at the time. You would think that you might appeal to two different audiences if you put a science-fiction picture with a romantic picture, but Jim simply found from experience that what audiences wanted was two-of-the-same kind of pictures; that went straight to the core audience. That whole idea is what really made AIP a success."[6]

According to Corman, there isn't a single movie in AIP's inventory that Sam could lay claim to. And that's coming from a guy who ought to know. Corman was there from the beginning. He was as much a part of AIP as Jim and Sam. It was his independently made movie, *The Fast and The Furious*, that got the American Releasing Corporation (which later became American International Pictures) started back in 1954.

Jim borrowed $3,000 from fellow exhibitor Joe Moritz[7] so that he, Sam and Roger could fly to New Orleans, Chicago and New York to screen Corman's film for the franchise holders. Jim knew most of these guys from his days as an exhibitor. He knew what they wanted, he knew how they bought their films, and he knew they were hungry for product. After they saw the film they agreed to pony up some money, anywhere from five to fifteen thou-

Dorothy Malone is kidnapped by escaped criminal
John Ireland in *The Fast and the Furious*.

sand dollars depending on the size of their territory. For their money they were promised two more films of comparable quality that would not be offered to their competitors. In those first few months, ARC was truly a family business, headquartered in the Nicholson household.

"My mother participated heavily," said Luree Nicholson. "She doesn't get the credit that she should. She did all the paperwork, kept the files; kept track of the films and the money. She was his partner and his muse. He ran everything by her."[8]

Luree's mother, Sylvia Svoboda, was an usherette at one of the theaters Jim Nicholson managed when he was living in Omaha back in the 40s. They'd only known each other for six weeks when they decided to tie the knot. They had three children—Luree, Loretta and Laura Lynn. The kids liked to hang around the sets and often traveled with their father on promotional tours. "[My dad] never raised his voice and he never spanked us. He was very philosophical, quoting Shakespeare, Plato, etc., and into spiritual beliefs like mind over matter and the continuation of the soul after death."[9]

As the company grew Jim and Sylvia took a small office in The Lawyer's Building at 6223 Selma Avenue, where Sam Arkoff had his office. Joe Moritz took over as treasurer, and his son, Milt, was the director of publicity and advertising. Leon Blender was their sales manager. Alex Gordon was in charge of casting, wrote copy for the pressbooks, and produced some of the movies. Sam Arkoff agreed to handle the legal work for a 25 per cent share in the company. By the end of 1955 ARC had four more features in release.

"The first few pictures were not great pictures," Leon Blender admitted. "The exhibitors wouldn't look at them because if they looked at them they wouldn't buy them. They would look at Jim's ad campaigns and press sheets instead."

Things got off to a rocky start. Most of the exhibitors used the movies to support bigger pictures, which meant ARC wasn't entitled to a split of the box office. Supporting features got a flat $25 rental fee. Jim gave a speech at a Theatre Owners of America (TOA) meeting in which he begged the exhibitors to give his company a fair shake. As far as they were concerned business

Apache Woman was the first of four westerns released by ARC.

was business. If ARC went belly up it was no skin off their noses. There'd be some other nitwit outfit to take its place soon enough.

Jim had to find a way to pry a percentage out of these people in order to survive. He did it by offering two films for a fraction of what the majors were asking for a single feature, a package deal so to speak, which gave ARC control over the program. He came up with two titles, *Day the World Ended* and *The Phantom from 10,000 Leagues* (both 1956). Lou Rusoff, Sam Arkoff's brother-in-law, wrote the screenplays around those titles.

The major studios had star power to help sell their films. ARC had to rely on the exploitability of the subject. Nevertheless, exhibitors wanted familiar

Marty the Mutant (Paul Blaisdell) is flanked by writer Lou Rusoff on the left and producer Alex Gordon on the right, on the set of *Day the World Ended*.

names for their marquees. In his role as the casting director, Alex Gordon chose people who'd been under contract to the studios, actors who never quite made it or supporting players. Later, when the company switched gears and made movies for young people, the need for name actors was no longer necessary. Newcomers were hired at SAG minimum.

Kent Taylor and Cathy Downs were chosen for the leads in *The Phantom from 10,000 Leagues*. Downs had been a Fox contract player and was coming off *The Joe Palooka Story* TV series when she appeared in *The Phantom*. Her co-star, Kent Taylor, was the star of TV's *Boston Blackie* and had made over 60 movies as a supporting player. Alex Gordon wanted Richard Denning and Lori Nelson for the leads in *Day the World Ended* because they'd recently appeared in The Creature series at Universal.

While Roger Corman was busy making *The Day the World Ended*, Jim cut a deal with a couple of film editors, Jack and Dan Milner, to make *The Phantom* for a 60/40 split in the profits. After watching their picture, Jim told the brothers they should stick to editing. One exhibitor said it was the "biggest clinker" of the year and hoped to God there wasn't anything worse coming his way.

At first the distributors wanted to split the package and use the movies as supporting features. Jim held his ground. A newspaper strike in Detroit saved the day. None of the studios wanted to open their movies without the support of newspaper advertising. A desperate exhibitor booked the two pictures and was happily surprised by the number of people who showed up. Before long the package was playing to packed houses in New York, Chicago, Boston, and Dallas. More prints were ordered to meet the demand.

"Those two pictures played at The Hollywood Theatre for four weeks!" Alex Gordon recalled. "The theatre never played any picture for longer than a week. That combination really put AIP on the map."

By March the company had a new name, American International Pictures, and a new address—8255 Sunset Boulevard. And Jim Nicholson had a partner—Sam Arkoff.

Luree Nicholson didn't know how Sam talked her father into making him a partner but I think I can guess. Taking care of the legal work had be-

Lori Nelson and Richard Denning.

come a full-time job once the company was up and running. Sam probably felt he deserved a partnership. Jim must have thought so too.

"My father kept the controlling interest," Luree told me. "I believe he had fifty-one percent of the stock and Sam had forty-nine percent, which is why my father's name is always listed first. Sam handled the legal and financial aspects of the company. My father had no interest in that part of the business. He didn't want anything to do with it. He was the good cop. He wore the white suit. Sam was the bad cop. He wore the black suit. They joked about it."

Jim Nicholson was working at Realart as Jack Broder's office manager when he met Sam Arkoff. Broder and his partner, Joseph Harris, had taken a ten-year lease on Universal's entire film library for $3 million bucks in 1948, when Universal was merging with International Pictures and needed some fast

Sam Arkoff and Jim Nicholson, partners.

cash. Broder's bargain rate, pre-packaged combo programs of horror pictures, comedies and dramas all but saved the independent exhibitors who were at the end of the food chain. Sometimes Broder would slap a new title on one of the old movies, to bring it up to date so to speak, and that's exactly what Sam Arkoff wanted to see him about. Sam's client, Alex Gordon, had left a script with Broder called *The Atomic Monster*. Broder rejected the script then used the title on an old Lon Chaney movie. Sam wanted some money. Jim didn't think he had a snowball's chance in Hell of getting it. He'd been with Broder long enough to know his boss would rather part with a finger than part with a buck. When Sam walked out with a $500 check Jim was impressed.

Before coming to work for Broder, Jim had taken a lease on four theaters. Once again it was Joe Moritz who loaned him the money to do it. Anyone who knew Jim well could have predicted he'd get into exhibition. His sister Betty told me, "When we were kids he turned our basement into a theatre. I sold the tickets for a penny and was in charge of the refreshments, usually a pitcher of lemonade. Jim ran the projector. He rented movies from the camera store. Some of them were home-made."

Jim would have been delighted to take advantage of Broder's pre-packaged genre double-features had they been available when he owned his theatres because that's exactly the kind of program he specialized in. And he'd done all right until some of his fellow exhibitors followed his lead. The competition was more than the market could bear and Jim lost his theaters, his home, and his car to back taxes.

In his quest to find his place in show business, Jim had been a spot man in a burlesque house, a radio announcer and performer. He and his family had always lived hand-to-mouth and when he lost the theatres Sylvia was fed up. She took the children, moved in with her mother, and filed for divorce. As soon as she landed a job with Lockheed Martin she and the children moved into an apartment owned by her grandmother. She'd hardly had a chance to settle in when all of the kids got the measles.

It has been my experience that when the universe decides to have its way with you, things usually go from bad to worse. Jim Nicholson was sinking into a state of depression over being broke and abandoned when he came down with pneumonia. Ill health had dogged the blue-eyed, brown hair ex-theatre owner all of his life. When he was seventeen a sinus condition forced him to quit his job at a theatre in San Francisco to seek the warmer climate of Southern California where he came down with scarlet fever. Now he was so sick he didn't have the strength to get out of bed.

Leon Blender heard that Jim was in bad shape and took up a collection to send him to the hospital. "He used to book films from me when I worked at 20th Century Fox," Leon said. "We got to be friends. Jim Nicholson was a very warm man. He used to come over to our apartment every once in a while for dinner. The place was a dump. After I adopted my daughter and went to work for Jim he said, 'Why don't you go find a house?' I told him I needed money. 'Find a house,' he said. 'We'll find the money.' And he loaned me the money."[10]

Fortunately Jim's parents (Percival and Esther) had moved to Los Angeles so he had a place to stay while he recovered from what turned out to be a collapsed lung. A guy has a lot of time to think when he's flat on his back and Jim came to the conclusion that it was time for him to stop *showing* movies and start *making* them. He wanted to open a production and distribution company but he needed some seed money to do it. One of the first people he approached was Sidney Pink, a fellow exhibitor who had co-produced a couple of films with Arch Obler, the creator of the popular radio series *Lights Out.* In his autobiography Pink said he turned Jim down cold because Jim had tried to steal his theatres while Pink was in the service. Frankly, that doesn't sound like something Jim would do.

The next person he approached was Leon Blender, who was working for Jack Broder at the time as Realart's branch manager. Leon didn't have the money but he had a job for Jim as Broder's sales manager. Leon had also secured a secretarial position for Sylvia at Realart.

Sylvia had decided not to go through with the divorce. She decided to move back in with Jim. It wasn't long before she wished she hadn't and blamed Luree for getting them back together.

"She could never take responsibility for anything," Luree told me.

"When she was dying from pneumonia after her stroke, her last words to my sister Laura, were: It was all your father's fault."

Jim became friends with a young ambitious fellow named Herman Cohen, who'd come to work for Broder as his assistant when Broder decided to get into film production. By the time Jim arrived Jack Broder Productions was on hold and Cohen was getting antsy. He entered into a co-production deal with Nat Cohen (no relation) at Anglo Amalgamated Films in England and finally left Realart in 1954 to produce his first stateside feature, *Target Earth*, based on a short story called 'Deadly City' by Paul Fairman.

"Jim Nicholson was with me when I found the magazine with the story in it at a newsstand on North Las Palmas," Cohen told Tom Weaver. "Jim took the story and started writing a treatment for it, and I bought the treatment from Jim, I think for two hundred fifty dollars."

Cohen used Jim's treatment to develop a script with writer Bill Raynor and took the project to Steve Broidy at Allied Artists. Broidy put up half the money; Cohen raised the rest. The modest $85,000 feature helped Cohen get a four picture deal with United Artists.

"Jim wanted me to be his partner," Cohen said. "Sam Arkoff would never have been around if I had been Jim's partner! Because Jim and I were close personal friends even after I left Broder. Jim told me his ideas and this and that, and I said, 'Jim, I can't come with you'—this was while I was in the midst of making those four pictures for UA. 'But anything you need,' I told him, 'my secretary, my staff and I will help you.' In fact, we did all his mimeographing and everything else at my offices!"

As one might assume from Cohen's remark, he had no use for Sam Arkoff, and the feeling was mutual. "We kept up what you might call a forced cordiality," Sam told me. He thought Herman was pompous. I agree. He was pretty full of himself. Whenever he quoted anyone, the quote usually began with his own name.

"Herm, do you think…?"

"Herm, could you make us a horror movie about a…?"

"Herm, I've got a problem. I don't know how to…"

Herm, do you ever get tired of hearing the sound of your own name?

However, to give him his due, and though Sam would have been loath to admit it, Herman Cohen played a significant role in AIP's history. His *I Was a Teenage Werewolf* (1957) was a huge money-maker. He also produced the company's first color and CinemaScope feature. Even more important, he brokered a lucrative distribution deal for AIP with Anglo Amalgamated.

Let's take a break from the narrative for just a moment to shine some light on a few of the other key players in AIP's success story.

Lou Rusoff was the company's resident writer. A moody, brooding individual who lived with his wife and son in a nice Laurel Canyon home, he had written for Canadian radio and television before coming to AIP. Sam said: "Often, he was working on five or six scripts simultaneously—not only his own but rewriting other people's screenplays when emergencies occurred and the original writers were unavailable. He also eventually produced some of the AIP movies he wrote."[11]

Rusoff's son Ted became a production assistant and often worked as an unpaid, uncredited extra. Eventually, he oversaw the dubbing of such movies as *War of the Zombies, The Last Man on Earth* (both 1963) and *Dr. Goldfoot and the Girl Bombs* (1966). "I knew nothing whatsoever about dubbing at the time," he told writer Harvey F. Chartrand, "but apparently just having someone from the home office breathing down their necks made the vocal actors tow the line and the dubbings improved."

Brooklyn born Edward L. Cahn joined the company in 1956 at Jim Nicholson's request. He'd spent most of his career directing short subjects at MGM during the 40s and graduated to B-movies in the early 50s. He directed Jack Broder's first feature, *Two Dollar Bettor* (1951). He was an imposing figure, full of bluff and bluster, dramatically waving his pipe whenever he was trying to make a point. When the pipe was in his mouth you couldn't understand half of what he said. His daughter, Judith, often worked as his script girl. Knowing that Cahn shared Alex Gordon's love of old movies, Jim put the two together as a producer-director team. Cahn made eleven features for AIP, nine of them produced by Gordon.

Alex Gordon had been a publicist for Renown Pictures in England before coming to Hollywood. He was acting as Gene Autry's publicist when he became involved in a low budget western called *The Outlaw Marshall* (1954) starring Johnny Carpenter. The picture went over budget and before it was finished there were labor claims and lab liens attached to it and the people who'd put money into the thing were screaming to get it back. "It got to such a state that I needed a lawyer," Alex told me. "Carpenter had once been involved with Sam Arkoff on something else so Carpenter said, 'I know a lawyer named Sam Arkoff.' So that's how I first met Arkoff. "

Bartlett A. Carre was AIP's production manager. It was his job to see to it that the movies never went over budget, something he'd been doing since 1930. He started in the business as an actor in 1924 and appeared in 41 features, one of which he directed. He served as an associate producer on a number of AIP films before he retired in 1963.

Ronald Sinclair also started in the business as an actor. Louis B. Mayer put him under contract for the sole purpose of using him as a threat to keep Mickey Rooney in line. Sinclair became a film editor hoping it would lead to his becoming a director, which it never did.

Ronald Stein supplied the music for almost every AIP film in the 1950s. "He was great," said Alex Gordon. "What we did, we'd give him $5,000 and that would be his and the score would be his—he insisted that he would retain the rights to his scores because he wanted to build up a music library, which he did. He would take the $5,000, he'd go to either Mexico or Munich and there he'd get a whole orchestra, twenty or more people, sometimes thirty, and give us a terrific score, for a price we could afford."[12]

After Stein fell out of favor, his old cues were used without his permission. Since he owned the publishing rights he felt he should receive some compensation. When he complained about it, Sam Arkoff showed up at his home one evening and the two men had a little tête-a-tête behind closed doors. Stein's wife, Harlene, said that when they emerged forty-five minutes later, her husband's face was ashen. And he never complained about anything again.

Les Baxter replaced Stein as the company's resident composer. Said Baxter: "Nicholson would give me a few ideas of what he wanted, and I would listen to them and give him everything he wanted. But most people don't realize that a composer has infinitely more technique at his command than the few suggestions that are given, and he can embellish those greatly. It's no problem to give a producer what he wants; I'm sure that some of the temperamental composers fight that and say, 'No, I don't wanna be told what to do,' or 'I wanna do just what I wanna do.' It's also a simple matter to give the producer what he wants and much more."[13]

Al Kallis was the guy responsible for the wonderfully lurid poster art that sold AIP's movies to the exhibitors, the distributors and to the public. One enthusiastic exhibitor said Kallis was worth his weight in gold, which he most certainly was. Another exhibitor said he wished they could put sprocket holes in his posters. Kallis was working for Saul Bass at Paramount when Roger Corman, who had just finished a feminist western called *Gunslinger* (1956), asked him what it would take to lure him away from Bass. "I told him that once we agreed on the approach the advertising would take, the rest was up to me. He had to leave me alone. He agreed, especially after I told him I'd give him a fixed rate."

Kallis was just what Jim Nicholson had been looking for. He asked him to join the team and the two men closed the deal on a handshake. Luree recalled many a morning when Kallis, Milt Moritz and her father would sit at the kitchen table spit-balling ideas.

"Jim had the best sense of exploitation I ever encountered in a distributor," Kallis said. "Jim and I would make up most of the titles and kick around what the advertising approach would be. That was a creative area everybody could get in on. Then, I'd make up an ad campaign. We'd send out 8 by 10s of the layouts to theater owners. If it looked like they were going to book the picture, we'd make it."[14]

In the early days, Kallis would watch the movies to see what elements he could exploit. He started reading scripts instead because the movies were generally so mundane they stifled his imagination. Ultimately, he found that it was better to simply work from Jim's titles, which occasionally backfired.

After raising the money to make a western called *Dead Man's Gun*, Mike Connors was asked to meet with Jim and Kallis. They showed him an illustration of the film's leading lady tied to a stake on an anthill, surrounded by Indians. The title had been changed to *Flesh and the Spur* (1957) "This is the way we're going to promote your picture," Jim told him. "Fellas, that's beautiful," Connors said, "but we got no Indians in the picture. There are no Indians, there's no anthill, there's nothing like that in the script." They said, "Well, that's the thing we're talking to you about. We're gonna have to put in a scene." Connors couldn't believe it. "You mean, right in the middle of the picture, suddenly a bunch of Indians appear and grab her and put her on this anthill and disappear?" They said, "That's right because this is how we're gonna promote the picture!"[15]

At least Connors had some advance warning. Roger Corman had completed a movie about an invisible alien called *The Unseen* when he was told that Jim had changed the title to *The Beast with 1,000,000 Eyes* (1955) and had sold the picture to the exhibitors with a very visible monster on the poster. Corman had to find somebody that could make a monster fast and cheap. And that's when Paul Blaisdell entered the picture. He became AIP's go-to guy for creepy creatures and unusual props. A shy man who lived with his wife, Jackie, in a house tucked away in Topanga Canyon, accessible only by a suspension bridge. Blaisdell created some of the most memorable monsters of the 1950s.

"[He] was a very nice man but a very strange person," Alex Gordon said of him. "He wanted everything *his* way and he felt that that was the correct way and, frankly, I think he was probably right."[16]

Blaisdell refused to deal with anyone but Jim Nicholson. He didn't want to have to answer to a bunch of people, especially Sam Arkoff. Naively believing that he was part of 'the family' and would ultimately grow with the company, Blaisdell continued to work for peanuts. When AIP moved into bigger productions the 'family' gave him the old heave-ho. From time to time, Jim would find some little something for him to do but it wasn't

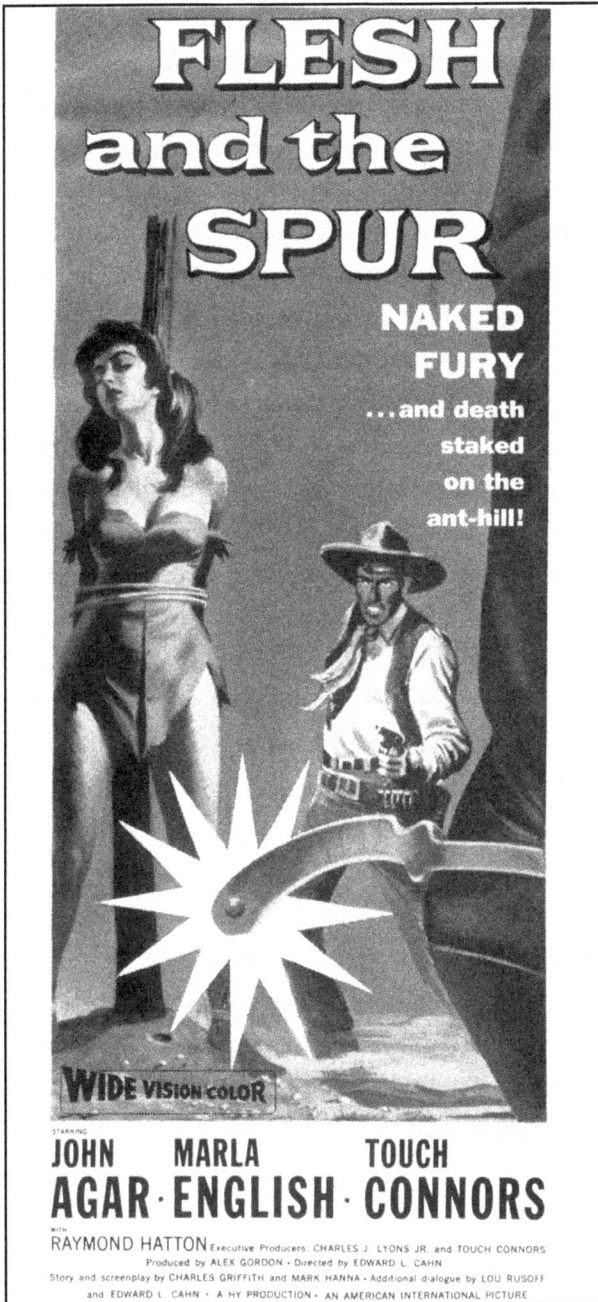

Flesh and the Spur (1957) artwork by Al Kallis.

enough to keep Blaisdell afloat. He paid the bills with carpentry work, becoming bitter and reclusive, losing touch with the few friends he had. When I telephoned him for an interview in 1983 he asked me to send him some blank cassette tapes and a list of questions. He wouldn't meet with me in person. When he died from stomach cancer that year, his passing caused nary a blip on Hollywood's radar. Five years later his home was all but destroyed by a mudslide and was condemned by the city. The neighbors naturally assumed that Jackie had moved out until they found her corpse in 2006. She'd been living in the house for seventeen years without plumbing or electricity.

Bert I. Gordon had been making commercials in Wisconsin before coming to AIP. His *The Amazing Colossal Man* (1957) was one of AIP's most popular movies and the first one to play New York's prestigious Broadway Theatre. Sam Arkoff told me that the reason Bert left the company was because he got too big for his britches and started making unreasonable demands which Arkoff blamed on his wife, Flora, whom he called "a ball-buster." But then Sam thought any woman who spoke her mind was a ball-buster. He didn't have a lot of respect for women, something he shared in common with Herman Cohen. He liked his women passive and silent. The truth was Bert thought he was being cheated and accused Jim and Sam in open court of diverting the profits from his pictures into their other companies, which was true. And here's the way it was done.

Sam set up a string of corporations. Roger Corman had a share in Palo Alto Productions. Nicholson and Corman owned Sunset Productions. Nicholson, Arkoff, Alex Gordon and Lou Rusoff were partners in Golden State Productions. And Bert Gordon had a stake in Malibu, Alta Vista and Carmel. Whenever a picture started to show a profit, Sam would dump another picture into that corporation, giving AIP a new write-off. This sleight of hand kept both the IRS and the profit participators at bay for years.

"Basically," said Corman, "depending on who you were, [AIP] had multiple statements... I was getting solid profit participation payments [on *Bloody Mama*] and Shelley Winters was saying: 'This picture is playing everywhere, it didn't cost very much to make. I can't believe it's never gone

Paul and Jackie Blaisdell at home.

into profit.'"[17]

Edward Bernds, Richard Matheson, Jack Rabin and Sidney Pink were just a few of the people who shared her astonishment. After going over the company's books, Sid Pink's lawyer came to the conclusion that a movie could play in every theater in the world and never show a profit the way Sam kept the books.

So what else is new? Hollywood is notorious for its creative bookkeeping. According to novelist and screenwriter Niven Busch, Jack Warner was the master of double-entry bookkeeping. "[Warner Bros.] had the most foolproof, plate-steel system in the world. I still don't know, and I don't think anybody else does, how they do it."[18]

Remember back in 1979, when the lines of people waiting to see *Alien* stretched for as far as the eye could see? It was one of the most success-

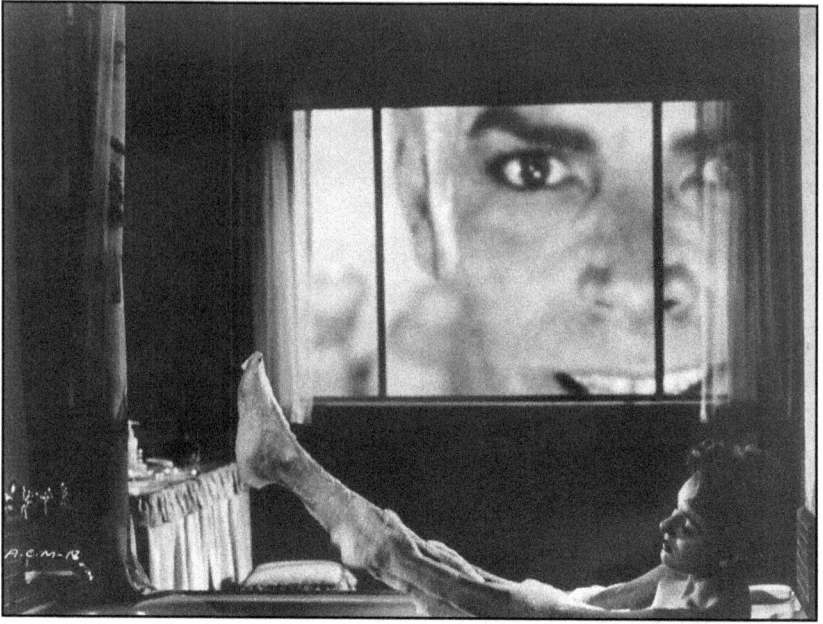

Above: Jean Moorhead didn't know there was such a thing as a 60ft tall peeping Tom. Below: Cathy Downs hopes that William Hudson and Larry Thor can drive that giant hypodermic needle into the ankle of her 60ft tall fiancé and stop him from growing any taller. From *The Amazing Colossal Man* (1957).

ful films that year and yet 20th Century Fox maintained, in spite of the evidence to the contrary, that the picture never broke even. Then there was the famous Buchwald vs. Paramount lawsuit that forced the studio to explain how *Coming to America*, which had earned a record breaking $288 million in revenues, had yet to turn a net profit. This practice of wholesale thievery is cynically referred to as "Hollywood Accounting" and it's all quite legal, though it shouldn't be. In a business that makes its fortune by manufacturing fantasies, bookkeeping is just another of its fantasies. Movies are made to generate income, not profit. Corporations sell their movies to companies they own for less than their worth. It's the old shell game. Forget the guy who steals a couple of bucks from the 7-Eleven. These are the people who should be behind bars. But the biggest thieves in this world rarely see the inside of a courtroom, much less prison. In the grand scheme of things Sam Arkoff was small potatoes. And it would be naïve, if not ridiculous, to believe that Jim Nicholson didn't know what he was up to.

Bert Gordon and June Kenney during a
rehearsal for *Earth Vs. the Spider* (1958)

Jim Nicholson, Dean Parkyn (in make-up created by Jack Young for *War of the Colossal Beast*), Sam Arkoff, and Leon Blender.

In the May 27, 1964 edition of the *Motion Picture Herald*, Raymond Levy wrote:

> One of the points of being able to make a quick decision whenever it may be advisable to do so, Jim Nicholson and Sam Arkoff derive a special kind of pleasure by revealing now the fact that many deals that seemed to be made by one of them in his office were actually agreed upon by the pair in quick consultation. Between the office of president Nicholson and the office of executive vice president Arkoff is a private washroom; when both men have visitors and a fast decision may be advantageous, the washroom serves as a place for all the 'conference' they need. There could be significance in their philosophy that 'too many cooks spoil the broth' in decision-making.

Any 'washroom' decision that might lead to an uncomfortable situation was always handled by Sam Arkoff. Confrontations were Jim Nicholson's worst nightmare. To put it bluntly, he had no backbone. Couple this with the fact that he wanted everyone to like him and you have a combination that would have crippled his efforts to build AIP into a thriving business had he not hooked up with Sam Arkoff. Jim's creative marketing sense and his public relations abilities were a perfect complement to Sam's ruthless business savvy.

"Sam Arkoff was the smartest negotiator that I ever met in the motion picture industry," declared Roger Corman. "In business, of course, you always try to get the edge. And I remember on one picture we were working out the budget, and we were $10,000 apart on my fee. I said, 'Sam, I'll flip you for the last $10,000.' We were all young at the time, and the dollar was worth maybe a fifth of what it is now. So for a couple of young guys who didn't have a great deal of money, this was an audacious proposal. And Sam immediately said OK. We flipped, and I won the $10,000. On every negotiation from thereon in, Sam somehow negotiated to the point where we were always $10,000 apart, and we'd always flip for it. And after my first win, he won every single time. I told him after a while that I wanted to examine the quarter."[19]

"Jim sat behind the immaculate desk in a big office, in a suit and tie and a smile," said writer Chuck Griffith. "He was the one that invited you in. He was the one who asked you to do the picture. He'd tell you how good it was going to be. Then you'd go see Sam in his shirttails with his coat off, and he'd start talking hard facts. 'Tits and ass. Sex and violence. That's all we need. Anything else is arty-farty.' Sam was the dynamo."

In their respective roles as good cop/bad cop it's only natural that Sam Arkoff would emerge as the villain of the story, especially in light of his campaign to drive his partner out of the company. It was a crummy thing to do. No question about it. But it was more than just a power grab as we will later see.

Jim and Sam get the credit for discovering the 'teen market,' but that honor goes to Sam Katzman, who blazed the trail with his low budget, teenage musical *Rock Around the Clock* (1956). Jim and Sam simply had the good sense to follow his lead. While the major studios continued to doggedly make the same sort of family friendly movies they'd always made, AIP stepped in with movies aimed at teenagers and children, or to quote Sam Arkoff, "children and morons." AIP's 1956 line-up included *Hot Rod Girl* ("teenage terrorists tearing up the streets"), *It Conquered the World* ("every man its prisoner… every woman its slave"), *The She-Creature* ("reincarnated as a monster from Hell"), *Shake, Rattle and Rock* ("rock 'n' roll vs. the squares) and *Runaway Daughters* ("they called her jailbait!").

The exhibitors were well aware of the shift in the age group of their customers. In his address to 150 top executives and theater managers, Norman Rydge, the managing director of the Greater Union Theaters, told his audience that young people were the motion picture industry's safeguard. "Every age group offers potential patronage for the movies," he said, "but our task from this moment onward is to concentrate on the young people, creating and developing in them regular picture-going habits. In this way the industry will not only safeguard today's attendances, but also build up insurance for the future."[20] He was singing Jim Nicholson's song. It would be safe to say that Jim was far more interested in what his children had to say about the pictures than the critics. He put a screening room in his home so they could watch the movies as a family.

"We didn't think the movies were very good but they were fun," said Luree.

One of Jim's daughters came up with the catchy title for Herman Cohen's *I Was a Teenage Werewolf*. She'd seen it in a piece of satire written for the May 1956 issue of *Dig*, a popular teenage magazine.

Cohen brought his werewolf script to AIP after the last of his four pictures for United Artists tanked. He went on a little road trip and discovered what Jim and Sam already knew—teenagers were the ones who were buying the tickets. So he and his friend Aben Kandel wrote a script with this new audience in mind. The story they concocted, a clever combination of the horror and juvenile delinquency genres, concerned a troubled teenager who is turned into a werewolf by the psychiatrist, who is supposed to be helping him curb his anger. The movie took seven days and $85,000 to make. It's easily the best movie that Herman Cohen ever produced and one of the best in AIP's canon as well.

"At first I wasn't sure I wanted to put my name on the film," Cohen said. "Then people from *Time* and *Newsweek* and *Life* started calling the office. They'd heard about the picture and wanted to know who was producing it. I didn't want to pass up the publicity. It was the title that made them so curious."

Released in June of '57, it grossed well over $2 million by the end of the year. Cohen and Kandel went to work on a follow-up—*I Was a Teenage Frankenstein* (1957). It was still in the butt-scratching stage when a chance conversation with exhibitor and theatre-owner R.J. O'Donnell threw everything into fourth gear.

Robert J. O'Donnell, known as 'The King of Texas Interstate' by his fellow exhibitors, and 'The Boss with a heart of Irish Gold' by his employees, was having lunch with Jim and Sam one afternoon around Labor Day and it didn't take him long to start bitching about being gouged by the major studios. "I hate to give those bastards Thanksgiving week," he grumbled. Thanksgiving week has always been one of the most profitable weeks of the year for exhibitors. Knowing that O'Donnell had done good business with *Teenage Werewolf*, Jim jumped right in. "We've got *I Was a Teenage Franken-stein* in the works." O'Donnell grinned. "If you can have it ready by Thanks-giving I'll give it The Majestic, but I'll need another feature to go with it."

The Majestic was O'Donnell's 2,400-seat Flagship Theater in Dallas. AIP could clean up in a theater like that. Jim Nicholson explained the situa-tion to Herman Cohen, who hammered out another script with Aben Kan-del, *Blood of Dracula* (1957), and the two pictures were shot back-to-back in four weeks. As promised, the pictures played The Majestic on Thanksgiving Day and opened in 75 Texas theaters on the 28th. Total domestic rentals for the package came in at $686,000, quite a bit less than *Teenage Werewolf*, but still a sizeable profit for such an unremarkable pair of movies.[21]

Harold Bell, an exhibitor in Quebec, sent an open letter to *Boxoffice* mag-azine praising American International. "We have finally found out that Cin-emaScope and all those other super ideas they are trying to sell us just don't work," he wrote. "Don't think for a moment we haven't tried them all. We have. Then, while gasping for air, we picked up what we think is a small com-pany going places with good pictures at prices we are able to live with. To all the small theatres that have not played these pictures, get on the band wagon and make yourselves enough for a steak dinner with a few of these—*Dragstrip Girl, I Was a Teenage Werewolf, Reform School Girl, The Amazing Colossal Man, Naked Paradise* and many others. They're all from American International."

As crazy as this may sound, one disgruntled exhibitor wrote a letter ex-pressing his displeasure with the AIP package he booked and was angry at his customers for packing the house. Fellow exhibitor Harold Smith wrote in response: "I think it's a shame that a person will criticize a company that goes out of its way to make pictures that will do above average business for both large and small town exhibitors. I appreciate AIP's showmanship and fair dealings with both large and small. Keep those money-makers rolling. I'm behind you all the way."

1957 was a golden year for AIP. *Teenage Werewolf* made a small fortune, *Teenage Frankenstein* played a flagship theater, and *The Amazing Colossal Man*

Herman Cohen and Aben Kandel.

(1957) was the first AIP movie to open in one of New York's prestigious Broadway theaters. While RKO and Republic were sinking into Hollywood history, everything seemed to be falling into place for AIP. Jim explained the secret behind the company's success to Ivan Spear at *Boxoffice*. "You have to talk to exhibitors about other things than terms. You can't sit in an ivory tower and force-feed them with product created without regard for the theatreman and his market. The exhibitor, humanly enough, wants what he thinks he can sell. The producer and distributor can find out what that is by meeting with him. The meeting can't be a quick 'Howdy,' either. It has to be for enough time to strive at something."

Feeling pretty good about themselves, Jim and Sam took over a master lease on Charlie Chaplin's old studio on Sunset and La Brea. They moved out of their Sunset Boulevard address into a 2,000 square foot office complex on the lot, only to discover it had been built on the cheap. There were no bathrooms. They couldn't have been happier when Red Skelton took the studio off their hands and let them stay there rent-free for a year while their new offices were being built in Beverly Hills.

Once AIP became a force to be reckoned with it became an easy target for frightened people and opportunistic politicians, who were always looking for someone to blame for the rise in teenage crime. Rock 'n' roll music, comic books and movies became the scapegoats.

On May 12, 1958 *The Evening Bulletin* (a Philadelphia newspaper) ran the following story: "Two young boys went to the movies yesterday and saw a picture called *Motorcycle Gang* [an American International picture], described by the exhibitors as a 'teenage hit.' After leaving the movies they stole an automobile and injured a woman so severely that she lost most of a leg."

The fact that the boys had stolen the car *before* they saw the movie was sort of glossed over in the *Bulletin's* account. Why spoil a good story with the facts?

A week later, when the incident had pretty well run its course, the *Upper Darby Times*, a suburban weekly, put the finger on the sloppy reporting when it discovered the key to the automobile had actually been taken a *week* before the boys saw the movie. Outraged, *Boxoffice* ran a scathing attack on all the people who were so quick to make hay of the story. They concluded by saying: "We're getting awfully tired of being blamed by pulpit, politicians and paper for everything bad in the world."

Estes Kefauver, a senator from Tennessee, was in charge of a senate subcommittee investigating the causes of juvenile delinquency. Kefauver pointed to the type of advertisements that AIP specialized in and declared they were "nothing but purplish prose, keyed to feverish tempo to celebrate the naturalness of seduction, the condonably of adultery, and the spontaneity of adolescent relations." Goodness! The committee did its best to tie real crime to reel crime but after grilling a number of Hollywood big wigs, the committee's 122 page report proved that their efforts had been a complete waste of time.

At a meeting of the Theatre Owners Association of America, during an AIP sponsored luncheon, producer Jerry Wald took the floor and accused his hosts of making movies that could destroy the industry. Rattling off a list of titles, Wald said: "These are not the sort of pictures on which we can build a market for the future. While they make a few dollars today they will destroy us tomorrow." Wald begged Nicholson and Arkoff to lift their horizons. Nicholson waited patiently for him to finish and then calmly reminded Wald that his most recent picture, *Peyton Place* (1957), was riddled with incest, rape and murder. "I'd rather my own children see one of our pictures than something like, say, *God's Little Acre* [1958]. Our monsters don't drink, smoke or lust." And none of them, as Wald had suggested, had ever been condemned by the Legion of Decency.[22]

"Our stories are pure fantasy, with no attempt at realism," Nicholson told the *New York Times*. "Because of this it is difficult to see how anyone could take our pictures so seriously that psychological damage could occur. In our concept of each of our monsters, we strive for unbelievability. Teenagers, who comprise our target audience, recognize this and laugh at the caricatures we represent, rather than shrink in terror. Adults, more serious-minded perhaps, often miss the point of the joke."[23]

In 1958 AIP released 13 combinations:

John Ashley was one of the stars of *Motorcycle Gang* (1958). "My sisters and I loved John Ashley," Luree Nicholson said. "He was such a nice guy... and gorgeous! My dad thought he was going to be a big star."

1. *Jet Attack*—"the most amazing story to ever hit the screen!"—plus *Suicide Battalion*—"To hell with the orders... WE ATTACK!"

2. *Dragstrip Riot*—"murder at 120 miles an hour!"—plus *Cool and the Crazy*— "Seven savage punks on a weekend binge of violence!"

3. *Machine Gun Kelly*—"without his gun he was naked yellow!"— plus *The Bonnie Parker Story*—"cigar smoking hellcat of the roaring thirties!"

4. *High School Hellcats*—"What must a good girl say to *belong*?" plus *Hot Rod Gang*—"Crazy kids, living to a wild rock 'n' roll beat!"

5. *How to Make a Monster*—"It will scare the living yell out of you!" plus *Teenage Caveman*—"Prehistoric rebels against prehistoric monsters!"

6.   *Attack of the Puppet People*—"Doll dwarfs versus the crushing giant beasts!" —plus *War of the Colossal Beast*—"The towering terror from hell!"

7.   *Hell Squad*—"The guts and gore of desert war!"—plus *Tank Battalion*—"Terrible in war... tender in love!" (Or was it the other way around?)

8.   *She Gods of Shark Reef*—"Beautiful maidens in a lush tropical paradise ruled by a hideous stone god!"—plus *Night of the Blood Beast*—"No girl was safe as long as this head-hunting thing roamed the land!"

9.   *Screaming Skull*—"The tortured ghost who claimed vengeance in the bride's bedroom!"—plus *The Brain Eaters*—"Crawling, slimy things terror-bent on destroying the world!"

10. *The Spider*—"will eat you alive!"—plus *Terror from the Year 5000*— "From time unborn... a hideous she-thing!"

11. *Submarine Seahawk*—"The secret sub that won the war!"—plus *Paratroop Command*—"Kids living to the deadly thrill of jump and kill!"

12. *Tank Commandoes*—"Battle born passions of defiant men at war!"—plus *Operation Dames*—"No fury like four girls trapped behind enemy lines!"

13. *Road Racers*—"Is it a sport or is it murder?!"—plus *Daddy-O*— Daring to live... daring to love!"

But a terrible thing had happened. The major studios, seeing the success that AIP was enjoying, began flooding the market with low budget, independently produced combo packages of their own. "So 1958 was not the triumphant summer it should have been," Arkoff said in reflection. "The pictures had done okay but not what they had done before. We couldn't even collect the money. We had a lot of outstandings and it was hard to get 'em. And we could see, too, that we could no longer go the combination route. That was the end of our combinations. I'm not saying that occasionally, when we had two weak ones, we wouldn't put two together or we'd pick up two, but fundamentally, that was at the end of the whole concept that everything had to be in combinations in order to get a percentage price. So we stood back and said, well, where do we go from here?"

The answer to that question appeared in the October 20 edition of *Boxoffice*: "American International Pictures, during 1959, plans to put an experimental toe into the waters of more costly production... the regular pictures on the organization's forthcoming slate will be allocated budgets of $250,000 to $500,000, which is from two to four times the average cost of AIP features." A few months later *Boxoffice* reported that Jim and Sam were going to curtail the combo programs in favor of single quality attractions, which necessitated the expansion of the company's distribution and publicity staff.

The first example of this shift in policy was Herman Cohen's *Horrors of the Black Museum*, released in April 1959, in CinemaScope and color. It was jointly financed by AIP and Anglo-Amalgamated in England at a cost of $400,000. Now the question was, could AIP make a movie for $200,000 that would be good enough to sell to the exhibitors as a single attraction? The answer of course was yes, and the picture that Jim and Sam decided to gamble on was *House of Usher* (1960), announced in a July '59 trade ad as *The Mysterious House of Usher*.

"It was my idea to make *House of Usher*," said Roger Corman. "It was something I'd wanted to make for a long time. I had been making low budget, black and white films and I felt the time had come for a change. So at a lunch meeting with Jim and Sam I said, 'Look, instead of making two ten day black and white films for $100,000 each, why don't we make one movie in fifteen days for $300,000?' They agreed." Corman said that Jim had some reservations. He wasn't sure the kids would pay to see a movie based on something they may have been forced to read in school. Sam had no reservations. He was against the idea. "At our final pre-production meeting I remember Sam said, 'There's no monster in the film.' I didn't want to lose the project so

I said, 'The house is the monster.' Now I don't know if Sam really went along with that but he agreed to make the picture anyway.'"

What other choice did he have? Sam *never* had veto power. Not yet anyway.

Corman seems to be taking credit for the company's decision to make bigger pictures, which is a little disingenuous. Jim and Sam had already decided to make bigger pictures back in '58. Corman simply seized the opportunity to make something he'd always wanted to make. And the Poe story was a practical choice, given that it was confined to a house with four characters. There would be enough money left to give the movie some production value, which was essential. To compete in the marketplace, the movie had to look better than the average television show. The addition of color and CinemaScope would help, though by 1959 most people didn't know the difference between CinemaScope and standard wide screen. As a matter of fact a lot of the exhibitors didn't give a hoot about CinemaScope. If it was a choice between CinemaScope and color, they'd opt for color every time. But it was a marketing tool and would help lend an air of prestige to the project.

Corman, Nicholson and Arkoff did agree on one thing, however, and that was the choice of Vincent Price for the lead role. A supporting player in contemporary dramas and costume pictures for years, Price's career had taken a turn in 1953 when he was cast as the mad sculptor in *House of Wax*, one of the top ten money-makers that year. In spite of the stigma attached to horror films in those days, the art collector, author and gourmet cook was able to side-step being typecast for a time but in 1959, after starring in four horror movies that year, it was obvious that he had become a successor to actors like Boris Karloff and Bela Lugosi. As Price's salary would take the largest bite out of *House of Usher*'s budget, Sam negotiated a deal whereby the actor agreed to have his $35,000 salary spread out in step payments. He was also given a piece of the picture. (Uh-oh!)

Richard Matheson, a major force in fantasy literature, was hired to write the screenplay. His *The Incredible Shrinking Man* (1957) had been a big money-maker for Universal and he was a regular contributor to the popular television series *The Twilight Zone*. Matheson had several meetings with Corman before he turned in his first draft of the script, then titled *The Haunted House of Usher*. Only then did he meet Nicholson and Arkoff. He'd been under the impression that he was working directly for Corman.

It was a tough assignment. Matheson somehow had to make a 90 page script out of a 14 page story. One of the ways he did it was to add a romance, which was something the banks usually insisted on before they'd finance a picture.

In Poe's story an old friend comes to visit Roderick Usher and his sister, Madeline. In Matheson's version the visitor is Madeline's lover. We are told they got engaged while she was in Boston. But as the story begins to play out one has to wonder what she was doing there. It must have been something pretty important or her brother wouldn't have allowed her to leave the house. Unless she slipped out without his knowledge. And why did Madeline agree to marry Winthrop when she knows the Ushers have a history of madness? Her brother is convinced she'll go crazy, which is why he's against the marriage, but more to the point she seems to believe it too. Yet Matheson makes no effort to address any of these issues. Eugene Archer, the critic for the *New York Times*, hit the nail on the head when he wrote: "Just why the handsome young visitor at the Ushers' residence didn't demand some logical explanation for the strange behavior of his fiancée and her mysterious brother is never satisfactorily explained. The young man—his own motivations as unclear as the nature of the curse of the Ushers—is rebuffed by the butler, ordered from the house by his brother-in-law-to-be and offered no explanations at all by his fiancée, who confines her conversations with her betrothed to a few vague syllables before vanishing into a handy secret passageway. When the hero manifests only polite bemusement, he seems less illustrative of well-bred Victorian manhood than just emasculated."

By injecting a romance into the story, Matheson opened the door to several dramatic possibilities and yet he takes advantage of none of them. Instead of meaningful, dramatic situations and insights into the characters and their motivations, the audience is treated to a series of repetitious exchanges between Usher and Winthrop, which I have distilled here for your reading pleasure.

Vincent Price as Roderick Usher.

Usher: "I'm afraid you're going to have to leave, Mr. Winthrop."

Winthrop: "I've come to see Madeline."

Usher: "You must leave this house now. It is not a healthy place for you to be."

Winthrop: "Would you permit me to light a candle so that…"

Usher: "I think you had better leave, Mr. Winthrop."

Winthrop: "I think you need some light in this house, Mr. Usher."

Usher: "For her own sake as well as yours, would you leave *now* please?"

Winthrop: "No, I will not."

Madeline: "Phillip!"

Usher: "Mr. Winthrop was just leaving."

Madeline: "Leaving?"

Winthrop: "I'm *not* leaving."

Usher: "Whatever consequences may follow your refusal to leave are upon you alone."

Madeline: "You'd better leave this place. Please leave. It isn't safe for you."

Winthrop: "I'm not leaving you, Madeline."

Usher: "I trust you will be prepared to leave tomorrow morning."

Winthrop: "If you wish. But if I do, I won't be alone."

Usher: "In the name of God, Sir, will you not understand? Leave my sister be."

Winthrop: "I mean to take her from this house tomorrow."

Usher: "I will not argue with you. Will you leave please?"

Butler: "Mr. Winthrop, you must leave."

Winthrop: "Madeline, get ready to leave. We're leaving. Now."

Butler: "Shall I prepare some breakfast before you leave?"

Usher: "Still here? I suggest you leave, Mr. Winthrop."

Matheson said he visualized the characters while he wrote his script. "So it was a shock to me when I first saw Vincent on the set with his hair bleached white, because I was so used to seeing Roderick with a beard and dark hair. It took me a little while to get used to it, but Vincent was absolutely right in shaving off his mustache. He was perfect for that role and was really great fun to work with; one of the nicest men I've ever met in Hollywood."[24]

Corman was given $200,000 and fifteen days to make the picture. He was still in pre-production when Jim and Sam flew to Europe, looking for films they could pick up cheap. Joe Levine, who had once been AIP's Boston distributor, had made a ton of dough with an Italian movie that he dubbed and spent a million dollars to promote called *Hercules* (1959). Jim and Sam

"You must leave," Myrna Fahey tells Mark Damon while Harry Ellerby and
Vincent Price wait for their chance to tell him to leave.

wanted a piece of that action. They discovered they could buy a film, dub it
and rescore it (Jim never cared for the original scores) for a lot less than it
would have cost to produce it themselves.

"We had a foreign department in New York with a guy in charge named
Bill Wright," Sam explained. "We went to Italy and that's where we met Fulvio Lucisano because Bill Wright knew him. Fulvio was a young producer
and he served as a liaison for us. On that particular trip we picked up two
pictures, one of which became *Sign of the Gladiator* (1959) and the other
was a Hercules picture. We made that *Goliath and the Barbarians* (1959).
And those two pictures revitalized the whole company."

One exhibitor opened *Goliath and the Barbarians* on Christmas Eve. Ex-
pecting an empty house, he gave everybody the night off. To his surprise he
took in $3,500 that night. He fired off a telegram to Jack Zide at Allied Films to
let him know it had been five years since he'd made that much money in a single

day. Leon Blender got a telegram from a guy who said he'd opened the picture in fifteen towns and it was doing blockbuster business in every one of them. To follow up on their success, Jim and Sam bought another Italian movie, *The Vengeance of Hercules*, added a sequence with a dragon, and changed the title to *Goliath and the Dragon* (1960). It was playing in theatres before the year was up.

Before leaving for Europe, Jim Nicholson told Corman's art director Dan Haller he could use the sets that had been built for *Ghost of Dragstrip Hollow* (1959) for the Usher mansion. Haller was appalled. He told Jim it was a bad idea and when Corman heard about it he agreed. "Let's make something good for a change," he grumbled, and without consulting with Jim or Sam, sent Haller to Universal with $2,000 to spend on flats.

Jim Nicholson hired Les Baxter, a well-known figure in pop music, to score *Goliath and the Barbarians* and *House of Usher* on the assumption that his name would add some respectability to the pictures. From that point on he replaced Ronald Stein as AIP's resident composer. This is the trap that people like Stein and Paul Blaisdell and Chuck Griffith find themselves in, once a producer has a little more money he wants to trade up. Stein could have written a good score for *Goliath and the Barbarians*, probably better than Baxter, as evidenced by his score for Corman's *Atlas* (1961). Stein's music for *The Haunted Palace* (1963) was more effective than any of Baxter's scores for the Poe movies. But Stein's name would have meant nothing on the poster. This is why the people at the bottom rarely rise with the tide of success.

The critics had always been tough on AIP movies but that had never been a problem because the market that AIP had been aiming at was the drive-in crowd, and that crowd didn't give a hoot what the critics thought. But this time positive word of mouth was essential to the success of the picture, so for the first time in its history AIP courted the press with a screening of the movie and a cocktail party in Palm Springs. "At the party people came up to me and told me how faithful we had been to Poe's story," Sam said. "Well, if you had read Poe's story, you'd realize if we had *really* been faithful to Poe, the movie would have been twenty minutes long, because the original story was only ten pages!"

Advertising artwork for *Goliath and the Barbarians* (1959),
one of the foreign imports that revitalized AIP.

The movie had its world premiere at the Paramount Theatre in Atlanta. There was a 'luncheon wake' held for the exhibitors as well as newspaper and radio people. An attractive young lady worked the room with a sash-type banner that read: "Miss Get in the Swim with *House of Usher* Grosses." There was a coffin on display with a hand extending from beneath the lid and a sign—"Bury the Blues… *House of Usher* Brings Boxoffice Grosses to Life."

In his letter to AIP's sub distributors, which contained a proof of the newspaper campaign designed to reach the widest possible audience, Milt Mortiz promised the picture would be "one of the top grossers of this year." And he was right. The picture played all summer, earning $3 million in revenue from over 10,000 engagements.

"All things considered," wrote the critic for *Variety*, "the fall of the House of Usher seems to herald the rise of the House of AIP."

Corman was asked to produce and direct another Poe picture with Vincent Price and this time he chose *The Pit and the Pendulum* (1961). The critics were divided. *The Hollywood Reporter* called it "a class suspense horror

Chelo Alonso from *Goliath and the Barbarians* (1959).

film," and *The New York Times* thought it was "Hollywood's most effective Poe-style horror to date," while *Variety* said it had a "reverse-twist ending that might well have pleased Poe himself." But the critic for the *Hollywood Citizens News* concluded that "when the dramatic histrionics evoke laughter rather than edge-of-your-seat suspense, then it must be admitted that this American International release is not up to much." And though the *Los Angeles Examiner* thought Vincent Price turned in "the acting job of his career," the critic for *The Los Angeles Times* complained that "Price mugs, rolls his eyes continuously and delivers his lines in such an unctuous tone that he comes near to burlesquing the role."

The Pit and the Pendulum was a huge success. Jim and Sam realized they had a gold mine on their hands. There was only one problem. Edgar Allan Poe was in the public domain. There was nothing to prevent some other enterprising producer from jumping their claim. Vincent Price signed an agreement which prohibited him from making Poe movies for any other company. The Price/Poe combination proved to be so successful that any costume picture that AIP made with the actor was in danger of having Poe's name attached to it.

Two cases in point. A story by H. P. Lovecraft became Edgar Allan Poe's *The Haunted Palace* (1963) and Ronald Bassett's *The Witchfinder General* was advertised as Edgar Allan Poe's *The Conqueror Worm* (1968).

Vincent Price stars in Edgar Allan Poe's House of Big Tits.

Oddly enough, Charles Bennett was asked to write a science-fiction picture called *The City in the Sea*, the title of a short poem by Poe. "It was simply horrid," said Bennett, "the worst thing I was ever involved in, I think. Jacques [Tourneur, the film's director], the poor devil, got the blame for it, but actually he was not to blame at all. I had written a good script, and I was asked to go to England to make alterations. The wretched American International Pictures came up with a lousy offer which my agent turned down, so they put on some other writer who completely annihilated the thing. It was dreadful. I should have taken my name off of it."[25]

Susan Hart backed up Bennett's claim that he'd written a good script.

Myrna Fahey, Mark Damon and Vincent Price
discuss the next scene with Roger Corman.

Louis M. 'Deke' Heyward was the one who trashed it. From time to time Vincent Price would look at the dialogue he'd written and complain that Deke was screwing his career into the ground. Co-star Tab Hunter had been looking forward to working on a new wave Italian movie but the deal fell through and he ended up in this picture instead. Hunter said it was like being tossed a soggy sandwich after being invited to a banquet.

Although the movie played in the U.K. as Edgar Allan Poe's *City in the Sea*, Jim Nicholson curiously changed the title to *War-Gods of the Deep* (1965) for the U.S. release and removed Poe's name from the advertising.

Deke Heyward was in charge of all of the British co-productions. He had a tiny office in London, filled with paintings and an organ. According to director Gordon Hessler, he was politically adept at handling things and would protect everyone from Nicholson and Arkoff when they came to town to make their suggestions. He produced or co-produced over twenty feature films, including *Those Fantastic Flying Fools* (1967), *The Oblong Box* (1969) and *Dr. Phibes Rises Again* (1972).

Between 1961 and 1962 American International released twenty-seven features, mostly co-productions, imports or pick-ups. Jim Nicholson said he was proud to be in the forefront of what he called a 'new wave' of production supply. "Today, with other so-called 'independents,' AIP offers the exhibitors a complete, year-round supply of saleable product... For exhibitors to take us and other independents for granted, to give lip-service support and

Jim Nicholson with Vincent Price and Barbara Steele
during the making of *The Pit and the Pendulum* (1961).

John Kerr and Anthony Carbone between scenes
on *The Pit and the Pendulum* (1961).

then sit back, pick and choose, and give second-rate treatment to us, this can only seriously hinder our efforts and will spell an eventual fatal blow to us and even to the motion picture industry itself."[26]

The sale of recent movies to television, often exacerbated by demanding bankers and their stockholders, was a constant threat to the exhibitors. In March of 1963, Jim Nicholson promised to withhold the sale of AIP films to television for at least five years after the release date, and challenged other companies to follow his example. (In 1958 he promised to wait ten years.)

"We alone cannot run with the ball," Sam added. "It is up to the other production-distribution companies to determine, each for itself, that to continue the present policy of some companies in playing a picture on television while it still has box office value, is disastrous to each company as well as to the industry as a whole."

Jack Armstrong, the president of National Allied Theater Owners Association, was thrilled. "Jim Nicholson and Sam Arkoff deserve the highest commendation from everyone in the motion picture industry for the positive and constructive step to save the industry from self-destruction. All producers and all film companies cannot be urged too strongly to provide theatrical releases with similar definite clearance over television."

TOA president John H. Stembler agreed. "TOA applauds American International on its precedent-making decision that offers some reassurance to exhibitors that motion pictures intended for theatrical showing will not, within a few short years, be seen on prime-time network TV shows, such as *Saturday Night at the Movies*."[27]

In 1967 CBS aired AIP's *How to Stuff a Wild Bikini* (1965).

We promise to keep our movies off television for five years… unless somebody wants to buy them.

The exhibitors had as much right to be angry at Jim and Sam as they had to celebrate. Who would have thought one of their pictures would ever play one of the networks!

How to Stuff a Wild Bikini was an outdoor anything goes vaudeville show, full of pop music, slapstick comedy and babes in bikinis, one of a series of films that began with *Beach Party* (1963). These films frustrated the critics, delighted the grateful exhibitors, and offered the promise of nirvana to young people everywhere who had the price of a bus ticket to California.

Surfing had become a popular pastime in Southern California and Hawaii during the 50s and 60s, creating its own language and lifestyle and music. Columbia's *Gidget*, released in the summer of 1959, was the first movie to introduce this subculture to a mainstream audience. Based on Frederick Kohner's novel about his daughter's brush with the surfing set, the light-hearted comedy was a huge hit, spawning two sequels and a television series. It also made a star out of its leading lady Sandra Dee. Unlike *Gidget* however, *Beach Party* never let parental concern or interference creep into the mix.

Luree Nicholson said: "My father wanted to make a movie about all-American kids on the beach and he asked Lou Rusoff to write the script. Lou had a couple of teenage sons of his own so he watched them and analyzed them, like Robert Cummings did in the film."

The target audience for *Beach Party* was, of course, the kids, but Jim Nicholson wanted to broaden the appeal by casting Bob Cummings and Dorothy Malone in the lead roles. Cummings plays a stuffy anthropology professor who comes to the beach to gather material for his book, *The Behavior Pattern of the Young Adult and Its Relation to Primitive Tribes*. As his love-starved secretary, Dorothy Malone patiently waits for the day he'll take time off from studying sex and start engaging in it.

For the film's younger leading lady Jim Nicholson had his eye on Annette Funicello, the popular singer-actress who got her start on Walt Disney's *Mickey Mouse Club*.

"For starters, Mr. Nicholson had no reason to think Mr. Disney would approve the project and agree to lend me," Annette recalled. "Apparently, many producers had approached Mr. Disney before about me, but he always found something wrong with the films they wanted to cast me in. Yet something about *Beach Party* appealed to him. One day as I was walking down Mickey Mouse Avenue, he approached and, script in hand, said, 'Annette, can I see you for a minute? I've read this. It's good clean fun, and I think you'll have a wonderful time doing it.'" His only reservation concerned her choice of beach attire. He didn't want her to expose her navel.[28]

And so thousands of hopeful young males were robbed of the pleasure of seeing Annette in a bikini. No navel. No cleavage. No nuthin'. She might just as well have worn a burlap bag. The movie would have probably grossed twice as much if she *had* worn a bikini.

Neither Sam Arkoff nor director William Asher wanted Annette. They wanted Sandra Dee, which may be the reason why Annette and Asher didn't get along. "When my father hired Annette, Asher was not supportive," said Luree who was one of the bridesmaids at Annette's wedding. "Though Annette didn't like him, being a professional, she never said she wouldn't work with him or request another director. She is not that kind of person."[29]

Annette's manager and soon-to-be husband Jack Gilardi had two clients who lobbied to be Annette's co-star—Bobby Vee and Frankie Avalon. Both Gilardi and Lou Rusoff thought Avalon was a better fit. Unlike Vee, he'd already made the leap from singer to actor. And Avalon had some history with AIP, having appeared in *Panic in Year Zero* (1962) and *Operation Bikini* (1963). He was also the voice of *Alakazam the Great* (1960). Besides all that, he and Annette were good friends.

Other members of the cast included Eva Six, John Ashley, Jody McCrea, Candy Johnson and Harvey Lembeck as Eric Von Zipper, the leader of a gang of numskull motorcycle bums. And in a surprise cameo, Vincent Price as Big Daddy.

"It's going to be a loser," Sam predicted from the outset. A later screening of the dailies from the first day's shooting did nothing to change his mind. "This won't work," he grumbled, giving director William Asher some cause for concern. Asher was worried that Sam might pull the plug until Jim Nicholson whispered in his ear, "Don't pay any attention to him."

Lou Rusoff was present at that screening, partially blind and wheelchair bound, dying from brain cancer. He insisted on coming to the set, which was more than Sam was willing to do. The picture was still in the editing stage when he passed away. AIP held a benefit premiere of the picture for the Variety Club children's charities in Winnipeg, Rusoff's home town.

AIP gave *Beach Party* its most aggressive publicity campaign. Jim Nicholson, Leon Blender, Milt Moritz and Annette Funicello flew to New York, Boston, Chicago, Dallas and Miami to screen the picture for the exhibitors and members of the press. In Dallas and Miami Jim and Annette made 142 personal appearances. Other cast members appeared on television talk shows and made public appearances at beaches, public swimming pools and theatre lobbies. Several drive-ins brought in truckloads of white sand to stage their own beach parties. *Life* magazine ran a six page laudatory article on AIP titled "Peek-a-Boo Sex—or How to Fill a Drive-In," with pictures of Jim and Sam and Frankie and Annette. AIP bought 5,000 copies and sent them to the top exhibitors across the nation.

"Four of our Houston drive-in theaters opened your *Beach Party* first run multiple to such outstanding business that first five day grosses were

Annette helps Bob Cummings with his research in *Beach Party* (1963).

well ahead of such outstanding grossing pictures as *Hud, Tammy and the Doctor, Nutty Professor* and *The Birds* to name a few," Brandon Doak wrote in a telegram to Leon Blender. Doak worked for the Stanley Warner Management Corporation. "[Those movies] were terrific grossers for our Texas drive-ins, so it looks like you have a definite winner in *Beach Party*. Eagerly looking forward to playing your *Beach Party* throughout our Texas zone of some thirty-seven drive-ins."

When AIP announced that *Muscle Beach Party* (1964) was in the works, 200 anxious exhibitors were biting at the bit before one frame of film had been shot. The critic for the *New York Post* thought *Muscle Beach* was more "abysmal" than its predecessor, but added it would be a big hit with "millions of morons." And it was. "This picture won't do anything but business," said Arkansas exhibitor Terry Axley. It out-grossed the first picture and *Bikini Beach* (1964)–which had its first showing at the New York World's Fair–and was so popular that AIP had to order 150 additional prints to meet the demand. And it still wasn't enough.

Sam's son, Lou Arkoff, said: "For a movie like *Beach Party* to come along with guys yelling 'cowabunga' and characters like Eric Von Zipper, the real surfers watching this thought: What a crock of shit." Lou was probably right but there are plenty of people who fondly remember the *Beach Party* films and if you asked those people to name the quintessential screen couple of the 1960s, they wouldn't say Rock Hudson and Doris Day. They'd tell you it was Frankie and Annette.

"Isn't it crazy how everybody remembers those movies?" Frankie Avalon said in a recent interview with Richard Ouzounian. "We shot all of them in about 15 days and we were just having a good time. We'd be laughing so much that our director, Bill Asher, would have to say things like 'OK, kids, quit fooling around so we can shoot the comedy scenes.'"

Jim Nicholson thought he could use *Beach Party* as a way of entering the television market and hired Stanley E. Dudelson, the former national sales manager of Columbia's Screen Gems, to make it happen. But Dudelson couldn't seem to interest anyone in anything. It took Ruth Pologe, the head of AIP publicity in New York, to sell a one shot special called *The Wild, Weird World of Dr. Goldfoot* to ABC. Written by Deke Heyward to promote *Dr. Goldfoot and the Bikini Machine* (1965), it featured Vincent Price, Tommy Kirk, Susan Hart, Aron Kincaid, and *Beach Party* regulars Harvey Lembeck, Patti Chandler, Mary Hughes, Sally Sachse and Luree Nicholson. It aired on November 18, 1965 in the *Shindig* time slot. The only other original piece of programming was *An Evening with Edgar Allan Poe* with Vincent Price, shot on tape for syndication.

AIP-TV made its money from Mexican horror movies and Italian sword and sandal movies, which the company bought cheap and sold in packages to stations hungry for product. They also produced a few new movies to dump into these packages, down and dirty no-budget junk that would have been impossible to sell to the big screen. Rock Stevens (aka Peter Lupus) went to Italy to make *Challenge of the Gladiators*, *Conquest of Damascus* and *Hercules and the Tyrants of Babylon* (all 1964), which were given a limited theatrical release before being bundled into a sword and sandal package for television.

Color movies made these packages more attractive to the buyers, so Larry

Frankie and Annette.

Buchanan was hired to produce and direct color remakes of some of AIP's old sci-fi films. Working out of Dallas, Buchanan was given one name actor, an old script, and $40,000. With such a small amount of money the only way he could make a color movie was to shoot it 16mm. John Ashley was in Buchanan's *The Eye Creatures* (1965), a remake of *Invasion of the Saucer-Men*.

"I was the only actor from Hollywood," said Ashley. "All the rest were local people from Dallas who had had little theatre background and that sort of thing. We shot it on Gordon McLendon's ranch. I think it took three or four weeks. I was going to do another one right after that, *Mars Needs Women* [1967] but I got tied up with something else and Tommy Kirk did it."

"What I was doing in those pictures, I don't know," Kirk told Kevin Minton in an interview for *Filmfax*. "The only thing I can say is that I had a drug problem then, and I didn't know what I was doing or what I was getting into. I was an idiot."

"Larry, God bless him, is a nice guy but he really was not a director," said John Agar. "He did the best he could, but he didn't even know enough not to 'cross the line,' which is one of the simplest things there is in direction."[30]

Buchanan didn't fret over whether his movies were any good or not. He just loved making them.

AIP didn't exactly make a big splash in the television market but they certainly had cause to celebrate as they rolled into their tenth year in business. They had 375 employees, 30 domestic exchanges and franchise holders (10 of which they owned), 15 foreign distribution outlets and over 130 films that represented over $200,000,000 in gross revue. They could boast that AIP stood for Always In Profit and get away with it. The secret of their success was no secret at all. They made the movies that the kids wanted to see. And they would keep growing so long as they kept an eye on what the kids were interested in.

"The tastes of youth in motion pictures vary and change quickly, just as they do in music," Jim told *The Film Daily* in June of '66. "Three or four years ago, surfing songs were popular. Today, ballads and protest songs are increasingly popular. It's as though the youthful audience has swerved from its interest in jiggling in the sand." So, like its audience, AIP 'swerved' away from comedies and began making protest pictures.

Jim Nicholson once stood before the International Catholic Film Office and delivered a sanctimonious speech about moral responsibility. "It is distressing," he said, "that some producers are content to fiddle with romanticism, puerile sex and glamorized brutality while the world around them burns with confusion, fear and incipient despair." It was time, he said, to put an end not only to the movies with morally objectionable subject matter but the leering advertising that promoted them. "At American International it is our studied conclusion that such productions are neither commercially profitable nor morally justifiable, but the fact remains that it is in the gray area between the legally permissible for profit's sake, and the morally reprehensible for the devil's sake that the producer's great responsibility falls."

Even before the credits rolled on *The Wild Angels* (1966), a disclaimer warned the audience that the picture they were about to see would shock them, maybe even anger them. "Although the events and characters are fictitious, the story is a reflection of our times." The audience was then treated to a gritty and unsavory account of some motorcycle thugs who would have eaten Eric Von Zipper and his gang for lunch, shoved Frankie's surfboard up his ass, and had their way with Annette. The year was 1966 and a lot had happened in America since Frankie and Annette hit the beach. President John F. Kennedy had been murdered in Texas. His successor Lyndon Johnson had escalated the war in Vietnam, increasing the need for fresh cannon-fodder at a rate of 5,000 soldiers per month. Draft dodgers fled to the safety of Canada and with each passing month antiwar sentiments grew as America watched its young soldiers slaughtered on the nightly news. African-Americans, fed up with their second-class citizenship, staged a series of peaceful protests, demanding the rights promised by the Constitution. More often than not they were hosed, tear gassed, and beaten with clubs and chains by local and state police. Many Americans who naively believed that racism and segregation was confined to the southern states were shocked when years of pent-up rage exploded in six days of arson and looting in the Watts ghetto of Los Angeles. Thirty-four people were killed and nearly 4,000 were arrested. Before the decade was over Martin Luther King, Jr., Malcolm X and presidential hopeful Robert Kennedy were murdered, causing the *Washington Post* satirist Art Buchwald to write: "To the rest of the world the U.S. must look like a giant insane asylum where the inmates have taken over."

Disgusted and disillusioned, young people turned their backs on the values of their parents. Small wonder that in this climate of pessimism, the nihilistic and totally unsympathetic James Bond emerged as the movie hero of the decade. In *The Wild Angels*, when Peter Fonda, serving as the spokesman for his motorcycle gang, demanded the freedom to get loaded and ride their machines without being hassled by the Man, there was an anti-establishment audience cheering him on.

"We picked up on things really fast," recalled Milt Moritz. "I remember seeing a gang of Hells Angels on the cover of the *Saturday Evening Post* and showing it to Jim Nicholson. Before you knew it, we'd made *The Wild Angels*."

The Hells Angels were a gang of long-haired drop-outs who'd been left behind by the Industrial Revolution. They wore sleeveless denim jackets and German Iron Crosses and were usually in need of a bath. Most of them had nicknames, tattoos and a preference for heavy-duty American-made motorcycles. Their club emblem was an embroidered patch of a winged skull wearing a motorcycle helmet. They hung out in low-life bars, drank to excess, raped women, beat up men, and lived off their women. Their activities were well known in the Oakland and San Francisco areas of California but it wasn't until 1964, when a mob of them gathered at Monterey on Labor Day weekend and set up camp at the seaward end of Beach Road in Marina, that their activities attracted the interest of the state attorney general and the public at large. Two young couples had the misfortune to stroll by the camp. The girls, ages 14 and 15, were taken from their male companions and repeatedly raped. Two of the rapists were later identified as the presidents of the North Sacramento and Richmond branches of the group. State Senator Fred S. Farr wanted the attorney general to investigate the outlaws. District attorneys, sheriffs and chiefs of police gathered information on 446 members of the gang. 151 had felony convictions, misdemeanor arrests were in the thousands, and 85 of these thugs had served time in state prison. By the time that the photograph of the Angels on their way to a funeral appeared on the cover of the *Post*, their reputation as mean sons of bitches had been well established.

George Chakiris had been Jim Nicholson's choice for the leader of the Angels, but Chakiris bowed out of the project when he was told he'd have to ride a chopper. Peter Fonda, originally slated to play the role that ultimately went to Bruce Dern, was moved into the starring role. Nancy Sinatra was his co-star. When father Frank heard that she'd be working with members of the biker gang, he let it be known that there'd be hell to pay if anything happened to her. In his autobiography Peter Fonda wrote that Nancy Sinatra earned the respect of the entire company because she could take care of herself. "Hell," he added, "she could have taken care of herself, Frankie Jr., Tina, Nancy Sr., and Frank!"

Five days after the picture went into general release, Peter Fonda was arrested for possessing marijuana. At his trial, the prosecuting attorney made repeated references to the film, believing it would bolster his case. If he'd been on AIP's payroll he couldn't have done a better job of promoting the film, turning Fonda into a cult hero. As a result, the exhibitors were willing to pay a higher rate for the picture.

The Wild Angels proved to be AIP's most successful movie to date. Made for $360,000, it took in more than $5 million in rentals in the first six months and created yet another franchise for the company—the biker movie. By the end of the following year *Devil's Angels, Hells Angels on Wheels, Born Losers* and *The Glory Stompers* (all 1967) were doing fantastic business in the Midwest and the South, once the prime targets for the Western.

The next hot topic that Jim Nicholson wanted to exploit was the hallucinogenic drug LSD (Lysergic acid diethylamide). It had been used in medical research for years but was virtually unknown to the public at large until a dropout Harvard professor named Timothy Leary began promoting it as Western Yoga. Leary was convinced that LSD could open people's minds and enable them to find a happier life. "Turn on, tune in and drop out" was his campaign slogan and once the kids discovered it could be manufactured in almost any chemistry lab, they were more than happy to comply.

"My daughters have been offered LSD on the grounds of their high school," Jim Nicholson told the press. "This is a fact of life, and we'd damned well better start discussing it out in the open so we can do something about it."

In *The Trip* (1967), Peter Fonda is undergoing a crisis in both his marriage and in his career as a director of television commercials. He drops acid in the hope of finding some meaning in his life. Written by Jack Nicholson and directed by Roger Corman, the film is an ambitious attempt to simulate an acid trip on a $300,000 budget. Of course it's impossible to render cinematically an internal experience for any amount of money, but the film does succeed in evoking a feeling of being *with* someone on the drug.

Unlike most of the drug-based movies of the period, the film's leading man, director and writer brought firsthand experience to the subject. Equally important, the film was objective. At the end, when Fonda returns to the 'real world,' he is left to wonder what he should do next. But Jim Nicholson, who was becoming more conservative, got an attack of cold feet. He added a foreword to the film, warning the audience that drug experimentation was dangerous. He also cut some scenes. But the thing that really pissed Corman off was the optically added cracked glass over Fonda's image at the very end of the movie. Corman's version of the film left it up to the audience to decide if Fonda's experience had been a good or bad thing. The cracked glass implied that the experience had shattered his life.

Jim Nicholson was much happier with producer-director Maury Dexter's take on marijuana use by the high school students in *Maryjane* (1968). The script by Richard Gautier and Peter Marshall echoes the outdated sentiments of *Reefer Madness* (1936). "It spreads, like cancer," a police officer tells a group of teachers. "First it's marijuana, then LSD and STP, then its heroin and cocaine." One of the teachers asks: "Are you saying that marijuana leads to the hard stuff?" The cop has to admit that "big-time scientists say no" but that his own statistics prove that *every* hardcore addict started with marijuana. To mention that they also started with mother's milk would not have altered the outcome of this sequence or the film's conclusion. For one brief moment it looked as if the film might be leading to an enlightened treatment of the subject when one of the teachers (played by Fabian Forte) admits that he smoked marijuana and it didn't hurt him any. But he comes around to the cop's point of view by the end of the movie.

The postwar 'boom' babies, having been raised on James Dean and Bob Dylan, thought *Maryjane* was a comedy. As they watched their parents wash down tranquilizers with martinis, it was not only hypocritical but ludicrous

Nancy Sinatra and Peter Fonda.

to make such a fuss about marijuana use. By 1968 the generation gap was never wider. As the futile war in Vietnam raged on, the insanity of being asked to die for a country that denied them the right to vote caused the teens to protest in mass. The unrest of the nation's youth reached its peak in August of 1968 at the Democratic National Convention in Chicago when old line Democratic Party bosses chose Hubert Humphrey over Eugene McCarthy, a candidate who was strongly opposed to the war. When thousands of protestors came to Chicago to express their opposition, Mayor Richard Daley dispatched the police to bash a few heads in. And if a few innocent bystanders happened to get in the way that was their tough luck. This gestapo-like display was televised by all three networks.

The release of AIP's *Wild in the Streets* (1968), in which a 24-year old president dumps everyone over 30 into concentration camps, could not have been better timed. When Major Daley heard the film contained a sequence in which Washington's water supply was spiked with LSD, he put a barbed wire fence and a 24-hour guard around Chicago's reservoirs.

Released in May, the *New York Times* called *Wild in the Streets* "the best American film of the year so far." Impressive when one considers that there was a time when an AIP movie didn't even rate a mention, much less praise from the New York paper. In all probability no one noticed or cared about the significant change in the company's credits. Prior to *Wild in the Streets* Jim Nicholson's name had always preceded Sam Arkoff's. Now it was Samuel Z. Arkoff and James H. Nicholson present. Although Jim was still the president of the company, Sam had gone from being vice president to Chairman of the Board. Likewise, Sam's name now appeared before Jim's in the articles written about them. And Sam had more or less taken over as spokesperson for the company.

"Jim was fundamentally, in many ways, a shy man," Sam told me. "He didn't like to speak particularly, which is one of the reasons that he'd say a few words to the exhibitors with whom he felt, you know… But I gradually became the one who did more of the speaking for the organization, partly because I had debate training and I enjoyed it, particularly at these exhibitors' conventions, telling them what thieves they were, in a humorous way."

The way Sam explains the situation, he makes it seem as if he did Jim a favor, doesn't he? It was probably Sam's concern over the delicate balance of his partner's nature that caused him to exclude Jim from meetings. Why trouble this poor shy man with silly business concerns? And it was probably why people were hired to do the creative things that Jim enjoyed doing, things he could do in his sleep, until finally there was nothing left for him to do but sit alone in his office and stare at an empty desk.

In the late 60s, during an interview for a television special, Sam made it clear that their relationship had deteriorated. He humiliated Jim by happily contradicting *every* remark that he made. Jim was so angry he wasn't able to hide it from the camera. And it all started in Columbia's screening room back in 1964, when Jim Nicholson and his buddy Mike Frankovich were watching the dailies of a movie being filmed in Hawaii called *Ride the Wild Surf*. Jim was smitten by one of the three young ladies in the cast, a 22-year-old brunette named Susan Hart. When she was on the screen he couldn't take his eyes off of her. He phoned her agent and a few months later her name was on a contract and she was in *Pajama Party* (1964), doing a dance that caused flowers to drop and volcanoes to erupt.

Things certainly erupted in the Nicholson household when Jim told Sylvia that he wanted a divorce. It shouldn't have come as a surprise. Their relationship had been a loveless, even hostile one for over a decade.

"My mother left my father once for a few months," Luree recalled. "She went off with some guy around the time that my daughter was born in 1961. She came back for that. They had a reconciliation of sorts. There were things they expected of each other if they were going to continue to live together. Everything looked fine on the surface, but underneath it was very unpleasant. She was always needling him. Always undermining him. Always some nasty little remark."

Even so, it wasn't like Jim to force this sort of confrontation. And why the urgency? Had he simply had enough, Sylvia wondered, or was there something going on that she should know about? Something that she could use against him? She intended to find out but she wanted him to think that she was as willing as he was to put an end to their wretched relationship. She agreed to a quiet Reno divorce, then hired a private detective to keep tabs on

Judy Pace and Christopher Jones from *Wild in the Streets* (1968).]

him. Once she had the proof that she needed, she charged Jim with adultery in open court. She put on quite a show as the injured party. She told the judge that her husband had been running around with some young starlet and she just couldn't take it anymore. She continued the charade in the hall outside of the courtroom in a tearful display for the press. It was pure soap opera.

In his countersuit, Jim maintained that Sylvia was the one who'd been unfaithful. She'd had five affairs that he knew about. Actor Richard Harrison (who married Jim's daughter Loretta in 1961) told me *everyone* knew about Sylvia's affairs, which wasn't true. Apparently, very few people were privy to the trouble in the Nicholson household.

"I was surprised when Jim divorced his wife and took up with that young actress," Mickey Zide told me. "Whenever we went to a convention Jim would always have us bring our wives because he didn't want anybody fooling around. And then *he* does it."

Luree didn't blame her father for wanting out of the marriage but she wished he'd gotten the divorce before he started seeing Susan and told him so. But then she could tell him things like that. They'd always been close. "If I was ever upset and I really needed to talk to him, I could go to the office and it didn't matter who he was with or who he was waiting to see, he'd see me first. He was always there for me."

After the divorce, Jim and Susan announced their engagement during a world-wide promotional tour for *Dr. Goldfoot and the Bikini Machine* (1965). Unbeknownst to everyone but the family, the couple had gone to Mexico, where they were secretly married a few months before. Susan put her acting career on hold to take care of their baby, a boy named after his father.

Susan's relationship with Sam Arkoff had been a good one. She and Jim did a lot of travelling with the Arkoffs because AIP had so many co-productions shooting in England and Spain. Susan thought Sam had a wonderful sense of humor and was fun to be around. That all changed when the terms of Jim's divorce was finally settled and the judge gave Sylvia half of Jim's AIP stock. That gave Sam the controlling interest. Now, for the first time in the company's history, *he* had the last word.

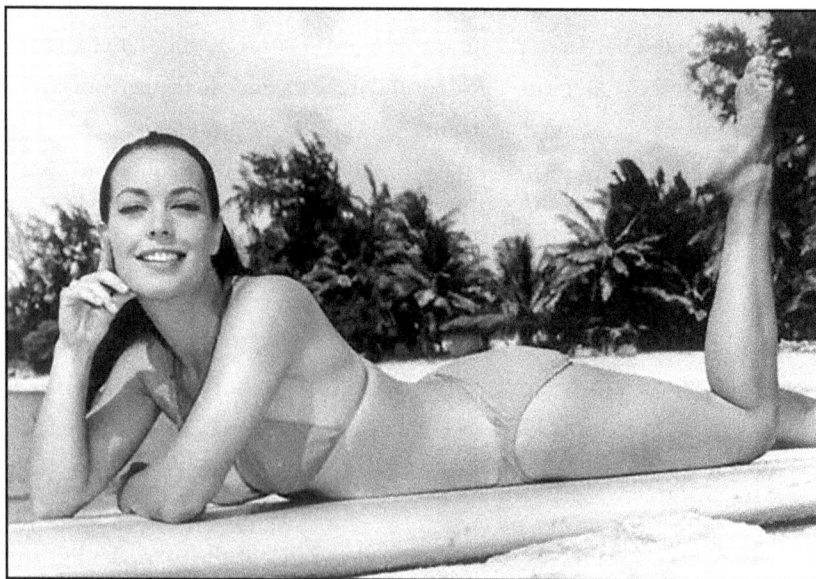

Susan Hart.

Susan was ready to fly to Italy to star in *Planet of the Vampires* (1965) and the sequel to *Dr. Goldfoot* when Sam fired the first shot in a war that Jim Nicholson never saw coming. Sam issued a memo that said there would be no more nepotism at AIP and then made his son Lou vice-president of the company. Of course nepotism had nothing to do with Sam's decision to keep Susan from working at AIP. He did it because he was angry at Jim for breaking up 'the family.' The Nicholsons and the Arkoffs had been like a family, spending holidays and vacations together, and Sam blamed Susan for messing everything up.

After Sam went on a diet and lost a lot of weight, he told a roomful of exhibitors, "From now on, Jim has the black car. *I* have the white car and *I'm* going to kiss the starlets." At that point Jim weighed more than Sam.

"Jim used to be skinny," Mickey Zide told me, "but he started taking steroids to keep up with this younger woman, and I'm afraid the steroids helped do him in."

Lack of exercise may have had something to do with it as well. When he wasn't at the office, Jim and Susan spent most of their married life at home. People showed up for dinner and a movie nearly every night of the week. "And sometimes two movies a night," Susan recalled. "We'd see up to five hundred pictures a year! His life really centered around motion pictures— watching them, making them, talking about them and showing them."[31]

In 1969 the company moved into a four-storey building in Beverly Hills, a far cry from its humble beginnings on Selma Avenue. The movies were costing more to make and the company had to go public to raise enough money to keep up. Sam called it the biggest mistake of his life.

As the company grew, Jim's participation diminished. He still had a say in selecting the films the AIP produced, but to anyone with half an eye open it was obvious that he was no longer in charge. He resigned in January of 1972 and died before the year was up.

For the first couple of years after his death, AIP continued to prosper, partly due to the success of a series of what came to be known as black exploitation pictures, a genre that Jim started with *Blacula*. But somewhere along the line Sam forgot what AIP was all about and the company went from being a major minor to a minor major and started sinking money into big budgeted movies—*The Wild Party* (1975) with Raquel Welch, *Force 10 from Navarone* (1978) with Robert Shaw, and *Meteor* (1979) with Sean Connery. Flops like these caused a 12 percent dip in the company's profits and Sam was forced to merge with Filmways to keep afloat. Once that happened he found himself in a situation similar to the one he had created for Jim Nicholson. His tenure with Filmways didn't last a year. He resigned and walked away with 4 million bucks plus most of AIP's pre-1960 film library.

Knowing that a judge would eventually rule that Susan Hart was legally entitled to some of the pictures, Sam quickly made a deal with Sony to the release the films on videotape. The first eight titles were the so-called cream of the crop, titles such as *I Was a Teenage Werewolf*, *It Conquered the World* and *Machine Gun Kelly*. But the $30 price tag proved to be a little too steep and the remaining titles were dumped on the market at $10 a pop, with unattractive black and white packaging. Years later, after ownership of some of the better titles was given to Susan, Lionsgate released what was left of the Arkoff library on DVD. They had the good sense to put two titles on a disc, modestly priced at $15. Even at that price the sales were so tepid that Lionsgate gave up and seventeen titles went unreleased.

Susan Hart is living in Palm Springs now, happily married to Roy Hofeinz Jr. She has yet to release any of the films she owns. She may think because she has some of the better titles—*I Was a Teenage Werewolf*, *I Was a Teenage Frankenstein*, *The Amazing Colossal Man*, *Invasion of the Saucer-Men*, *It Conquered the World*—that she's sitting on gold. Past performance indicates otherwise. Once the children who grew up with these movies die, the little interest there is in these films will probably die with them. Hopefully, Jim Nicholson won't suffer the same fate. If nothing else I would like to see his name precede Sam Arkoff's in the history books, and that he will be remembered as the guy who, against all odds, created the biggest little film company in Hollywood history.

Selected Filmography

THE FAST AND THE FURIOUS aka **CRASHOUT** (1954) with John Ireland, Dorothy Malone, Bruce Carlisle, Jean Howell and Marshall Bradford. Written by Jerome Odlum and Jean Howell. Produced by Roger Corman. Directed by Edward Sampson and John Ireland. Black and White 63 minutes. A Palo Alto Production. An American International Release.

Roger used two cameras to film the racing scenes in this picture. "I decided to get behind the camera and direct myself," he said. "I knew immediately that this was what I wanted to do." He also got behind the wheel to play the driver that Ireland passes to win the race. Only Roger got carried away and wouldn't let the car pass. He claimed the guy who was doubling for Ireland wasn't going fast enough. It wouldn't look right if he had to hit the brakes to let him win. The truth was Roger didn't want to lose the race.

The Critics: "During the first couple of reels it looks as if it is going to pay off in a top-flight, low budget production. But unfortunately the script fails to deliver a concentrated love story."—*Hollywood Reporter*; "Sports car enthusiasts may get more satisfaction than other people out of the principal novelty in the picture …"—*Motion Picture Herald*; "Distributors of Jaguar automobiles should have subsidized this woefully weak feature inasmuch as a car of that make commands more attention and screen time than anything or anybody else in the film. In fact, before the picture reaches its tortuous end, ticket buyers will have seen so much of the sleek jag that quite possibly they will all be of the opinion that it's well-nigh time to turn it in on a new one."—*Boxoffice*; "Energy-sucking excitement."—Mark McGee.

The Exhibitors: "For us, it could not finish fast enough. As for the furious part, we couldn't find it."—Harold Bell, Canada; "We put this on as a free Christmas show for the kids. Picture not so hot. Couldn't even fill the house for free."—Michael Chiaventone, IL.

DAY THE WORLD ENDED (1956) with Richard Denning, Lori Nelson, Touch Connors, Paul Birch and Adele Jergens. Written by Lou Rusoff. Produced and directed by Roger Corman. Black and white, SuperScope, 81 minutes. A Golden State Production for American Releasing Corporation.

Richard Denning was paid $7,500 for his starring role in this movie, plus a half percent of the net profit.

Alex Gordon: "I'm sure he never saw a dime. Occasionally there would be a question about it and I'd ask Arkoff, and he'd say, 'Oh, yeah, I'm sending him checks.' Which he wasn't. I never did find out much about Arkoff's accounting practices except that he was the only one who got rich!"[32]

Lori Nelson: "It was a slow period for me after I left Universal, kind of hard going because when you leave a major studio, you sort of have to hustle and about all you can get are low-budget films until you're able to come back up again. So that's what I did. My agent sent me on interviews here and there, and some I got and some I didn't. *Day the World Ended* was one of the first ones I got. It was really a second-rate, low-budget film, though later I came to realize that practically every actor or actress in Hollywood who wasn't under contract to a studio did a low-budget Roger Corman film before they went on to become famous."[33]

Paul Blaisdell: "I played the monster, Lori's three-eyed, four-armed fiancée. I knew there was going to be a problem when the time came for me to carry [her]. She was five feet tall and I think she weighed a hundred pounds. I weighed a hundred and forty-two pounds."

Lori Nelson: "Paul was rather a small guy and he fit the suit to himself. It was funny looking and had these little arms that came out from his shoulders, and when he walked they would wiggle, which made everyone laugh. With the suit on and me being kind of heavy, he was always dropping me or falling back, and I'd fall on top of him and we'd die laughing."[34]

The Critics: "… *Day* comes off far, far better than its companion piece."—*Los Angeles Times*; "… seven persons survive an atomic holocaust and hole up in a valley. None of them is very interesting…"—*Los Angeles Examiner*; "With all of its story faults and production inadequacies, its design hits the science fiction trade near perfectly… Ronald Stein's music deserves special mention."—*Hollywood Reporter*; "On the assumption that no situation can be too imaginative for the rabid science-fiction addicts… this rather radical approach to that category should prove effective as a sup-

Lori Nelson and the Mutant from *Day the World Ended* (1956).

porting feature."—*Boxoffice*; "A moderately interesting science-fiction melodrama. The direction is adequate and so is the acting."—*Harrison's Reports*; "A bit overlong in the telling and sometimes too incredible even as science-fantasies go, the film does have imagination and scenic entertainment value."—*Citizen News*.

The Exhibitors. "This show was not for a college town. Students not much interested in this sort. I agree. They have been overdone of late."—Ken Gorham, VT; "A super boring (if I am allowed to use that word) picture. It was really a headache. People waited for over 75 minutes to see a two-minute scene of the monster. Had to drag on this poor picture for a week to almost empty houses."—Agha Rafique Almed, West Pakistan.

SHAKE, RATTLE AND ROCK (1956) with Lisa Gaye, Touch Connors, Sterling Holloway, Raymond Hatton and Douglas Dumbrille. Written by Lou Rusoff. Produced by James H. Nicholson. Directed by Edward L. Cahn. A Sunset Production for American International Pictures.

Rhythm and blues icon Fats Domino was paid $1,500 to sing 'I'm in Love Again,' 'Honey Chile,' and his classic 'Ain't That a Shame.' His sequences were shot months ahead of the rest of the production to accommodate his busy schedule. Five days before the cameras were set to roll his manager told producer Alex Gordon he was backing out of the deal. 20th Century Fox was willing to pay Fats $25,000 to sing *one* song in *The Girl Can't Help It* (1956). Sam Arkoff intervened and reminded Domino's manager that he'd signed a letter of agreement, which Sam could and *would* use to get an injunction to stop Fats from working for Fox.

The Critics: "A rather hasty little black and white pudding…"—*Los Angeles Times*; "For the rock and roll crowd this light entry should show good response."—*Variety*; "There are some rock and roll artists involved whose names will aid in the marquee dressing and the picture itself is deftly enough done to please the younger fans."—*Hollywood Reporter*; "Strictly for the teenagers…"—*Boxoffice*; "The film's conclusions are arrived at in a singularly unpersuasive manner."—*Monthly Film Bulletin*.

The Exhibitors: "If you haven't used it, you'd better do it pretty soon. It seems like this type is what the people want these days." S.T. Jackson, AL; "We pleased a few youngsters with a very nice little picture which should do more for others than it did for me…"—Harold Bell, Quebec; "This was my first picture from an independent company and I must say I like doing business with someone who isn't always begging me for playdates. This is a wonderful rock and roll show."—Harry Hawkinson, MN; "We played this with *Runaway Daughters* and drew our biggest Sunday and Monday crowd of the year. If you book this when 'Fats' has a record on top, as we did, it cannot miss."—O.M. Shannon, TX; "Grownups came out to see this as well as the teenagers and small fry. Everyone seemed to like this picture and we made some money clear on this one."—W.M. Finley, AR; "I doubled this with *Motorcycle Gang*, both repeats, to my highest weekend gross in months."—Victor R. Webber, AR; "Played a trio of rock 'n' rollers—*Rock Around the World, Rock All Night* and *Shake, Rattle and Rock*—all oldies. Even the teenagers couldn't take them... They came out holding their noses but the boxoffice came out smelling like roses, so we can't complain."—Skip and Marie Fletcher, AK.

RUNAWAY DAUGHTERS (1956) with Marla English, Gloria Castillo, Mary Ellen Kaye, Anna Sten and John Litel. Written by Lou Rusoff. Produced by Alex Gordon. Directed by Edward L. Cahn. Black and white, 77 minutes. A Golden State Production for American International Pictures.

Marla English.

Alex Gordon chose Marla English, a former Paramount contract player, for the lead in this foray into teenage angst and juvenile crime. For three years English was relegated to bit parts at Paramount. When the studio finally offered to send her to Europe for a more substantial role in *The Mountain* (1956) she turned it down. She'd fallen in love with Bud Pennell, another Paramount contract player and didn't want to leave him. She asked the studio to give him a part in the picture and when they refused she threw a hissy fit and refused to do it. "It was the dumbest thing I ever did," she told *Parade Magazine*. Paramount let her contract lapse and she found herself in a succession of B-movies, first at United Artists and then at AIP. Seeing that her career was on a fast track to nowhere, she retired from acting in 1957, moved to San Diego and married Paul Sutherland, the owner of a large parking complex.

The Exhibitors: "Doubled with *Shake Rattle and Rock* to good business for a change."—S. T. Jackson, AL; "Very good for bottom half."—Harold Bell, Canada.

I WAS A TEENAGE WEREWOLF (1957) with Michael Landon,
Yvonne Lime, Whit Bissell, Tony Marshall and Dawn Richard. Written by Ralph Thornton. Produced by Herman Cohen. Directed by Gene Fowler. Black and white, 76 minutes. A Sunset Production for American International Pictures.

"I think Michael Landon was the only actor I know who could pull off playing a werewolf and do it so convincingly that it wasn't corny," said actress Cindy Robbins. "The movie *was* corny, let's face it. He gave such a fabulous performance. In the hands of anyone else, it could have been a real bomb."[35]

Landon was living in a one room apartment with a young lady, her child from a previous marriage, and five or six cats when producer Herman Cohen signed him for this picture. Cohen took Landon to the market and bought him a load of groceries. "I got a big hug and a kiss in the parking lot when I drove him home, because he had no money at the time—he was broke, he was in tough shape."

"I was working over at Hal Roach Studio and my wife was doing another picture over there that was being produced by Herman Cohen, and Herman was the kind of producer who was really a micromanager," recalled the film's director, Gene Fowler, Jr. "He would give a list of changes to Margie, and then he would wait patiently for her to finish. He wandered in to my cutting room—I knew him, I had been introduced to him already (and knew he was a producer)—and we would talk about pictures. Time went by, and he called me and said, 'How would you like to direct a picture?' I said 'Very much.' He said, 'Well, I've got a script here. The title is strictly exploitation.'" So I picked up the

Newspaper ad for *I Was a Teenage Werewolf/Invasion of the Saucer-Men* combo.

script and I read it. I said, 'Marge, I can't do this goddamned thing. It's just plain crap… and she said, 'Who the hell will ever see it?'… I agreed to do it because I did want the experience. I had to rewrite the script and we made it in six days."[36]

Seven days actually, and since the script had been written by Cohen and Aben Kandel using a pseudonym, there is some question as to just how much re-writing the micro-managing producer would have tolerated. However, a lot of the dialogue in *Teenage Werewolf* is more convincing than usual for a Cohen film, as are the performances. When I asked Cohen why he never worked with Fowler again he said he had a few problems with him, "so I personally felt he was not the director for me." Which suggests that Fowler *did* tamper with the script. And he can certainly take credit for the performances. There was, however, at least one instance where Cohen was right and Fowler was wrong. Michael Rougas played the first victim of the werewolf. Cohen told him that he'd be the only one in the sequence. The *camera* would be the werewolf. But Fowler shot the sequence with the werewolf in it. "The following day, when we were doing the last day of shooting, I asked Herman how the rushes looked, and he just waved me off," Rougas said. "I thought, Oh God, what's that about? He came back to me later and said, 'We have to re-shoot it, but please don't take it personally, it has nothing to do with you.' He said, 'I told you the death scene was yours and Michael was not to be seen chasing you.'"[37]

As it stands the sequence plays like something out of one of Val Lewton's horror melodramas and makes the werewolf's later

Dawn Richard is about to get more exercise than she bargained for.

attack on the young gymnast, played by *Playboy* playmate Dawn Richard, all the more effective.

"Michael had to jump over a stack of folded chairs to get to me on the stage, and when he did, he misjudged and landed right on top of them," Richard said. "He cried out in pain and limped around for a few minutes, then we went back to filming. The next day, he came in and showed us his black-and-blue legs. They were really bad."[38]

Although Yvonne Lime was the co-star of the film, Richard was the one who ended up in the advertising, cowering in her black leotard with a furry claw slashing a bloody trail across her image.

Michael Landon in make-up created by Phillip Scheer.

"The element of the bloody claw gave it a design look which piqued the interest and lifted the picture by not doing the obvious," said Al Kallis. "In my advertising, there was always an understanding of the elements of what we were playing *with* and whom we were playing to."[39]

The film was reissued on a double bill with *I Was a Teenage Frankenstein* after Michael Landon became the star of TV's *Bonanza*.

The Critics: "Michael Landon delivers a first class characterization as the high school boy constantly in trouble and has okay support right down the line."—*Variety*; "To take first things first, the title is a magnificent piece of composition. It has a haunting quality about it, and I ought to caution you that if you let it pierce your consciousness it will echo in your brain in a constant refrain."—*Los Angeles Examiner*; "...excessively familiar material ... emerges as shallow entertainment."—*Motion Picture Herald*; "The next step in low, lowbrow cinema was a marriage of the undead and the underdone..."—*Time Magazine*; "Despite the preposterous story, Fowler has handled his scenes with crispness and punch. Young Landon is an interesting and sensitive actor and lends considerable value to his role."—*Hollywood Reporter*; "...despite rather good acting, Ralph Thornton's decent script and Gene Fowler Jr.'s largely competent direction, the picture comes apart like a wet tissue."—*Los Angeles Times*; "It's a lot better than anyone had the right to expect!"—Mark McGee.

The Exhibitors: "Played with *Invasion of the Saucer-Men*. This is an okay double bill that did nice business for us, partly due to a good date and partly due to eye-catching paper and good trailers. This is the unusual and that seems to be what the people want these days."—Mickey and Penny Harris, TX. "...this combo did more business than anything I've played in a long time. It pleased, too."—S.T Jackson, AL. "It was an all-around good job of making a picture on very little cash."—Victor R. Webber, AR.

INVASION OF THE SAUCER-MEN (1957) with Gloria Castello,

Steve Terrell, Frank Gorshin, Lynn Osborn and Raymond Hatton. Written by Robert Gurney, Jr. based on "The Cosmic Frame" by Paul W. Fairman. Produced by James H. Nicholson and Robert Gurney, Jr. Directed by Edward L. Cahn. Black and white, 68 minutes. A Malibu Production for American International Pictures.

Steve Terrell has the distinction of being the first teenage science fiction movie hero. Usually middle-aged scientists or doctors were in charge of things but in this film all of the authority figures are bungling nitwits and it's up to the kids to thwart the invaders from Mars. According to Bob Burns, who worked with monster-maker Paul Blaisdell, this movie began as a serious melodrama until everyone realized it should be played for laughs. Co-producer-writer Robert J. Gurney claimed he wrote it as a comedy and that the only reason nobody laughed at the sneak preview was because the editor, Ronald Sinclair, had cut all of the funny stuff out of it. So Gurney took over the editing, put all of the funny stuff back, and presto! A vacuum of comic delight.

Paul Blaisdell's Martians from *Invasion of the Saucer-Men* (1957).

The Critics: "Edward L. Cahn directed with attention to the little details that means the difference between mediocre science fiction and audience appealing entertainment."—*Motion Picture Herald*; "... an especially diffused storyline with many characters and incidents that have no bearing at all on the main theme."—*Hollywood Reporter*; "... suffers from poor use of attempted comedy and is further handicapped by a haphazard sort of yarn which makes the film's 69-minute running time seem twice as long."—*Variety*; "... weak in all departments."—*Boxoffice*; "... it hovers somewhere between pure hoke and a vaguely attempted satire on the genre."—*Los Angeles Times*.

The Exhibitors. "More comedy than anything else, but to look at the advertising one would never think so. Anyway, it got by alright and the crowd seemed to enjoy it. "—Victor R. Webber, AR; "This is fair only. Got by on a double bill."—S.T. Jackson, AL; "... everyone seemed to enjoy the laughs between the scares."—Mickey and Penny Harris, TX; "Mediocre entertainment. If people have other places to go, they won't stop for this picture."—Harland Rankin, Canada.

THE AMAZING COLOSSAL MAN (1957) with Glenn Langan, Cathy Downs, William Hudson, Larry Thor and James Seay. Written by Mark Hanna. Produced and directed by Bert I. Gordon. Black and white, 80 minutes. A Malibu Production for American International Pictures.

In 1928, *Amazing Stories* published a short story by Homer Flint called "The Nth Man," in which a two mile tall giant gives the president of the United States six months to straighten out the broken economic system that has favored a few at the expense of the majority. (We need that giant now more than ever.) Jim Nicholson read the story and wanted to make a movie about a giant man sans the politics. A 1956-57 AIP brochure announced that Roger Corman would be making *Colossus* (Jim's new title for the film) in SuperScope. Corman hired Chuck Griffith to write the screenplay. He turned it into a comedy for Dick Miller. His script was rejected.

About that time Nicholson became aware of a young filmmaker from Kenosha, Wisconsin named Bert I. Gordon, whose specialty was low budget special effects movies. Nicholson thought he seemed like a better fit for the project and turned it over to him. Gordon and Mark Hanna developed a new script that was more to Jim's liking. Gordon shot the live action in two weeks, then spent three months on the special effects.

"I made *The Amazing Colossal Man* because I wanted to make a very human story," Gordon said. "It was very difficult to show the warm, human relationship between the girl and the man she loved, grown to giant size, without becoming ludicrous."

"Bert Gordon knew nothing about actors and didn't care at all, he just wanted to do his special effects and so on," said Alex Gordon, who was in charge of casting. As a favor to Adele Jergens, Alex gave the lead role to her husband. "When I brought in Glenn Langan, Bert Gordon thought he would be fine because he was tall and nice-looking and everything, and there'd be such a contrast."[40]

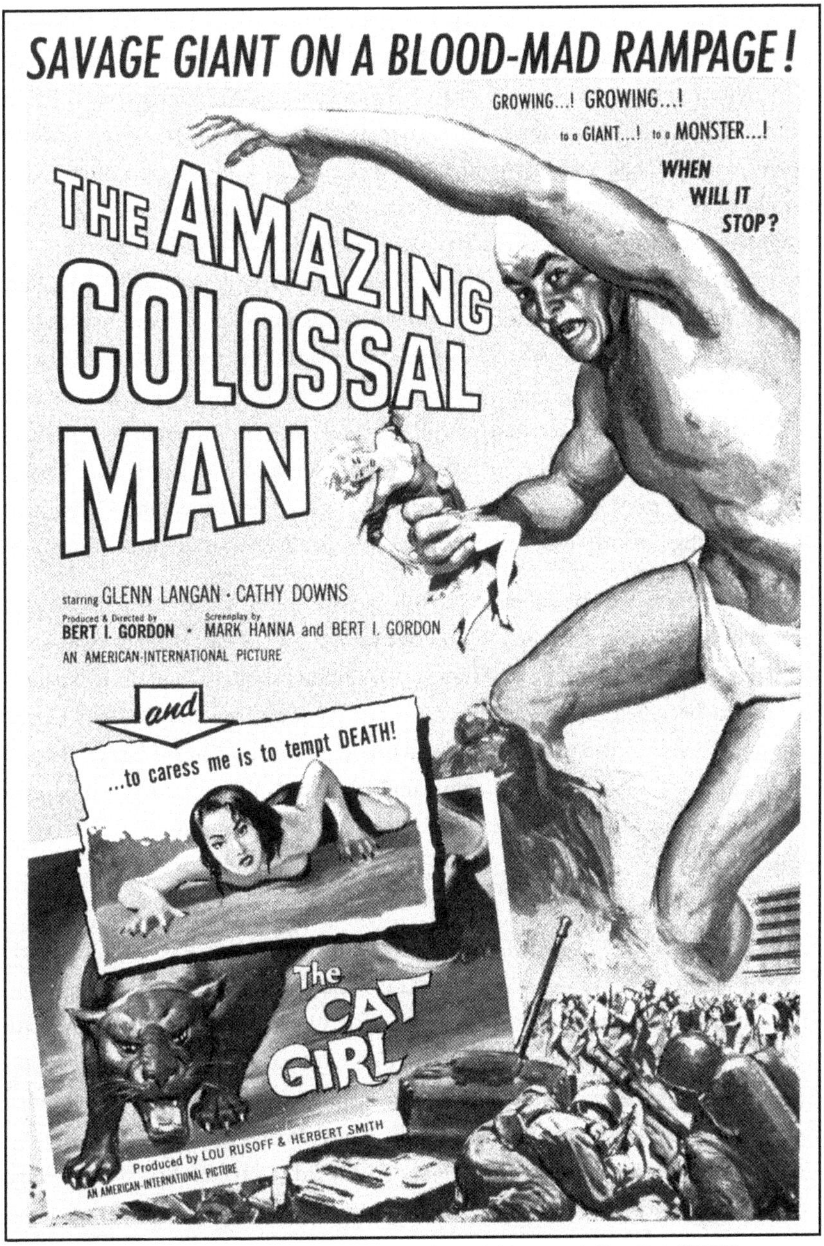

Newspaper ad for *The Amazing Colossal Man* and *Cat Girl* (1957).

The Critics: "Glenn Langan delivers persuasively in title role ... and Cathy Downs as his fiancée ... is likewise convincing."—*Variety*; "The Globe downtown was packed to the rafters yesterday afternoon when I saw the picture. Not all teenagers, either. Fans of all ages who like action movies, no matter how weird the scenario."—*Mirror News*; "A science-fantasy presentation, *The Amazing Colossal Man* is a pretty good one although it dissipates some of its effectiveness by running on too long and attempting to sustain a climax after it has passed its peak."—*Hollywood Reporter*; "The film has quite a good script, but is let down by poor trick photography."—*Monthly Film Bulletin*; "Although the story is incredible, it is put over by expert special effects work."—*Harrison's Reports*; "... boasts more plausibility than most and without sacrifice of excitement and suspense."—*Boxoffice*; "Special effects here deserve an A for effort, although the discerning patron may look with considerable skepticism at a few odds and ends along the potted path to the fadeout."—*Motion Picture Herald*; "The picture is somewhat too long, but it manages to generate some excitement before the king-sized monster is cornered at Boulder Dam."—*Los Angeles Examiner*.

The Exhibitors: "The special effects in this picture are okay and it is of a different type that will get people in just to find out what it's all about. Business was good and if the grownups would be a bit more open-minded about such pictures business would have been better. The teenage crowd came in fairly well and the small kids in large numbers. Doubled with *Cat Girl* and *Colossal Man* is by far the better. But as I said business was okay and I can't complain."—Victor R. Webber, AR; "... did better business than any big picture I've played lately."—S.T. Jackson, AL.

CAT GIRL (1957) with Barbara Shelley, Robert Ayres, Kay Callard, Paddy Webster and Ernest Milton. Written by Lou Rusoff. Produced by Lou Rusoff and Herbert Smith. Directed by Alfred Shaughnessy. Black and White 69 minutes. An Insignia/Carmel Production for American International Pictures.

AIP's first co-production with a British film company is a dull and confusing rehash of Val Lewton's 1942 classic *Cat People*. Writer Lou Rusoff was sent to England to co-produce the picture to make sure it didn't get "too British." For some curious reason Rusoff didn't object when director Alfred Shaughnessy re-wrote his script. In Rusoff's script, the title character actually transforms into a cat-monster but Shaughnessy didn't like that and in his version she uses a leopard to murder her victims. Barbara Shelley, making her film debut as the cat girl, thought Shaughnessy's changes were an improvement. Jim Nicholson and Sam Arkoff disagreed.

They wanted what they'd asked for—a monster movie. Jim placed a frantic call to Paul Blaisdell and told him they needed a cat-monster ASAP. "How much time do I have?" Blaisdell asked. "Two days," Jim told him. "You're kidding, aren't you, Nick?"

"The part where the girl woke up in the insane asylum, took a look in the mirror and thought she was changing into some kind of a leopard—that was the makeup AIP wanted me to do for the movie," Blaisdell recalled. "It involved the head and the paws and of course the rest of me had to be wearing pajamas because, frankly, when I take my shirt off, I don't look too much like a girl."[41]

The Critics: "…sub-standard even for quickie exploitation pictures."—*Hollywood Reporter*; "[A] rather weak picture of its kind and leaves much to be desired."—*Harrison's Reports*; "…all of the horrification—and there is aplenty thereof to satisfy the seekers of chills—doesn't seem to ring true when handled in the polite, restrained

Sam and Hilda Arkoff at London Airport to meet with Nat Cohen and Stuart Levy to discuss further co-productions.

manner characteristic of oversea troupers."—*Boxoffice*; "Lou Rusoff's competently-developed screenplay gives an onlooker ample entertainment in a compact 69 minutes…"—*Motion Picture Herald*; "…screenplay fails to fulfill the promise of [the] idea through blurry writing, and Alfred Shaughnessy's direction is too rambling and distorted to count for much."—*Variety*; "It stinks."—Mark McGee.

JET ATTACK aka **THROUGH HELL TO GLORY** aka **JET ALERT** (1958)

with John Agar, Audrey Totter, Gregory Walcott, James Dobson and Leonard Strong. Written by Lou Rusoff. Produced by Alex Gordon. Directed by Edward L. Cahn. Black and white, 68 minutes. A Catalina Production for American International Pictures.

AIP made four war packages and each picture followed the same formula. A handful of soldiers are sent on a dangerous mission and after a few brief encounters with five or six enemy soldiers, and a liberal dose of stock footage, the mission is accomplished. This one was produced by Alex Gordon, who had always wanted to work with Audrey Totter and was delighted when he learned that the actress's price had finally dropped to $3,000 a week. He ran her name past the exhibitors and they approved. But when he told Sam Arkoff he wanted to hire her Arkoff snapped: "Anybody *but* Audrey Totter." Gordon went ahead and hired her anyway.

"Jim, Sam, Eddie and I had just eaten dinner at the Ivanhoe and we were walking back to the office when Sam asked what was happening with the picture," Gordon said. "I told him I'd signed Audrey Totter. He got furious and he shoved me, and the next thing I knew I was on the ground. I wasn't hurt really. I was more shocked than anything. I went to my office. Eddie poked his head in to see how I was. He said, 'I never dreamed he would do anything like that.' A little later Arkoff came in and he apologized. He said, 'I know I shouldn't have hit you but sometimes you make me so goddamn mad.' And I said, 'But Sam, over Audrey Totter!'"

AIP usually held their sneak previews at the Cornell Theatre in Burbank, but *Jet Attack* was shown at the Uptown in a Korean and Japanese neighborhood. The audience booed and hissed throughout the picture. The beleaguered manager phoned Jim Nicholson and read him the riot act. Nicholson was furious. "You know a lot of exhibitors may not want to play the picture if the word gets out it got a bad reaction from that audience," he told Gordon. Frankly, the picture is so low on entertainment it would have more than likely gotten a bad reaction from *any* audience.

Radio Spot. *Announcer*: "It's take-off time for jet-jockeys, smashing space and the enemy with cannon and rocket and the newest secret weapons. Thrills as old as outer space. Thrills as new as our most secret weapons. Thrills as jagged as a sky battle as jet smashes jet, whipping death across the blazing sky. Never before such action in the world of the air. Never before has the camera dared such close brushes with the air roar of rocket and machine guns. Never before the astounding battle of a jet interceptor versus a helicopter in JET ATTACK. Plus SUICIDE BATTALION. They had no place to hide and they were outnumbered. But their orders said no surrender. On they smashed with gun and flamethrower though they knew it was a one-way road to death. Every stinking tree, every rotten swamp held the enemy. It was all the way and die for the soldiers of the SUICIDE BATTALION. Don't miss this battle-jammed double feature… JET ATTACK and SUICIDE BATTALION.

The Critics: "…a good war feature and much stronger film fair than *Suicide Battal-ion*…"—*Boxoffice*; "A pretty good little war feature despite superficial characterizations in the screenplay."—*Variety*; "has plenty of action and should appeal to adults and teen-agers."—*Film Daily*; "…badly written, poorly directed and acted."—*Motion Picture Exhibitor*; "…everyone but John [Agar]… bites the dust. Yes, even Audrey [Totter]; she didn't seem to be nicked anywhere but in the arm but the big struggle with the Russian accent probably so exhausted her that she just couldn't make it."—*Los Angeles Times*.

SUICIDE BATTALION (1958) with Michael Connors, John Ashley, Russ Bender, Jewell Lain and Bing Russell. Written and produced by Lou Rusoff. Directed by Edward L. Cahn. Black and white 79 minutes. A Zuma Production. An American International Picture.

"I was Cho Cho, the Polynesian jungle girl that John Ashley married," said actress Jackie Joseph. "I had a sarong and long hair and patent leather high heels, running through the jungle during the war. I think I worked longer on *Suicide Battalion* than I did *Little Shop [of Horrors]* because no one could figure out how to write Polynesian. It was a funny job. I was working in Las Vegas with Mitzi McCall when the movie opened at the Palace. I took her to see it and when it was over she said, 'You dragged me here in the middle of the afternoon to see *this?*' I was so excited to be in the movies it never occurred to me that I should have been embarrassed about it."

The Critics: "…for its class is a well-produced little feature… The picture's greatest weakness is a confusion about action and motivations that is never entirely cleared up, but the cast performs capably…"—*Variety*; "The story starts off fairly well but gets lost either through cutting or inadequate direction."—*Film Daily*; "The good basic idea is hopelessly messed up with tritisms."—*Los Angeles Times*; "Weak on story... throws in a lot of action which does not always seem convincing."—*Motion Picture Exhibitor*; "...proves good fare for the action-seeking customer and for its class is a well-produced little feature."—*Boxoffice*; "Suffers from battle fatigue."—Mark McGee.

MACHINE GUN KELLY (1958) with Charles Bronson, Susan Cabot, Morey Amsterdam, Jack Lambert and Wally Campo. Written by R. Wright Campbell. Produced and directed by Roger Corman. Black and white, Superama 84 minutes. An El Monte Production. An American International Picture.

This film is loosely based on notorious gangster George Francis Barnes Jr., better known as Machine Gun Kelly. The entire film is built around his final words to the federal agents who tracked him to his hideout. When they asked Kelly why he didn't put up a fight he replied, "Because you would have killed me." One of the Hollywood trade papers announced that Corman regular Dick Miller would be playing the title role.

"I can't remember, maybe a week before we were supposed to start, they told me I was out," Miller said. "I had a contract so they had to pay me, but I really wanted that part because it was a good part. And I didn't find out why until years later, after Jim Nicholson left AIP and went into independent production. He had a little office on Sunset and I stopped by one day to drop off some scripts. Now he and I had never been buddies or anything like that but we started talking about the old days, you know, and he said, 'You want to know why you didn't get that part?' I said 'Sure.' It turned out that Bobby Campbell wanted his brother in the part. Bobby was living in New York at the time, and he started sending telegrams and making phone calls, saying that I wasn't right for the part. Now, understand, Bobby was supposed to be my friend. Finally, he says only his brother can play the part, that he's tailored the script for his brother. So Roger gets all upset and he finally says, 'Pay Dick off and get me the names of three actors available to play Kelly by tomorrow.' And they ended up giving the role to Charlie Bronson. And that really made me mad. I thought about it many times. I walked away from a lot of parts but this one walked away from me and I really wanted it. I think it would have done for me the same thing it did for Charlie."[42]

Corman was informed by someone from the Production Code office that J. Edgar Hoover and the FBI were concerned that a new cycle of gangster movies might have a negative effect on our image abroad, to say nothing of offering a blueprint to would-be criminals. Corman promised not to make any more gangster movies then turned right around and made *I Mobster* that same year.

The Critics: "The solving of this case was such a masterpiece of detection that one wonders why the producer-director, Roger Corman, didn't make some use of it."— *Hollywood Reporter*; "Convincing, accurate, rapidly-paced action-laden biography of one of the hardest hombres of his hectic era."—*Boxoffice*; "... a first-rate little picture ... Script is remarkable for the crisp flavor of the dialogue and takes the trouble to sketch briefly, but effectively, minor characters and incidents that give weight and meaning to the otherwise sordid story."—*Variety*; "... comprehensive, compact and paced for dramatic effect."—*Motion Picture Herald*; "The acting in this film, which would be a lot better with less footage and a general tightening all the way around, is excellent."— *Citizen News*; "Kelly (Charles Bronson) hefted a big gun, but this screen memorial to him is exceedingly small bore. Besides, it shoot blanks."—*Los Angeles Examiner*.

HORRORS OF THE BLACK MUSEUM (1959) with Michael Gough, June Cunningham, Graham Curnow, Shirley Ann Field and Geoffrey Keen. Written by Aben Kandel. Produced by Jack Greenwood. Executive Producer Herman Cohen. Directed by Arthur Crabtree. Eastmancolor, CinemaScope, HypnoVista, 95 minutes (82 min UK). A Carmel Production for American International Pictures.

Jim Nicholson must have been a little nervous about sending this film out as a single attraction, even though that was the whole point of making a more expensive movie. He asked Herman Cohen to whip up a black and white cheapie to pair with it. Then he added a thirteen minute prologue in which a hypnotherapist demonstrated the power of suggestion. Jim called this silly piece of hype HypnoVista. "It actually puts YOU in the picture!" the advertisements claimed. "You FEEL the chilling fog... the piercing blade... the acid vat of death!"

"When Jim told me what he was writing and working on, I was reluctant to permit it to be tagged on, but I let Jim talk me into it," Cohen said. "He said, 'Herm, if it's really that bad, we'll take it off.' We tested it in a few theaters and the audience went for it like crazy, hokey as it was."

The film's opening sequence, inspired by a real life incident, is easily the most effective and disturbing moment in the film. A woman receives a pair of binoculars in the mail and when she adjusts the focus a pair of nasty spikes pokes her eyes out. Ruth Pologe, AIP's head of publicity in New York, told Cohen to bring the trick binoculars with him when he returned to the U.S. and then tell the people at the airport that he'd lost them. Anything for some free publicity.

Cohen's first choice to play the maniac who writes best-selling books about the murders he commits was Vincent Price, but he couldn't afford him. "Anyway," Cohen said, "under British Eady, you're allowed to bring X-number of Americans in, but Nat Cohen said, 'Herm, why can't you use a British actor?'" The part was given to Michael Gough who delivers a scene-chewing performance worthy of Price on his best day.

In his book, *Monsters in the Closet*, author Harry Benshoff examines the homosexual and misogynistic tone of Cohen's films. Apparently, having surrounded himself with like-thinking people, Cohen was a little taken aback when asked about the homosexual implications of *The Black Museum*. When questioned about Gough's little speech to his impressionable young assistant, where he states that women are a vicious unreliable breed, the producer had to admit Gough did sound a little gay but then, unable to control himself, added: "Mind you, there's a lot of truth to what he's telling him."

Herm, you'd better let me have that shovel before you dig yourself in any deeper.

"Cohen was a showman first, last, and always; his manner was always overbearing and his opinions sacrosanct," Michael Gough told historian David Del Valle. "During the filming of *Horrors of the Black Museum*, he would show up unannounced on set and tell our director, Arthur Crabtree, how to direct a scene and the actors as well ... as a result, Arthur began to loathe Cohen on sight."

During a discussion about the picture in one of the major universities, a young student asked Cohen why Hollywood didn't make more pictures for intellectual audiences. Cohen asked the class how many of them had seen *Black Museum*. Nobody raised their hand. Cohen turned the professor's back to the class and asked the question again. A lot of hands went up. "Then I asked about *Face in the Crowd* [1957], and practically no one had seen it—there were so few hands it was ridiculous," said Cohen. "For *Sunrise at Campobello* [1960] there were even fewer."[43]

The Critics: "This is probably one of the slickest, best written, best produced and best directed horror films to come out in a very long time."—*Los Angeles Times*; "In virtually every category of craftsmanship, this picture bares evidence of only an ounce of thought for every pound of CinemaScope footage ... dialogue shows a convenient disregard for motivation and dramatic technique."—*New York Times*; "The producers have relied on sensationalism without subtlety of characterization, situation, or dialogue. As a result, this rather distasteful item is likely to gather more misplaced laughs than shudders among discriminating audiences."—*Variety*; "Has a way of making

This is the scene everyone remembers, Dorinda Stevens getting her eyes poked out by a trick pair of binoculars.

its points as a spine-chiller."—*New York Herald Tribune*; "Director Arthur Crabtree extracts the mood of brooding evil… with commendable skill…"—*Film Daily*; "… Gough is in constant contact with Scotland Yard… and it is almost impossible to believe that the fabled institution could not have tripped him up sooner than it does."—*Motion Picture Herald*; "Michael Gough… is the type of obvious villain who, in a realistic story, would be the first man collared by any precinct captain. But he has a gaudy Bela Lugosi quality that is perfect for a make-believe chiller."—*Hollywood Reporter*; "The intellectual audience-pleasure derived from a subtle exercise in crime detection gives place to the offensive, charnel-house gluttony of mass butchery…"—*Cue*; "… ladles out the gore with such a heavy hand, I think Cohen can confidently expect to get a few angry notes from parents."—*Mirror News*; "The gore at times is quite nasty. Equally offensive is the way the story is told—without style, dramatic suspense or understandable motivation."—*Los Angeles Examiner*.

The Exhibitors: "Scope and color made this one beautiful. And if your small town is like our small town, they will talk this one up, because it is something different in the line of horror movies."—Harold J. Smith, NY; "Worst piece of nonsense I ever

Michael Gough will see to it that June Cunningham loses
her head before *Horrors of the Black Museum* is over.

saw. Has long 'intro' the kids hate. Rest of film is an insult to the intelligence and, worst of all, is a bore."—Charles Burton, MO; "...a good story, interesting first reel and kept all satisfied. Had average Saturday, poor Sunday."—Arlen W. Peahl, OR.

*SIGN OF THE GLADIATOR aka SHEBA AND THE GLADIATOR aka SIGN OF ROME (1959) with Anita Ekberg, George Marshall, Folco Lulli, Chelo Alonso and Jacque Serrias. Written by Sergio Leone, Guido Brignone, Giuseppe Mangione and Francesco De Feo. Produced by Vittorio Musy-Glori. Directed by Guido Brignone. Eastman Color, Dyaliscope 80 minutes. A Glomer Film Production released by American International Pictures.

One puzzled critic noted in his review of this film that no matter how hard he looked there was no sign of a gladiator anywhere. Where did he go? What happened to him? Nothing. He was never in the film to begin with. The original title of this Italian film was *Sign of Rome*. Jim Nicholson thought *Sign of the Gladiator* was a better title but they had to have a gladiator in the film. "So we conceived that this man, this Roman consul, had been a slave tossed in the gladiators' ring," Arkoff said. "When the Roman blood got thin, which happened along about 300 A.D., they brought people who had been successful gladiators and put them in the Roman Army. Whether or not anybody ever got up to the position this Roman consul did in our picture ... Anyway, the queen of Syria, played by Anita Ekberg, gives this Roman consul the old sex play to get him to betray himself. If he doesn't overcome the Queen, who he's in love with, he could wind up back in the gladiator ring. Now there was a gladiator in the story." A little dubbing can solve just about any story problem.

The Critics: "Just when we thought the movies were beginning to show some improvement, along comes *Sign of the Gladiator...*"—*Citizen News*; "...a fatuous costume spectacle which deals with political hanky-panky in the Roman Empire in 217 A.D. It looks and sounds as if it were made just about that time."—*Los Angeles Examiner*; "Let's fervently hope that whoever supplied the English titles on this American International release had a sense of humor. The unwary spectator will need one. And so will the hefty Anita Ekberg if she doesn't start easing up on contemporary bread and potatoes."—*Los Angeles Times*; "The deepest thing about it is Anita Ekberg's cleavage. That's about all anyone will talk about."—*Variety*; "The one asset that might help this Italian-made film duplicate the surprise business done by *Hercules* is the presence of a robust girl, Anita Ekberg, with dimensions not easily overlooked ..."—*Hollywood Reporter*; "The plot is as thin as some of the costumes Miss Ekberg wears."—*New York Herald Tribune*.

The Exhibitors. "Not enough action to please our patrons, and especially the kids— what else have you these days? Did all right but am staying away from this type of show for a while."—A. Madril, CO; "Spectacular scenes—quite colorful and in CinemaScope. High school kids caught on right away that it was dubbed in English, so gave us a bad time over the dialog. Anita Ekberg... WOW!"—Carl W. Veseth, MT; "This has Scope and color, but was just not enough for us. In one of the later issues of *Boxoffice* I saw running time of 104 minutes. We got 82 minutes of it here. This could have been the reason for dissatisfaction."—Harold Bell, Quebec.

GOLIATH AND THE BARBARIANS aka THE TERROR OF
THE BARBARIANS (1959) with Steve Reeves, Chelo Alonso, Bruce Cabot, Giulia Rubini and Livio Lorenzon. Written by Gino Mangini, Nino Stresa, Giuseppe Taffarel and Carlo Campogalliani. ColorScope 88 minutes. An Alta Vista Production for American International Release.

This is not a scene from *Sign of the Gladiator*. It's from Columbia's *Zarak* (1956) but doesn't Anita Ekberg look fabulous?

Jim and Sam were in Europe to buy movies and found one called *The Terror of the Barbarians* with Steve Reeves. The producer had run out of money. Jim and Sam gave him $20,000 to finish it in exchange for the U.S. distribution rights. They dubbed it, Les Baxter scored it, and after struggling with the title—*Goliath and the Golden Horde, Colossus and the Golden Horde*—it did fantastic business.

The Critics: "It's not intended as comedy, but that's how [it] projects in the shallow, silly telling. It has the panoply of a big spectacle, but the disguise barely conceals the actual poverty of values in nearly all departments."—*Variety*; "Only occasionally in its brief passage does this Italian-made, English-dubbed film pull up to the intelligence level of an 8-year-old, and seldom does it manage to be more than conventionally dull ... The sooner it is forgotten, the better for the movie industry."—*New York Times*; "It is a lusty, brawling spectacle, full of deeds of derring-do and of danger, excitement and fair maidens."—*Los Angeles Examiner*; "The primitive little scenario ... is designed to give Reeves the maximum opportunity to flex. And that's about it. Some of the stilted love scenes, however, did provoke snickers from the juvenile audience."—*Los Angeles Times*; "The acting throughout is reminiscent of a serious High School dramatic effort."—*New York Herald Tribune*; "... a sprawling travesty of the historical spectacle."—*Mirror News*; "Little can be said for the story, acting or directing ... Summed up, a film for small fry—and adults with juvenile minds."—*Citizen News*.

The Exhibitors. "The picture is simply action-filled and the girl is reminiscent of Gina Lollobrigida. Don't worry. Play it."—Paul Gamache, VT; "Terms a little too high ... just average business."—James Hardy, IN; "A lot better than *Sign of the Gladiator*. Enough said."—Harold Bell, Quebec; "There is a lot of entertainment in this show and the business it does will surprise you."—Jim Fraser, MN; "This is not a blockbuster but they come to see it. I can't figger 'em out."—C. H. Crenshaw, TX; "I think that these spectacles starring Steve Reeves ... though somewhat silly, are what people want and wow what business they gave us. So what's to complain about?"— Paul Fourner, NB; "... opened in Dallas, Houston, San Antonio, Fort Worth and Galveston ... to the biggest grosses of any picture in the history of our company pre-Christmas time."—Raymond Willie, Vice President of Interstate Circuit; "Has lots of action, good color and drew a good turnout from the kids."—Mel Danner, OK.

THE ANGRY RED PLANET (1960) with Gerald Mohr, Nora Hayden, Les Tremayne, Jack Kruschen and Paul Hahn. Produced by Sid Pink. Written and directed by Ib Melchior. Eastman Color, Cinemagic 94 minutes. A Sino Production. An American International Release.

This ambitious little film about a trip to Mars was the brainchild of Sid Pink, a former theatre owner. Pink was convinced that a commercial artist named Norman Maurer could make his picture the talk of the town. Maurer was developing a lens that he hoped would make live action figures look like line drawings. "A positive 35mm black and white, and a negative were sandwiched together, printed on a third film through a specially built and designed pair of small Lucite lenses to bend the

Steve Reeves and Chelo Alonso.

light," Maurer explained. "The film was then exposed in red onto color film."[44] The effect that Maurer and Pink hoped to achieve was a seamless blend of live action, puppets, and cartoon backgrounds. What they got was something similar to a process called solarization and after a while it was quite annoying.

The picture went into production in September of 1959, on the largest stage at Hal Roach Studios. Pink ran out of money before they could complete the film and told writer-director Ib Melchior they'd have to scrap the sequence where a giant amoeba attacks the spaceship, even though everything leading up to and away from the sequence had already been photographed.

"We had to have the sequence," Melchior said, "so I bought five packages of Jell-O, some finger paint and a plastic spaceship. We froze the Jell-O, put the spaceship into the middle of it, and put it on a hotplate. We shot the Jell-O melting and it was printed in reverse. We didn't have any money so we had to use our imagination."

Pink went $50,000 over his budget and had to sell the picture to AIP to get the creditors off his back. He told writer David C. Hayes that he and Sam Arkoff didn't trust each other, "which worked out well because I wouldn't touch him with a ten foot pole. Jimmy Nicholson was the brains of that operation. With Arkoff, you never got a straight count."

Radio Spot. *Announcer*: "A great new motion picture in the world's newest motion picture process, Cinemagic, the wonder of the added fourth dimension. With Cinemagic you are actually on the first rocket ride to Mars in THE ANGRY RED PLANET. You'll FEEL the dizzying heights of their fantastic mile-high buildings! You'll SHIVER as you ride the river of the dead! Your depth perception will increase a thousandfold as you look into the water that lead into foreverness! And the ter-

The rat-bat-spider-crab is blinded by Jack Kruschen's ray gun.

Jack Kruschen, Nora Hayden, Gerald Mohr,
Les Tremayne and a people-eating plant.

rors you meet on Mars are beyond man's imagination. The rat-bat spider, so real in Cinemagic you'll feel the crazed stare of its blinded eyes, the tearing shock of its iron claws. The giant amoeba, like an earth germ only a hundred million times larger. Thrills! Shocks! Terrors! And your first glimpse of the world and the life of Mars are all yours to experience in THE ANGRY RED PLANET in Eastman 52-50 color from American International."

The Critics: "...the spectacle of the thing gets you even as you find the dialogue among the space travelers somewhat inane."—*Los Angeles Herald Examiner*; "While it may take considerable ingenuity to produce [Cinemagic], the result isn't really worth it."—*Variety*; "The Martian landscape looks like a risible collection of cardboard cutouts, photographed in a kind of infrared light against which the human figures blur like ink on a blotting paper."—*Monthly Film Bulletin*; "... warns its audience not to go to Mars. Stubborn patrons who ignore the advice will discover that the planet looks like a cardboard illustration from Flash Gordon..."—*New York Times*; "...simply embarrassing..."—*Los Angeles Times*.

The Exhibitors. "...it flopped. Funny, we always get taken on these so-called advertising campaigns..."—Paul Gamache, VT; "Only fair, and too much talk. This is about the worst big budget science fiction of the year. I was sure 'angry red' when I saw it."—Paul Fourner, NB.

CIRCUS OF HORRORS (1960) with Anton Diffring, Erica Remberg, Yvonne Monlaur, Donald Pleasence and Jane Hylton. Written by George Baxt. Produced by Julian Wintle and Leslie Parkyn. Directed by Sidney Hayers. Eastmancolor 92 minutes. An American International Release.

Herman Cohen was the executive producer on this picture and it's very much like something he would make. Written by George Baxt, the story is silly and most of the women meet a violent end, but unlike Cohen's films this one has an adult sensibility and is executed with style and wit by a director who obviously knows what he's doing.

"Off the top of my head," recalled writer George Baxt, "I told [Julian Wintle and Leslie Parkyn] a terrible story about a circus run by a plastic surgeon who turned criminals into beautiful people. The ones that weren't beautiful became freaks. They said, 'Okay, you have a deal,' and I almost fainted right in front of them."[45]

Anton Diffring is perfect as Rossiter, the brilliant but homicidal plastic surgeon who orchestrates fatal 'accidents' for the performers who want to leave his circus. In Baxt's script, and in the novelization of it by Tom Owen, the character's name is Dr. Goethe. The name was changed to Bernard Schuler to match the initials plastered all over Billy Smart's circus.

In the British version of *Circus of Horrors*, the credits are presented in the traditional way at the beginning of the film. AIP made the decision to hold the bulk of the credits until the end of their movies, a common practice today but AIP more or less led the charge. New, shorter credits were shot and Franz Reizenstein's main title was replaced by an instrumental version of 'Look for a Star,' sung throughout the film by Gary Mills. After the titles in the British version we see an establishing shot of a house. Inside we find Colette Wilde going from room to room, smashing every mirror in the joint. Because she's parading around in her undergarments, the American version cuts directly from the titles to the tail-end of this sequence. Throughout the film snips were made in all of the scenes where women were shown in their underwear but this one at the beginning is sloppy and jarring. Fortunately, the original version is the one available on the DVD release.

The Critics: "Blood and horror against a background of the big top are not new to hor-

Donald Pleasance, Kenneth Griffith and Jane Hylton anxiously
watch Anton Diffring remove Carla Challoner's bandages
in this tense moment from *Circus of Horrors* (1960).

ror picture fans but seldom have they been combined in the quantity and with the skill
that pervaded this British-made production..."—*Motion Picture Herald*; "...a pageant
of color, a triumph of 'Big Top' entertainment, and a parade of crimes that culminate in
one of the most suspenseful scenes the screen can offer."—*Los Angeles Times*; "...a neat
little package of movie melodramatic entertainment—with a story not too slick in its
writing and just ingenious enough to disarm criticism."—*Cue*; "...maintains a fast, hor-
rific pace and winds up with a satisfying, if grisly, fade out."—*Boxoffice*; "...the crispest,
handsomest, and most stylish movie shocker in a long time."—*New York Times*; "*Circus
of Horrors* is horrible. Not spine-chilling horrible. Just horrible, horrible."—*New York
Herald Tribune*; "...a better-than-average chiller-diller..."—*Citizen News*; "Director
Sidney Hayers has kept the proceedings moving briskly and absorbingly."—*Film Daily*;
"...an edge-of-the-seat picture... For teenagers and adults it is excitement plus, and
highly recommended..."—*Los Angeles Examiner*; "Lots of fun."—Mark McGee.

The Exhibitors. "This company certainly has arrived. The last two or three attractions
of theirs have been exceptional grossers for us and this is no exception... a real crowd

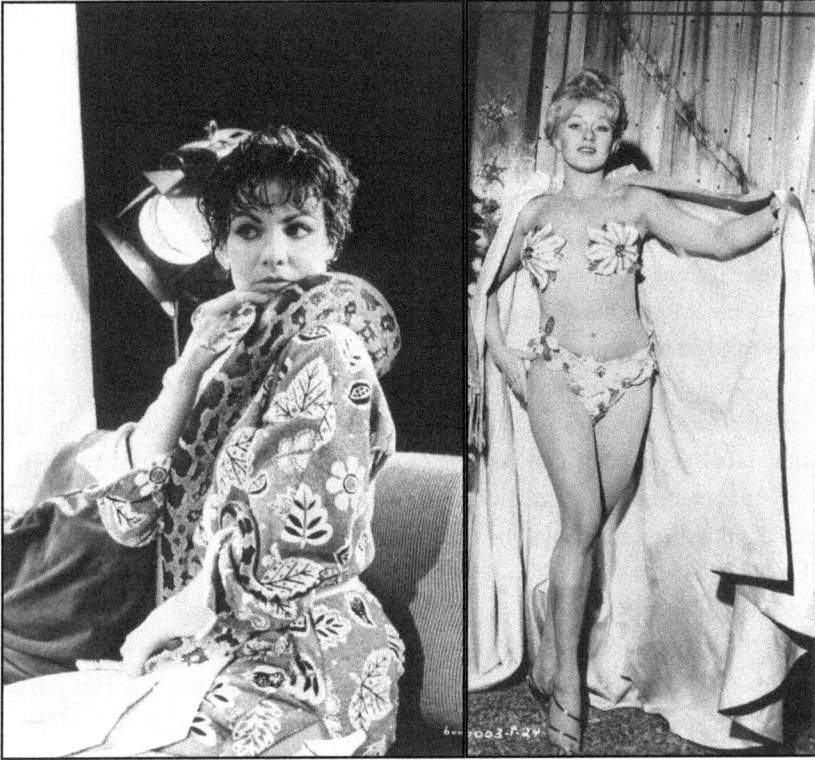

Left: Erica Remberg. Right: Vanda Hudson.

pleaser…"—Jim Fraser, MN; "As we have said before, this company has the recipe for horror and teen shows."—Harry Hawkinson, MN; "This was a very good picture and was packed with suspense. Color was beautiful but wish it had been in Scope too. Business was satisfactory."—Harold J. Smith, NY; "…did good business for us. Good show of its type and I would say play it, especially in small towns."—Terry Axley, AR.

HOUSE OF USHER (1960) with Vincent Price, Myrna Fahey, Mark Damon and Harry Ellerby. Written by Richard Matheson based on a story by Edgar Allan Poe. Produced and directed by Roger Corman. Pathecolor and CinemaScope 80 minutes. An Alta Vista Production for American International Pictures.

"When we first started the film," said Dan Haller, "Roger wanted to make a really good picture, but we saw right away we were going to go way over what AIP had initially approved for the budget. So we worked 24-hour days. What we'd do is shoot all day long, and then Roger and I [and assistant director Jack Bohrer] would go out to dinner… Then, afterwards, we'd go back on the set and stay there until we had the next day's work all planned out. We'd go over all the shots and say 'Where would John Ford put the camera?' or 'Where would Alfred Hitchcock put the camera?' Sometimes we'd stay as late as midnight or 1:00 a.m., so I always knew what Roger was planning to do the next day. Then I was able to get with the grips and let them know what we needed for the upcoming shots. That was especially good when we needed cranes or anything else that would require a lot of advance set-up time. So, whenever Roger finished a shot and said, 'Print,' we were already in position and ready to go on to the next shot."[46]

Corman heard about a fire in the Hollywood Hills on his car radio and drove directly to the scene. He caught the tail end of the blaze and returned the next day with Mark Damon, a horse, and a skeleton crew to film the opening scene of the picture. The actor rode past the blackened trees and the ash covered ground, a terrain more atmospheric than anything Haller could have created on a soundstage with the skimpy money he had to work with. Once Damon steps into the house the film never leaves the soundstage.

The climax of the film shows the Usher mansion engulfed in flames as it sinks into the mire. Corman found an old barn in Orange County that was going to be levelled and paid the owner $50 to let him burn it. He used two cameras to film it.[47]

On the last day of production, Corman and his crew were racing the clock to shoot a scene of the house collapsing around Vincent Price. They had five minutes before they'd slip into overtime. Floyd Crosby announced that he needed to pull a light, which meant the doors had to be opened so the wind machines could blow out the smoke. That was going to take at least five minutes. As he often did when he was frustrated, Roger threw his baseball cap on the floor and stormed out of the building. Crosby finished sooner than he or anyone else expected him to and the doors were quickly locked; the bell went off. Crosby looked at Dan Haller and said, "Come on, Dan—say Action!" So he said it and Vincent Price did what they'd rehearsed and they got the shot, without going into overtime.

The Critics: "…a restoration of finesse and craftsmanship to the genre of the dead."—*New York Herald Tribune*; "It is a film that should attract mature tastes as well as those who come to the cinema for sheer thrills."—*Variety*; "…a film that kids will love that never once insults adult intelligence."—*Los Angeles Examiner*; "…better than average horror film if that's saying much."—*Los Angeles Times*; "It is in the grand tradition of the horror film, with rich and lavish settings, a great horror of a

Vincent Price and Myrna Fahey as Roderick and Madeline Usher.

house slowly disintegrating, guttering candles flickering in the wind, murky secret passageways, and cobwebbed burial crypts."—*Hollywood Reporter.*

The Exhibitors. "Well acted—nice color."—Jim Fraser, MN; "The story was all dragged out and couldn't hold people's attention. Deserves a playdate, but would suggest adding another action picture with it. After all, this company is giving us the pictures that go across today. So they should be supported."—Harold J. Smith, NY; "This company is really turning out some honeys and this is one in Cinema-

Scope and color."—Harold Bell, Quebec; "…will out gross some of your so-called 'super pictures,' if your situation is like mine. Pleased all."—Terry Axley, AR; "If you haven't played it yet, book it for your weekend change, as it will make money."—Larry Thomas, WV; "My patrons who enjoy spook shows liked it and told me so on the way out."—Mitchell Kelloff, CO; "Could have been scarier. Color helped a lot, but deadpan acting of Vincent Price too high class for this."—Paul Gamache, VT.

BLACK SUNDAY aka THE MASK OF SATAN aka MASK OF THE DE-MON aka REVENGE OF THE VAMPIRE (1961) with Barbara Steele, John Richardson, Ivo Garrani, Andrea Checchi and Arturo Dominici. Written by Ennio de Concini, Mario Bava, Maracello Coscia and Mario Serandre. Black and white 84 minutes. A Galetea-Jolly Production. An American International Release.

AIP trimmed over three minutes of 'objectionable' material before they dared release this richly atmospheric Italian horror film, and it was still more gruesome and violent than American audiences were used to.

"It's supposed to take place in Russia, because it's taken from a story by Gogol but I must say, the film feels incredibly Nordic," said leading lady Barbara Steele. "It was very familiar, this landscape Mario Bava drew, because it reminded me of where I grew up in Scotland and Wales, a wild Gothic environment with wild storms. Looking at it, it's just impossible to imagine that this film was shot in Italy. It's just inspired, really."[48] The actress said she didn't like the fangs they gave her. "I had them changed three times. I loathed my wig—I changed that four times. I couldn't understand Italian… I certainly didn't want to allow them to tear open my dress and expose my breasts, so they got a double that I didn't like at all, so I ended up doing it anyway—drunk, barely over eighteen, embarrassed, and not very easy to be around."[49]

The picture made a horror icon out of Steele. She is, perhaps, the biggest female horror star in screen history.

The Critics: "A classic quality permeates this gruesome, shocking, horrifying story of a vengeful, blood-thirsty vampire. Effectively photographed in low key black and white against rich setting of macabre design… achieves frightful elements of surprise through clever makeup and performances."—Motion Picture Herald; "The technicians and artisans… are to be highly commended for creating moods and illusions with skilled sets, props, costumes, cinematography, musical score and particularly editing."—Hollywood Citizen News; "…a piece of fine Italian handiwork that

Barbara Steele as the vengeful witch Asa Vajda.

atones for its ludicrous lapses with brilliant intuitions of the spectral."—*Time*; "...as large a dose of spine-freezer as the motion picture screen has ever offered."—*Boxoffice*; "There is sufficient cinematography ingenuity and production flair... to keep the audience pleasantly unnerved."—*Variety*; "...a honey of a horror."—*Los Angeles Examiner*; "As a setting for unadulterated horror, it will leave its audiences yearning for that quiet, sunny little motel in *Psycho*."—*New York Times*.

The Exhibitors: "...the type of picture the parents tell us not to show—and every kid in town shows up. Rather oddball and certainly weird. The kids all ran for the doors, but they came back the next day for another look. This has been our most requested film and it did swell."—Al Zarzana, Ray Boriski, TX; "It was a 'Black Weekend' for me. Very little business on this one."—A. Madril, CO; "Play it and don't be afraid of it."—Harold J. Smith, NY.

MASTER OF THE WORLD (1961) with Vincent Price, Charles Bronson, Henry Hull, Mary Webster and David Frankham. Written by Richard Matheson based on *Robur le Conquerant* by Jules Verne. Produced by James H. Nicholson. Directed by William Witney. MagnaColor, 104 minutes. An Alta Vista Production for American International Pictures.

This was one of Jim Nicholson's dream projects. Sam Arkoff thought it was a bad idea and for a change it turned out that he was right. It was simply too big for its low budget britches. The seams are showing every step of the way. But Jim had high hopes for it, as evidenced by the roadshow-style stereo overture that opens the picture. And he was so happy with Richard Matheson's screenplay that he gave the writer a bonus. Jim wanted Roger Corman to helm the project but he was too busy and the assignment was given to William Witney, a prolific but artless director. His disdain for the project triggered a heated argument with Matheson that forced Jim Nicholson, who hated confrontations of any kind, to intervene.

The centerpiece of the film is Robur's flying machine, The Albatross. It was the creation of Project Unlimited, the company responsible for the Academy Award winning effects in George Pal's *The Time Machine* (1960). Project sent a letter to the Academy in the hope of winning another nomination for this picture, highlighting the intricate detail that went into the Albatross—39 rotating propellers, mechanized trap doors, rocket devices, controls, etc. Apparently the Academy was not impressed although the film did receive a Special Merit Award from *Parents Magazine*. Anytime *Parents Magazine* liked something it was a safe bet that the kids wouldn't.

There were a lot of merchandise tie-ins for this picture, a first for an AIP movie. Les Baxter's score was released on VeeJay Records, there was an Ace paperback novel and a Dell comic book.

The Critics: "The paper airplane crowd may find the ethics of the film a bit confusing, but they are bound to get a bang out of The Albatross, which is indeed a gorgeous gadget."—*Time*; "Adults dragged in to watch the American International release will find it devoid of artistic pretensions, but a lot more sufferable than they would suppose."—*New York Times*; "It's not so much the inevitable grotesquerie of the picture's mechanical marvels, but the drabness of the characterization and dialogue that keeps it well below the level of interest adult moviegoers would expect."—*New York Herald Tribune*; "...there is a certain element of monotony and repetition about the long ride in the air, a suspended lethargy that director William Witney has not been able to disturb too frequently."—*Variety*; "...watered down Jules Verne, in which generally unexciting acting and lethargic direction take second place to the astute special effects and art direction..."—*Monthly Film Bulletin*; "...engrossing, actionful science fiction drama..."—*Boxoffice*.

The Exhibitors. "This was okay, but was not the big superduper I thought it would be." S. T. Jackson, AL; "This one is really very good. Business average. I like American International. Seems like a fine company. They treat me pretty good anyway."—Don Stott, MD; "Vincent Price always is a draw, but somehow we did only average on this."—Ray Boriski, TX.

Ad art from *Master of the World* (1961).

Charles Bronson.

BURN WITCH BURN aka **NIGHT OF THE EAGLE** (1962) with Janet Blair, Peter Wyngarde, Margaret Johnston, Anthony Nicholls and Colin Gordon. Written by Charles Beaumont, Richard Matheson and George Baxt based on the novel *Conjure Wife* by Fritz Leiber. Produced by Albert Fennell. Directed by Sidney Hayers. Black and white 86 minutes. A Julian Wintle-Leslie Parkyn Production released by American International Pictures.

One night over drinks Richard Matheson and Charles Beaumont decided to write a script based on Fritz Leiber's novel *Conjure Wife*. Universal owned the story rights and had made a miserable version of it back in the 40s as part of the studio's Inner Sanctum series. Matheson wrote the first half of the script and Beaumont finished it. They jointly polished it and gave it to Jim Nicholson. Nicholson paid them each $5,000 and would have paid them more if he hadn't had to buy the rights from Universal. George Baxt, who receives a screen credit in the British version, said their script was an embarrassment and that director Sidney Hayers was near tears when he read it. Baxt claimed that he wrote 90 per cent of what was on the screen. Director Hayers said otherwise. "No, Richard Matheson and Charles Beaumont wrote the script, and George didn't have a lot to do with—I can assure you."[50] Hayers also put to rest the rumor that he had to keep his camera close on Peter Wyngarde to avoid showing his tight-fitting pants. Incidentally, Wyngarde wasn't the first choice to play Janet Blair's skeptical husband. It was Peter Cushing.

The Critics: "The many supernatural happenings should please the diehard lovers of the horror film."—*Motion Picture Herald*; "... has suspense and intriguing episodes to hold the most discerning audiences, as well as those who like their shudders in large doses."—*Boxoffice*; "... quite the most effective 'supernatural thriller' since *Village of the Damned* [1960] several seasons ago... growing chillier by the minute, and finally whipping up an ice-cold crescendo of fright... Excellently photographed (not a single 'frame' is wasted) and cunningly directed by Sidney Hayers..."—*New York Times*; "... fresh and exciting, skillful in its reliance on suggestion, naggingly effective as a study of psychic attack."—*The British Film Institute*.

The Exhibitors. "This drew quite well and was real scary and very well acted... Naturally, we had to play it on a double bill, but it could have played alone."—Paul Fournier, NB.

BEACH PARTY (1963) with Bob Cummings, Dorothy Malone, Frankie Avalon, Annette Funicello and Harvey Lembeck. Written by Lou Rusoff. Produced by James H. Nicholson and Samuel Z. Arkoff. Directed by William Asher. Pathecolor, Panavision, 101 minutes. An Alta Vista Production for American International Pictures.

William Asher was one year away from his successful television series *Bewitched* when he was asked to direct this film. He claimed that Lou Rusoff's script was full of violence and drugs, and that *he* was the one who convinced Jim Nichol-

Janet Blair.

son to turn it into a comedy. With all due respect to Mr. Asher, that's a lot of crap. Look at the record. AIP stopped making juvenile delinquency movies in 1959, the same year that Lou Rusoff wrote *Ghost of Dragstrip Hollow,* a slapstick comedy with songs, a blueprint for *Beach Party.*

"I broke into writing with the Annette Funicello/Frankie Avalon beach pictures," said Stanley Ross, a regular contributor to *Batman* and *The Man from U.N.C.L.E.* "My job was to come in and 'youthen' the scripts. They paid me $1,000 a script just to read them and change the dialogue to make it more contemporary."[51]

"When we did the beach pictures, AIP was more cognizant of an image," John Ashley recalled. "It was a lot different from the old days. I can still remember going to sneak previews of those pictures like *Motorcycle Gang* [1957] and *Dragstrip Girl* [1957] and when the audience saw that damn AIP logo they groaned. Of course, those pictures were made in ten days, sometimes less. But Bill Asher, the director of the beach pictures, wanted to maintain an image. We depicted the California surfing crowd as a bunch of fun-loving kids. Always Cokes. No beers. Nobody smoked. They even asked us not to smoke between takes."[52]

Gary Usher, Roger Christian, Guy Hemric and Al Simms wrote the songs for *Beach Party* and some of them were quite good. Simms was the head of AIP's music department and Hemric was his right-hand man. Usher and Christian had written songs for The Beach Boys, the chart-busting group who gave surfing its musical identity. Because of their association with the group, Simms assumed that Usher and Christian knew how to surf, so they were given parts in the picture. Simms was right about Christian but Usher didn't know the first thing about surfing. But since it was the middle of winter (who in their right minds would shoot a beach picture

It doesn't look like a very good day for a Beach Party
but Frankie and Annette are determined to have fun anyway.

in the winter time?) he assumed he'd have six months to learn. Panic set in when he was told to be at Malibu beach at the end of the week. It was cold and foggy when he and Christian paddled into the water. After a couple of hours, Usher turned blue, lost the feeling in his legs and couldn't stop shaking. "I was so embarrassed," he said. "They stopped the shooting, dragged me up onto the sand, wrapped me in blankets and gave me some hot coffee while they called the paramedics. The whole time I was dying a hundred and one humiliations."[53]

Al Simms felt Bill Asher played a crucial role in the success of the film. "If he was shooting a scene and something hit him, he didn't have to stop and write it down. He'd just tell Floyd Crosby, our cameraman, to set up over there and shoot. Even though it wasn't in the script, the scene would work every time."[54]

"I went over schedule," Asher admitted. "And at the end of one day's shooting, I suddenly noticed a lot of people around. I'd been so involved in what I was doing that I didn't realize that there was something out of the ordinary for a long time. Then I found out that all of the people were part of the wrap party. Sam [Arkoff] said, 'If nothing else comes in on schedule, the wrap party will.' So we had a wrap party. We had about three more days to shoot. I didn't have the time to go through the editing process that I wanted to afterward because I'd done a television pilot with Patty Duke that had sold, and we were shooting it in New York. I had to go back there and get started. Sam said, 'If you go to New York that's it. We haven't got time to fool around.' I told him I needed one weekend to tighten the editing, which meant double time pay. He said, 'You can have the weekend but as far as I'm concerned the picture is finished. So you'll pay for it.' So I paid for it. Not begrudgingly, because he was right."

Beach Party took off. When Asher got a check in the mail, reimbursing him for the money he'd spent, he expected the phone to ring any minute.

"Sam finally called and asked if I would meet with Jim on his boat in Miami to talk about another picture," Asher said. "We met Jim in Miami, Bob Dillon and I, and we concocted another story that weekend."

The Critics: "As a study of primitive behavior patterns, *Beach Party* is more unoriginal than aboriginal..."—*Time*; "It moves quickly and easily and has been dressed with handsome production values, including spankingly clean camera work by Kay Norton."—*Variety*; "...looks ready-made for the teenage crowd, whose numbers are legion, and also looks like lots of box office for the exploitation-minded showman."—*Motion Picture Daily*; "The real trouble is that almost the entire cast emerges as the dullest bunch of meatballs ever, with the old folks even sillier than the kids... Jody McCrea, Harvey Lembeck and Morey Amsterdam, as sideline comics, are downright embarrassing. Mr. Cummings has to be seen to be believed and Miss Malone had better hold tight to that Academy Award."—*New York Times*; "…made-to-order for youthful patrons, who make up the largest part of today's moviegoers, and it will also score with the older patrons."—*Boxoffice*; "…gets by with a serviceable plot, and fizzles out before there is any question of higher citations."—*New York Post*; "Everything is overworked—too many variations on the twist, too much slapstick, too many inanities."—*New York Daily News*; "A sappy bit of seashore nonsense in which an abundance of twisty turns and wiggles are set to puerile jungle rhythms and a foolish plot."—*Cue.*

The Exhibitors. "My Thursday gross was the largest for ten years! Friday's gross was the largest in history, and that includes *Ben-Hur* and all the super specials… AIP's a big winner here and this picture belongs in the best houses and on preferred playing time."—J. C. Weddle, IN; "Teenagers, of course, eat it up. This company will be seeing more of me from now on."—Jim Fraser, MN; "…is just suited for our best patrons, those 10 to 25 years of age, which are all we have left. Many more like this, please."—Leonard J. Leise, NE; "Good business at terms where I can show a profit."—Terry Axley, AR; "Did great business, and a great movie." Richard Allen, KS; "Played late to excellent crowds… Not much story; but who cares!"—Paul Fournier, NB.

X—THE MAN WITH THE X-RAY EYES (1963) with Ray Milland, Diane Van Der Vlis, Harold J. Stone, John Hoyt and Don Rickles. Written by Robert Dillon and Ray Russell. Pathecolor, Spectarama 88 minutes. An Alta Vista Production for American International Pictures.

As Roger Corman started preproduction on this film, he sent Sam Arkoff a polite reminder that he had yet to see the profit participations on at least a dozen movies, and if they wanted him to make this picture there'd better not be any more foot-dragging. Sam quickly settled the account.

Ray Milland played the doctor obsessed with expanding the limits of human eyesight. When one of his colleagues tries to prevent him from experimenting on himself, the man is accidentally killed and Milland takes it on the lam. He hooks up with Don Rickles, a sleazy carnival barker.

"Don Rickles was famous for his one-liners and comebacks to hecklers," said Jonathan Haze. "So Roger hired Dick Miller and me to sit in the audience and heckle Rickles when [Milland] is doing his act. The scene wasn't rehearsed. Rickles and

Vincent Price has a cameo role as Big Daddy in *Beach Party*.

Milland started doing the act, with Dick and me heckling Don. Suddenly Don says, 'Wait a minute! That's not in the script! Who are these bums? What are they doing, tryin' to horn in on my act?' And he wouldn't let us do it. So we just sat there! That was the last film I ever did for Roger, or anybody else. I was out of favor with Roger for whatever reason. I don't even know what it was, but he wasn't using me. And it was kind of an insult to have to come in there and do a one-day thing. I was just an extra in that movie."[55]

"The original idea to do a picture about a man who could see through objects was Jim Nicholson's and then the development of the basic idea was mine and Ray Russell's," Corman said. "I almost didn't do the picture for two reasons. One, I felt the script had not turned out as well as I had expected and, two, the more I got into it the more I felt we were going to be heavily dependent on the special effects. The picture was shot in three weeks on a medium low budget [$300,000] and I felt we were not going to be able to photograph what Xavier [Ray Milland] could see, and that the audience would be cheated. The picture turned out reasonably well but I think, when finished, it did suffer from that. The effects just weren't there."

The Critics: "... terrifying fare to delight the millions of horror devotees."—*Boxoffice*; "... poised uneasily between science fiction and horror, and only the occasional humorous touches and gory details are likely to appeal to Corman followers ..."—*Films and Filming*; "... surprisingly level-headed and persuasive in its restraint and succinct dialogue ... Mr. Milland's curtain speech in a church is both moving and a wrenching eye opener."—*New York Times*; "While I never expected to see Ray Milland starring in such a picture, he gives it the old college try to earnestness."—*Los Angeles Times*.

The Exhibitors: "American International is starting to come up, even if they are getting as commercial as Disney."—Chukk Garard, IL; "Guess I don't know pictures as I had the best Friday and Saturday I have had in weeks."—Paul Wood, FL; "This was a good movie in color, and should do well in any small house."—Benny Levitan, GA.

DR. GOLDFOOT AND THE BIKINI MACHINE (1965) with
Vincent Price, Frankie Avalon, Dwayne Hickman, Susan Hart and Jack Mullaney. Written by Elwood Ullman and Robert Kaufman. Produced by James H. Nicholson and Samuel Z. Arkoff. Directed by Norman Taurog. Pathecolor, Panavision 88 minutes. An American International Picture.

Jim Nicholson *supposedly* spent over a million dollars on this spy spoof which

Roger Corman, Don Rickles and Diane Van Der Vlis.

he hoped would make a star of his wife, Susan Hart, but if he did spend that much it certainly doesn't look it. Originally titled *Dr. Goldfoot and the Sex Machine*, it was written by Robert Kaufman as a musical comedy for William Asher to direct. Deke Heyward rewrote Kaufman's script after Asher stepped away from the project. Veteran director Norman Taurog, who'd been out of work for almost a year, took over the project and had Elwood Ullman rewrite Heyward's script. Somewhere along the line all but one of the songs were removed and the one that remained, which featured Vincent Price singing about his bikini machine, was cut by Sam Arkoff because he (Price) looked too fey. Susan Hart thought Sam made a big mistake. She said Price was wonderful, "right on the money" as she put it. It could well have been the highlight of this otherwise dreadful picture.

It was shot on location in San Francisco, MGM's backlot and Producers Studio. Miss Hart played one of Goldfoot's beautiful robots and she was quite good in a somewhat difficult role. She recalled a scene where milk was supposed to shoot out of her.

"I was connected with tubing," she said. "And I was wearing a trenchcoat. Well if you notice in the picture, I look about ten pounds heavier. And I recall, it wasn't even plastic tubing, it was metal tubing that they used, and there was a guy standing twenty feet away, and as I was drinking the milk they simply pumped, pumped—it was very primitive actually, just pumped the milk through my pipes, and out it spurted."[56]

Luree and Laura Nicholson played two of the robots, along with China Lee, Deanna Lund, Marianne Gava and Beach Party alumni Sally Sachse and Patti Chandler. Annette, Harvey Lembeck, Deborah Walley and Aron Kincaid appeared in cameo roles. Gumby creator Art Clokey provided the Claymation main titles during which The Supremes sang the film's title song. The movie had its premiere at the Golden Gate Theatre in San Francisco.

The Critics: "...a thrill-packed but completely fantastic spoof of the James Bond films... a sure-fire boxoffice hit."—*Boxoffice*; "...has enough fresh, amusing gags to make it entertaining... Price is splendid."—*Los Angeles Times*; "The expensive looking production runs the comedy gamut from high to low... Susan Hart is very good in a role which demands several dialects, human warmth and robot inanimity, often in rapid sequence."—*Variety*; "Highly imaginative from start to finish... All players performed well, but Vincent Price, as always, stole the show."—*Hollywood Citizen News*.

The Exhibitors. "This picture is the crazy-man-crazy type... Business just fair for this one."—Bobby Mayo, TX; "Stupid, ridiculous picture. Actors didn't play their parts and Price should not have been in it. Business good though."—Rick Clover, IA; "Crazy, but the kids loved it."—Leon Kidwell, OK; "Okay for weekends. Very humorous. Book it."—Paul Gamache, VT; "Did good business and teenagers came from all around."—Terry Axley, AR; "...no complaints on this one, because it did more than some of the big ones."—Harold E. Thompson, OH; "...screwy, but they liked it. The Mack Sennett chase at the finish always pleases."—Arthur K. Dane, NH.

Jack Mullaney looks on as Vincent Price inspects one of his robots.

THE T.A.M.I. SHOW (1965) with The Barbarians, The Beach Boys, Chuck Berry, Billy J. Kramer, James Brown, Marvin Gaye, Gerry and the Pacemakers, Leslie Gore, Jan and Dean, The Rolling Stones, Smokey Robinson, The Supremes. Produced by Lee Savin. Directed by Steve Binder. Black and white 113 minutes. A Screencraft Production released by American International Pictures.

Teenage Awards Music International was an incredible concert held at the Santa Monica Civic Auditorium on October 28 and 29, 1964, featuring one of the most incredible assemblages of talent in pop music history. As originally conceived by executive producer William Sargent Jr., TAMI was to be an annually televised non-profit concert with proceeds going toward music scholarships and other programs benefiting teens worldwide. Sargent had a lot of great ideas, according to Steve Binder, but he always ran into money problems and this turned out to be the only TAMI concert. The auditorium was filled with local high school students who got in free. Jan and Dean hosted the show. It was shot by Steve Bender and his crew from *The Steve Allen Show*, using Bill Sargent's 'Electronovision,' a high definition kinescope. It was the first time that James Brown did his now famous bit while singing 'Please, Please, Please,' where, as if overcome by passion, he dropped to his knees as if he were on the verge of collapse and had to be consoled by an offstage aide. "What I was up against was pop artists," said Brown. "I was R. & B. I had to show 'em the difference, and believe me, it was hard." Watching from the wings, Mick Jagger and the rest of The Rolling Stones had their worst fears realized. Being the most popular of the star-studded line-up they were slated to close the show but as Brown said, "Nobody follows James Brown!"

The Critics: "…is probably the noisiest show ever put on film and undeniably headed for a multi-million dollar gate…"—*Variety*; "…a veritable Who's Who of the teenage entertainment world."—*Boxoffice*; "It is amazingly close in feeling to the excitement usually reserved for live appearances!"—*Film Daily*; "Never have so many teen-agers heard so much of their favorite music from so many of their stars at one sitting in all history."—*Motion Picture Herald*; "Despite the state of uncontrollable hysteria some of these young patrons seem to get into during the show, when it is over, most of them walk out clear-eyed and alert. The observer is given the impression that they are secretly amused at adults who worry over what ultimate effect this banging beat will have upon their future lives."—*Citizen News*.

The Exhibitors. "Played a week first run here with promising results for more of these shows in the future."—Skip and Marie Fletcher, AK; "Went over really big with the local Negro people, because there were plenty of Negro stars and we advertised heavily on a local radio station."—Art Richards, SC; "…it pulled in the teenagers like a house afire. Why our young folks go for such stuff is beyond me! But they do, and in a whopping big way."—I. Roche, FL; "I don't want to discredit this show any, because it drew our teens in, but had to take sedatives afterwards."—Arthur K. Dame, NH; "My customers really ate it up. I don't know why anyone would not play this picture."—Harold J. Smith, TN; "Did not hold a week very well."—Thomas Cuddy, CT.

THE GHOST IN THE INVISIBLE BIKINI (1966) with Tommy Kirk, Deborah Walley, Aron Kincaid, Harvey Lembeck and Jesse White. Written by Louis M. Heyward and Elwood Ullman. Produced by James H. Nicholson and Samuel Z. Arkoff. Directed by Don Weis. Pathecolor, Panavasion 83 minutes. An American International Production for American International Pictures.

When the *Beach Party* series began to taper off at the box office, Jim Nicholson tried to vary the formula with *Pajama Party* (1964) and *Ski Party* (1965), which were both fairly successful. This one not so much. It began as *Beach Party in a Haunted House*. That was when Frankie Avalon and Annette Funicello were going to star in it. When they bowed out Jim changed the title to *Pajama Party in a Haunted House*, then to *Slumber Party in a Haunted House*. But a rose by any other name…

Tommy Kirk and Deborah Walley were cast in the lead roles. Walley, once married to AIP regular John Ashley, called Basil Rathbone (who played the villain in the piece) her soul mate. She said: "He was practically old enough to be my grandfather, but it was like a love affair, we were so enraptured with each other. During the whole shooting of the film we were inseparable; we had lunch together, talked theater. God! I just adored him! After the picture was over, he and I kept up a correspondence and he wanted to do *Romeo and Juliet* on Broadway. He wanted to direct it, and also play Juliet's father, and he wanted me to play Juliet. So, again my hopes go soaring. Finally my turnaround is here! I was moving forward, he had a producer lined up… And then he died."[57]

"That was one of the greatest joys in my life, making that film, because [Basil and I] hit it off and we talked a lot," said Kirk. "We talked about philosophy, talked about writers and literature and art. He shared himself, and I was fascinated by him, 'cause I'd seen all his great classics and I asked him about them all and what it was like to make them. I loved him."[58]

The film was a troubled one from the outset. On the first day of the shoot, a grip fell to his death from a catwalk. And it might have been a good idea to have a script. Louis M. Heyward was writing it as it was being shot, which worked for the writers of *Casablanca* (1942) but Heyward was not in their league. In an interview years later, he said the picture shouldn't and wouldn't have been made if Jim Nicholson hadn't been trying to make a star out of Susan Hart, a dubious remark since the woman wouldn't have been in the picture if Heyward hadn't made such a mess of it. She and Boris Karloff were added *after* the thing proved to be unreleasable. Jim concocted a frame story to help save it. These new scenes were directed by AIP's film editor Ronald Sinclair.

The Critics: "It should prove quite popular with the younger set notwithstanding some standard routines and trite dialogue."—*Film Daily*; "…offers visual thrills and chills, as well as slapstick humor, to keep the film moving at a fast and entertaining pace."—*Motion Picture Herald*; "…as limp and pointless as an unfilled bikini."—*Hollywood Reporter*; "…pure escapism aimed toward the teenagers and is great fun."—*Los Angeles Herald Examiner*; "…a flop."—*New York Times*; "Old timers give the picture some class."—*Los Angeles Times*; "All in all, a good try but short on script and inspiration."—*Variety*.

Tommy Kirk and Deborah Walley.

The Exhibitors. "This seemed to satisfy, albeit less entertaining than most of the kind. The title is good and you will no doubt do all right with it."—Arthur K. Dane, NH; "A fair comedy that should have been better. The 'beach gang' brought in their usual fans."—John Heberle, NY.

THE WILD ANGELS (1966) with Peter Fonda, Nancy Sinatra, Bruce Dern, Diane Ladd and Norman Alden. Written by Charles B. Griffith. Produced and directed by Roger Corman. Pathecolor, Panavision 90 minutes. An American International Picture.

Roger Corman based this movie on the stories that he and Charles Griffith heard at some of the Hells Angels parties. "We always brought some marijuana so we would always be welcome," Corman said. He didn't care for Griffith's screenplay and asked his production assistant Peter Bogdanovich to rewrite it. Bogdanovich lifted the plot from an old Howard Hawks movie and "turned it into that very corn-ball prototype of all the motorcycle movies," Griffith said with disdain.

Although they held no copyright on their name, Jim Nicholson was going to offer the Oakland branch of the Hells Angels a token payment to use the name until Sam Arkoff told him that a payment to one chapter would mean they'd have to pay them all. So Bogdanovich was asked to remove all references to the Hells Angels from his script. The president and vice president of the group's Venice chapter did receive $1,500 for their services as a group and each member was paid $22 a day plus an additional $10 for their choppers. Much of the film was shot on location in Mecca, a little town near the Salton Sea. The local police were poised to arrest any of the Angels they had warrants on but Corman's production manager Jack Bohrer held them at bay. "They're earning an honest day's pay for a change," he told them. "Why arrest them now?" Fearing the worst from the outlaw gang, assistant director Paul Rapp paid a couple of the toughest members to keep the others in line. Good that he did. During a scene in a restaurant with Nancy Sinatra, one of the bikers hoped that she would land on her behind during a take by pulling her chair too far back. Rapp threw the biker against the wall, praying that he would get some help from the guys he'd hired to keep peace, which he did. The biker was taken out back and had his clock cleaned.

Short on extras, Corman told Peter Bogdanovich to participate in a fight sequence between the bikers and the townspeople. Before he knew what was happening, Bogdanovich found himself on the ground being kicked for real, bleeding from ear to ear. As one could have predicted it was a troubled shoot.

Bogdanovich was surprised to hear that Corman intended to wrap on schedule as there were so many scenes left to shoot. "Second unit will do that," Corman told him. "Who's gonna direct second unit?" Bogdanovich asked. "It doesn't matter who directs the second unit," Corman replied. "My secretary could direct the second unit! Anybody can direct the second unit!"

Once the picture started pulling in the money, the Angels sued Corman for defamation of character to the tune of $2 million. One of them, Big Otto Friendly, threatened to kill Corman until he realized it would be rather difficult to collect from a corpse.

Corman's raw and rugged film was both damned and praised by the critics. Made for a modest $360,000 it grossed over $5 million in its first six months of release and over $10 million when the smoke cleared. In his column for the *Hollywood Reporter*, Jack Bradford wrote: "Roger Corman opens his own Swiss bank with a million plus deposit, courtesy of *The Wild Angels*."

The Critics: "Machiavelli would have adored the final, feeble, transparently hypocritical attempt at a moral posture when hero Peter Fonda, whose buddies, including his girlfriend (Nancy Sinatra), have just hightailed it out of town, unaccountably decides to wait for the cops…"—*Newsweek*; "Some advance spectators were completely repelled by it, but let this reviewer go on record as saying that [it] is a masterpiece and the controversy surrounding it is all to the good… AIP heads Nicholson and Arkoff deserve credit for the tremendous courage involved in financing so strong and outspoken a motion picture."—*Independent Film Journal*; "…an exciting, original film that captures an authentic slice of contemporary American life that speaks volumes for the world we live in today."—*Los Angeles Times*; "This preoccupation with violence for its own sake, which many American critics described as bad taste, is in fact the essence of a film which concerns the springs of violence and the fascist instinct in society…"—*Take One*; "Engrossing entertainment, it is well made and astonishingly honest and it's recommended with reservations."—*Los Angeles Herald Examiner*; "…carries shock impact of the sort that occasionally stuns."—*Variety*; "This is a brutal little picture that was shown at the Venice festival as an American entry (by invitation) and caused quite a few diplomats to mop their brows. It is an embarrassment all right—a vicious account of the boozing, fighting, pot-smoking, vandalizing and raping done by a gang of sickle riders."—*New York Times*; "It is precisely because nothing is shown of psychological or social background, that the film is faulty and, in a sense, irresponsible."—*The Saturday Review*; "…a thoroughly inept cast, without even the context of good cycling sequences."—*New York Herald Tribune*.

The Exhibitors. "May I add that in some 27 towns where we have played or are playing the picture it is so far, and cannot help but be for the remainder of the season, the number one attraction box-office-wise that we have had from any film company."—Arthur Stein, Central States Theatre Corp, IA; "…is exactly what the teens want. I agree it's poor entertainment, but a helluva lot of business."—Charles Burton, MO; "Okay, so I'm stupid, but the kids went for it a second time and by now I like it too. I plan to play it next year."—Charles Burton, MO; "A repeat of American International's *The Wild Angels* did outstanding business. All this company's headliner product can be repeated to better than average business. This company knows what goes!"—Charles Burton, MO; "I had shown this in my other theaters and expected business on it. Sure, they came to see it and the kids ate it up, but I wish they would come out to see the good pictures as they do this kind."—Leon Kidwell, OK; "You won't be proud you ran this picture, but it's probably true and will get you some curiosity seekers plus teenagers."—Terry Axley, AR; "Play it, the youngsters will love it!"—John M. Bailey, KS; "…this is the worst picture I have ever played… Sorry, but I can't recommend this picture for anyone."—Peter Silloway, VT; "Real wild, but it was the biggest grosser of the summer here. AIP is doing a good job."—Paul Gamache, VT; "It is too bad that Roger Corman has not made a more serious study of the subject matter. To me, he has piled too much sensationalism (despite some good acting and photography) that ruins the whole story."—Paul Fournier, NB; "We didn't want to play this type but the salesman talked us into it and it turned out to be one of the best grossers of the season. Apparently, 'the masses' like violence and raw action as we had many who never come otherwise."—Russell and Evelyn Burgess, ND.

THE TRIP (1967) with Peter Fonda, Susan Strasburg, Bruce Dern, Dennis Hopper and Salli Sachse. Written by Jack Nicholson. Produced and directed by Roger Corman. Color 85 minutes.

When Peter Fonda read Jack Nicholson's script he wept and told his wife he thought it would be the greatest motion picture ever made. He and Jack Nicholson and Charles Griffith all take credit for persuading Corman to take LSD before he made the movie.

Frances Doel: "I was instructed to take notes on his LSD trip. We went up to Big Sur— Roger, Chuck Griffith, Sharon Compton, who worked for Roger in the art department, and a couple of other people. Roger stayed at the Big Sur Inn. The rest of us camped out."[59]

Charles Griffith: "On the morning of [Roger's] trip I was to take a tiny bit and I was to be the link with reality and the beyond. And Sharon was there, pregnant, to be completely real. Roger took acid with some milk and we hung around in the woods. Nothing happened. 'I've been swindled,' he said with a rage about how he'd bought this acid and nothing was happening and it was a rip-off and he'd come all this way out here for nothing. He finally ran down. He was sitting there, sort of staring. 'Excuse me a moment,' he said. He lay down on his face on the ground and was gone."

Frances Doel: "I don't know where they got the LSD, but I think Roger's trip went very well for him. I know it did for me. It was one of those classic 'Oh, my goodness, everything's breathing' experiences!"[60]

Roger Corman: "I came up with an interesting concept while I was lying on the ground. I believed that simply touching the ground you could create art in your mind and it would be transferred to the mind of anyone who was touching the earth anywhere in the world. You could have an audience larger than a television audience."

Charles Griffith: "He would say things like 'I'm humping the earth. The earth is a woman.' Boy Scout troops went by. Nuns went by. They would all see him groveling in the dirt and they were all disgusted. I thought it was very funny."

Roger Corman: "At one point, I saw this old clipper ship coming toward me. It turned out to be a woman's body and I knew it loved me. When I was coming down, the thought occurred to me that there was no particular reason to go back to Hollywood. No particular reason to exist in the real world at all."

The Critics: "...Corman had made his best picture to date."—*The Saturday Review*; "The real impact and import… is that, for the first time, Hollywood has tuned into the vibrations—good and bad—humming hallucinogenically throughout the nation."—*Playboy*; "Is this what it's like to take a trip? If it is, then it's all a big put-on… And I would warn you that all you are likely to take away from the picture is a painful case of eye-strain and perhaps a detached retina."—*New York Times*; "Is [Corman] simply exploiting a new horror avenue or is this an honest attempt to reproduce by film an actual hallucinatory experience?"—*Variety*; "…a psychedelic tour through the bent mind of Peter Fonda, which is evidently full of old movies."—*Time*; "… pulls no punches."—*Boxoffice*; "…Roger Corman has made his best picture to date …"—*The Saturday Review*; "…it can be said that *The Trip* is technically and visually one of the most spectacular pictures ever made."—*American Cinematographer*; "…a definitive commercial for acid …"—*Chicago Reader*.

The Exhibitors. "This picture did above average business. But some scenes are not too good for small towns. There is a lesson in this for the teens. The 'wild color' is something else. Again I say it's for adults."—Leon Kidwell, OK; "This one is strictly for the birds—the ones that fly 'way out' that is. Some scenes are hard to take for the kids. It attracts a pretty good crowd in spite of itself."—Raymond St. Romain, LA; "Good boxoffice on a very sorry picture. A lot of walk-outs with very bad comments."—Larry M. Smith, GA.

THE BORN LOSERS (1967) with Tom Laughlin, Elizabeth James, Jeremy Slate, Jane Russell and William Wellman Jr. Written by James Lloyd (Elizabeth James). Produced by Tom Laughlin and Delores Taylor. Directed by T.C. Frank (Tom Laughlin). Color 113 minutes. An American International Picture.

A few years before actor-writer-producer-director Tom Laughlin made the mega-hit *Billy Jack* (1971), he was seen as the same character in *Born Losers*. AIP bought out the investors on the picture when Laughlin ran out of money and needed $300,000 to finish it. When AIP reissued the picture as "the original Billy Jack," Laughlin sued the company for $5 million in damages. The judge ruled that AIP was well within their rights so long as they clearly indicated in the advertising that the picture was a re-release. Pauline Kael called *The Born Losers* the most amateurish bad movie that ever ended up on *Variety*'s list of highest grossing films. It made even more money the second time around but Laughlin's lawsuit cost him his share of the profits.

The Critics: "The picture vividly and with powerful dramatic impact hits out of the fear of the public to become involved in the fight against crime."—*Film Daily*; "Here is a disgusting, repelling, and at times revolting film once again showing one of the scourges of modern-day society, the motorcycle gang in action..."—*Motion Picture Exhibitor*; "...a sickening little motorcycle melodrama from American International Pictures that is also a trailing catchall of most motorcycle film clichés to date."—*New York Times*; "Somewhere along the line the film gives way to shock for its own sake, ultimately and ironically merging as an apology for vigilante action."—*Hollywood Reporter*; "Director T. C. Frank builds mounting tension and suspense and draws sock performances from his entire cast..."—*Variety*; "...a bloody, sadistic, shocking and harrowingly authentic motion picture. It is not for the kiddies."—*Los Angeles Examiner*; "...while decrying violence, the film takes every opportunity to show it, doing it garishly, spreading the catsup so liberally, that the most voracious teenager is bound to be satisfied by it."—*Saturday Review*; "It is made all the more distasteful by the hypocritical attempt to cloak it in an anti-violence viewpoint."—*Cue*; "...the most pointlessly violent picture seen in a year in which violence has been the overwhelming rule rather than the exception."—*Los Angeles Times*; "...a picture which will shock even veterans of celluloid savagery and which will make mature adults turn from it in sick dismay..."—*Citizen News*; "Though the biggest losers will be those who pay to see the film, old movie buffs may want to get a glimpse of Jane Russell, who appears to have been thickened by the picture, and to hear one of the class clichés in cinema history articulated by a cowardly cop: 'Where did we go wrong?' From the beginning, baby."—*Time*

The Exhibitors. "What can you say about this company's product, except $ $ $."— Jerry Drew, CA; "Good business on a film that is brutal and even sadistic. I hated it. My teens loved it."—Charles Burton, MO; "We did above average business on it and everyone liked it."—Leon Kidwell, OK; "Too brazen for kids on Saturday. Well made."—Terry Axley, AR; "Brutally frank and tough, but it should have taught some of our teenagers something, if they are interested in learning. Didn't come up to expectations at the boxoffice, however."—H. E. and C. W. Rowell, VT; "Our regulars (6 to 16) seem to enjoy these violent pictures. No walkouts. No talking. No complaints."—Mrs. W. A. Windschitl, MN; "Lowest Friday-Saturday on record. Doubled with *Devil's Angels*."—Jack Frost, BC; "The kids came back to see it the second time."—James Trowbridge, NY; "Well acted and plenty of action for the motorcycle fans. Business was good for this time of year."—John McKinnon, Canada; "This one drew more adults than usual. They said, 'Why such a picture?' Why such a picture?—because it did business. Best weekend in months."—Ken Christianson, ND.

WILD IN THE STREETS (1968) with Christopher Jones, Shelley Winters, Diane Varsi, Hal Holbrook and Millie Perkins. Written by Robert Thom. Produced by James H. Nicholson and Samuel Z. Arkoff. Directed by Barry Shear. Pathecolor 94 minutes. An American International Picture.

Made in 20 days at a cost of $700,000, *Wild in the Streets* was one of the most ambitious films that AIP ever made and only they would have had the balls to make it. It was nominated for an Academy Award for Best Film Editing. Richard Pryor is in a supporting role. Rumor has it he showed up on the set naked just to get a rise out of Shelley Winters. There's also a boatload of celebrities who make cameo appearances including Army Archerd, Melvin Belli, Dick Clark, Louis Lomax, Pamela Mason, Bobby Sherman and Walter Winchell. And somewhere in the crowd is Gary Busey.

The Critics: "It's a silly film, but it does communicate in the simplest, most direct terms."—Roger Ebert; "…a kind of instant classic, a revved up *La Chinoise* or *Privilege* for the drive-ins in summertime. Blunt, a little preachy… the movie is philosophy with dual exhausts and a very clear logic about where things lead."—*New York Times*; "Some pictures are put-ons that seem to lead for a tacit agreement with their audience: what is to be viewed is beneath contempt, therefore it is beyond criticism."—*Time*; "It will stir up controversy and keep theatre turnstiles spinning."—*Boxoffice*; "…assumes a look several times its budget through extensive and diverse set-ups, admirably researched and utilized newsreel footage and the presence of a sizable recruitment of authenticating media personalities."—*Hollywood Reporter*; "Barry Shear, handling the directorial reigns… has gotten some fascinating performances from his cast."—*Film Daily*; "…a neat package."—*Variety*.

The Exhibitors. "This is a way out picture that brings in the teenagers. Well received and to some good business."—Charles Burton, ND; "I had great expectations for this, but 'no dice.' Only fair business."—Terry Axley, AR; "The kids seem to like it and it's worth a playdate. The adults probably will not like the subject matter, but the end might strike their fancy."—Ray St. Romain, LA.

THE CONQUEROR WORM aka **THE WITCHFINDER GENERAL** (1968) with Vincent Price, Ian Ogilvy, Rupert Davies, Hilary Dwyer and Robert Russell. Written by Tom Baker, Louis M. Heyward and Michael Reeves loosely based on *The Witchfinder General* by Ronald Bassett. Produced by Louis M. Heyward. Directed by Michael Reeves. Color 87 minutes. A Tigon British Film Production for American International Pictures.

Director Michael Reeves was angry at being saddled with Vincent Price as his leading man and told the actor so in no uncertain terms when they first met. Their relationship remained contentious throughout the production and all because the chip on Reeves' shoulder was so heavy it caused a breach in his communication skills. It came to a head one afternoon when Price had had enough. "Young man I've been in 84 films. How many have you made?" Unflinching, Reeves replied: "Two good ones." Price stood in awe for a moment then broke out laughing. After they'd finished the picture, Price realized that what Reeves had wanted all along was a low-key, restrained performance, which he got, but had Price understood that he wouldn't have been fighting him every step of the way.

The Critics: "A disgrace to the producers and scripters and a sad commentary on the art of filmmaking."—*Hollywood Citizen News*; "Vincent Price has a good time as a materialistic witch hunter and woman disfigurer and dismemberer and the audience seemed to have a good time as well."—*New York Times*; "Not since *Peeping Tom* has a film aroused such an outcry about nastiness and gratuitous violence as this one."—*Monthly Film Bulletin*; "…is quite happily and deliberately a horror film: that is to say, it has no particular pretensions of being anything else."—*London Times*; "…has no explicit 'Message'; but it does say something about the springs of despair, and it says it forcefully. It is a very frightening film."—*Films and Filming*; "…principals are hampered by Michael Reeves' mediocre script and ordinary direction."— *Variety*; "The film is aimed squarely at the sex and sadism market for which it is a natural."—*Boxoffice*; "Whether it is 'good' Bassett he'll have to decide. It isn't Poe at all."—*Variety*; "…the film should enjoy a long and profitable life… which is more than can be said for the characters who inhabit the tale."—*Hollywood Reporter*; "… the sickest picture in commercial release since that penny dreadful *Blood Feast*…"— *Los Angeles Times*; "…a piece of perfectly proportioned atrocity that moves along

Vincent Price as Matthew Hopkins, the Witchfinder General.

in a measured fashion as a grisly gavotte."—*Motion Picture Herald*; "Whatever you might think of it, it's effective."—Mark McGee.

The Exhibitors. "Teens ate it up. Yes, they like violence and sex. They won't buy purity!"—Charles Burton, MD; "...too much for some people but for the horror fans, it was just right."—Evelyn and Russell Burgess, ND; "We had the best turnout we have had all month and you could have heard a pin drop after the first ten minutes. Vincent Price, as always, is terrific. Only four girls walked out."—Mr. and Mrs. Windschitl, MN; "If your people like a rough movie, this will fill the bill."—Mel Edelstein, MN; "We did very good business with the teenagers on this. Price is at his very best. The kids like to be scared anytime so it should do well in almost every situation."—Terry Axley, AR.

DE SADE (1969) with Keir Dullea, Senta Berger, Lilli Palmer, Anna Massey and John Huston. Written by Richard Matheson. Produced by Samuel Z. Arkoff and James H. Nicholson. Directed by Cy Endfield. Color 113 minutes. An American International Picture.

In the late 1960s, mainstream movies were tackling subjects that had previously been forbidden—homosexuality, hedonism, sadism. Nudity was so common it was almost expected. Nevertheless, there was still the production code to deal with and the people in charge of rating films were more lenient with talk than they were with visuals. Show too much and they'd slap an X-rating on a film, which was the kiss of death to anyone but the producers of pornography, because it meant that nobody under 21 years of age could see the picture.

Louis M. Heyward was the one who got the bright idea to make a film about Donatien Alphonse Francois de Sade, the libertine French aristocrat, politician, and philosopher who wrote about his violent sexual fantasies. Heyward was working on *The Witchfinder General* when the idea struck him (no doubt he was inspired by some of the sadistic goings on in that movie) and it seemed to him like a perfect subject for exploitation. Jim Nicholson thought so too. He believed they could 'Roadshow' the thing if Richard Matheson and Roger Corman could successfully walk the sexual tightrope and produce a film that would satisfy the expectations of its audience without inflaming the sensibilities of the censors. Corman stayed with the project through the first draft.

"I went to lunch with Jim and told him that I wanted to step off the project," he recalled. "I was supposed to get some development money but I said I would walk away and give him the benefit of the work I'd done. I thought the picture was a trap. If we tried to show what De Sade did, or as Dick Matheson and I did, some of his fantasies, or more specifically what De Sade *did* in his fantasies, we'd be arrested. And if we *didn't* show it, the audience was going to be cheated. They were going to be cheated because of the title and because of the way I knew American International would sell the picture."

Cy Endfield, a victim of the Hollywood blacklist, agreed to direct the picture with Gordon Hessler acting as producer. Hessler and Endfield couldn't get along so Hessler was taken off *De Sade* and given another picture to produce (and direct) as a sort of consolation prize. "It was the greatest piece of luck that I was fired from it," he told George Reis, in his interview for DVD Drive-In. "When I did *The Oblong Box* [1969] they left me alone, there was nobody there. The day I started, Nicholson came on the set and said, 'Good luck.' That's it, and he was off."

De Sade was shot in Berlin, at a studio owned by Arthur Brauner. A good cast was assembled—Senta Berger, John Huston and Keir Dullea as the Marquis de Sade.

Dullea's fiancé was a pain in the ass according to Louis Heyward. He said: "I could not bar her from the set, but for her to sit there through the nude scenes was very hard. She would always go over to Keir at the end of a take and say, 'Keir, you don't have to be so close!' or 'Keir, you're touching her!' It got to be a bit of a problem."[61]

In Richard Matheson's script, which Heyward said was one of the best scripts he'd ever read, the audience is shown what de Sade is thinking as he dies, via a series of fantasy flashbacks. But Endfield didn't like that. He wanted a straightforward, non-fantasy narrative. "And yet," Matheson said, "he kept shooting scenes that I wrote, scenes that (except in a fantasy context) made no sense at all."[62]

Endfield was uncomfortable with the orgy sequences so he shot around them until there was nothing left to shoot. That's when he put on some headphones and listened to music while a bunch of naked women sat around waiting for him to call action. And when he couldn't stall any longer he got sick with the flu. Jim Nicholson asked Roger Corman to bail them out.

De Sade was two hours long, a first for the company. Jim Nicholson had hopes of making it a 'Roadshow' attraction, hopes that were flattened when the movie was condemned by the Catholic Legion of Decency and given an 'X' rating by the MPAA. Six minutes were trimmed in an effort to appease the MPAA but it was no soap. It took another seventeen minutes of editing to get the 'R' rating they were after. It was the biggest flop in the company's history.

This is just the kind of shenanigans that Keir Dullea's fiancé frowned upon as she watched De Sade being filmed.

The Critics: "It successfully reduces one of the most fascinating figures of world literature to the role of not-so-straight man in a series of naughty tableaux vivants... Orgies occur at regular intervals throughout the film, like toe-tap numbers in a Busy Berkeley musical, but the only shocking thing about them is the pink color in which they're photographed."—*New York Times*; "Keir Dullea appears as the troubled marquis and his vulpine, immobile face helps him to range between anger and painful pleasing with indifference. The orgies are only slightly more titillating than a *Playboy* centerfold and a good deal less polished."—*Time*.

The Exhibitors. "This is a poorly edited picture that is not entertainment and not good for business."—Charles Burton, MD.

*COUNT YORGA, VAMPIRE aka THE LOVES OF COUNT IORGA

(1970) with Robert Quarry, Roger Perry, Michael Murphy, Michael Macready and Donna Anders. Produced by Michael Macready. Written and directed by Bob Kelljan. Color 93 minutes. An Ericka Production. Released by American International Pictures.

Bob Kelljan and Michael Macready had made one skin flick before they decided to make a soft-core vampire movie. Robert Quarry persuaded them to lift their horizons and do it straight. They enlisted the help of friends who were willing to work for scale and deferments. Props and equipment were borrowed or stolen. Macready said he was overwhelmed by everybody's enthusiasm and grateful for their willingness to help get the picture off the ground. "Funny as this may seem, we approached *Yorga* with the same integrity we would have had if we'd been making a *Lawrence of Arabia*. I think it's a vital approach for anyone making exploitation pictures."[63]

The film was shot at night so that Quarry could work on a Paul Newman picture during the day. On the first night of the shoot, Quarry was told to be on the set at midnight. He sat around eating cold pizza for four hours before they got around to filming a shot of his legs walking across a lawn, after which the director sent everyone home. Quarry left in a huff and got lost driving home. The producer and director found him parked by the side of the road, fuming. They asked if he needed a lift. "No," Quarry said, he was going home and never coming back. They apologized and promised not to waste his time again. He agreed to press on to the bitter end. He was pleasantly surprised by the reaction of the audience at a test screening. They thought the film was pretty good and, more important, they thought *he* was good.

When it was sold to American International Quarry agreed to promote it. He was appalled by some of the fans, who were without question some of the strangest people he'd ever met. Quarry put his arm around the shoulders of one young chap who had, to Quarry's horror, filed all of his teeth to look like fangs. Quarry told *Psychotronic Magazine*, "Two years from now, this kid's going to be the Vampire Killer of Chicago and they're going to find the picture of me ... with my arm around him."

Count Yorga grossed $160,000 in the first week of its release in Los Angeles. It became one of the highest grossing films in AIP's history. Ultimately, Kelljan and Macready walked away with $2 million and gave Quarry a $350 bonus, which he thought was an insult. He was going to tear up the check but decided to take a couple of friends to dinner instead.

The Critics: "It adds nothing new..."—*Boxoffice*; "Bob Kelljan's direction, often resourceful, does especially well by Quarry's disdainful civility... There are other pleasures. Count Yorga's rented mansion features a gothic basement complete with three toothsome female vampires breathing heavily in diaphanous gowns while waiting to do their master's bidding."—*New York Times*; "A flimsy budget dooms this independently produced horror film to second feature status."—*Motion Picture Exhibitor*; "...the film has a calculated camp appeal to more sophisticated audiences. Robert Quarry in the title role has a very aristocratically handsome look and plays the part with a certain sinister intelligence, even a sly humor that befits a guy who has been around for several hundred years."—*Variety*; "...a curious mixture of near camp with a serious attempt at horror melodrama."—*Hollywood Reporter*.

THE ABOMINABLE DR. PHIBES (1971) with Vincent Price, Joseph Cotton, Hugh Griffith, Terry-Thomas and Virginia North. Written by James Whiton and William Goldstein. Produced by Louis M. Heyward and Ronald S. Dunas. Directed by Robert Fuest. Color by Movielab 93 minutes. An American International Production.

Vincent Price was in top form in what turned out to be one of AIP's most successful films, both critically and commercially. The script was handed to Jim Nicholson by Ron Dunas, who co-produced the film with Louis M. Heyward. Heyward claimed that his uncredited rewrite turned it into a parody, although several writers had a hand in the screenplay, including Brian Clemens, the creator of the tongue-in-cheek television series *The Avengers*. The film's director, Robert Fuest, directed several episodes of that series.

A writer for *Newsweek* noted that Price, an urbane actor and avid art collector, had "quite literally hacked out a niche, however clammy and cobwebbed," in the horror market. Price responded by saying: "The best parts are the heavies. The hero is usually someone who has really nothing to do. He comes out on top, but it's the heavy who has all the fun."

The Critics: "…a well-coordinated film, directed with a light touch…"—*Variety*; "…an amusingly stylish cliché of horror, loaded with fun for devotees."—*Cue*; "Good performances, strong direction, an imaginative script and outstanding production values should make this a solid box office success."—*Motion Picture Herald*; "The plot, buried under all the iron tinsel, isn't bad. But the tone of steamroller camp flattens the fun. Price finally climbs into his own grave to the tune of 'Over the Rainbow.' Up the creek is more like it."—*New York Times*; "…it is Price who carries the film in stunningly conceived settings which like the story, are both horrible and hilarious."—*Miami Herald*; "…never really frightening but bursting with ingenious shock values and projected with classy wit."—*Los Angeles Herald Examiner*; "A little decadent but lots of fun…"—*Los Angeles Times*; "The script by James Whiton and William Goldstein, who camp it up a bit, sometimes play it with tongue in cheek and sometimes place the tongue wetly between the lips and blow hard spraying an old-fashioned raspberry over the London countryside."—*The Hollywood Reporter*.

Footnotes.

1. Tom Weaver, *It Came From Weaver Five*, McFarland & Company, North Carolina, 1996, page 35.

2. Tom Lisanti, *Drive-In Dream Girls*, McFarland & Company, North Carolina, 2003, page 61.

3. Tom Weaver, *Double Feature Creature Attack*, McFarland & Company, No. Carolina, 2003, page 140.

4. Tom Weaver, *Eye on Science Fiction*, McFarland & Company, North Carolina, 2007, page 24.

5. Tom Weaver, *Science Fiction Stars and Horror Heroes*, McFarland & Company, North Carolina, 2006, page 156.

6. Lawrence French, "California Gothic," *Video Watchdog*, No. 138, 2008, page 18.

7. In 2001, Joe's son Neal produced a movie called *The Fast and the Furious*, which

Richard Wilson, Yvette Mimieux and Jim Nicholson.

turned into a highly successful franchise.

8. William Wharo, "James Nicholson," *Filmfax* No. 74, 1999, page 48.

9. *Drive-In Dream Girls*, page 55.

10. Jim Nicholson was famous for his no-interest loans. His employees also had medical coverage.

11. Samuel Z. Arkoff and Richard Trubo, *Flying Through Hollywood By the Seat of My Pants*, Birch Lane Press, 1992, page 130.

12. Tom Weaver, *Earth vs. the Sci-Fi Filmmakers*, McFarland & Company, 2005, page 130.

13. *It Came from Weaver Five*, page 27.

14. In an article that appeared in the May 4, 1984 edition of *L.A. Reader* titled 'Confessions of a Hollywood Hitman,' Burt Wilson described the fun of creating radio spots for AIP from the mid-60s through the early 70s. He said Jim and Sam never

looked at a film for quality or storyline or great acting (if any of those things existed it was a plus), they wanted to know if they could sell it. Did it lend itself to an ad campaign that would turn people on? And if it didn't, could anything be changed around to make it saleable? Wilson cites the example of a movie called *God Bless the Bomb* (1972), the story of three prisoners who steal a B-52 loaded with H-bombs, which they threaten to use on Fort Knox if the President doesn't end the war in Vietnam. When it didn't make any money the first time out it was pulled and given a new title—*Wild in the Sky*—and reissued as a comedy. That didn't work either, partly because AIP thought they could find an audience by running the movie near southern Air Force bases. Their target customers didn't take kindly to a movie with a homosexual base commander. Then one of the film's players, George Stanford Brown, became a regular on *The Rookies* TV show and the film was given yet another title, *Black Jack*: "He's got the man on the pan and he's gonna fry him good!"

15. *Eye on Science Fiction*, pages 28-29.

16. *Earth vs. the Sci-Fi Filmmakers*, page 126.

17. Lawrence French, *Video Watchdog*, page 26.

18. Scott Eyman, *John Wayne*, Simon and Schuster, New York, 2014, page 284-285.

19. Chris Nashawaty, *Crab Monsters, Teenage Cavemen, and Candy Stripe Nurses*, Abrams, New York, 2013, pages 11 and 12.

20. *Boxoffice*, August 24, 1957, page 18.

21. In an interview with Tom Weaver, Herman Cohen takes the credit for engineering this engagement with R. J. O'Donnell. According to Cohen, during a personal appearance tour with *Teenage Werewolf*, he talked with O'Donnell about making *Teenage Frankenstein*. He did say that Jim Nicholson was the one who suggested that he make a companion feature to go with it. Believe what you will. It doesn't really matter. In my experience, and Tom would probably agree with me, everyone wants to take the credit for just about everything.

22. In Arkoff's version of this story *he* was the one who had this exchange with Wald, but that's not what the record shows.

23. Rubine, Irving, "Boys Meet Ghouls, Make Money," *New York Times*, March 16, 1958, section 2, page 7.

24. Lawrence French, *Visions of Death*, Gauntlet Press, 2007, page 40.

25. *Double Feature Creature Attack*, page 25.

26. *Boxoffice*, January 21, 1963, page 13.

27. *Boxoffice*, March 25, 1963, page 5.

28. Annette Funicello and Patricia Romanowski, *A Dream is A Wish Your Heart Makes, My Story*, Hyperion, New York 1994, page 138.

29. *Drive-In Dream Girls*, page 59.

30. John Agar and L. C. Van Savage, *On the Good Ship Hollywood: The John Agar Story*, BearManor Media, 2007, page 96.

31. *Attack of the Monster Movie Makers*, page 136, 1994.

32. *Earth vs. the Sci-Fi Filmmakers*, page 131.

33. Vaughn, Don, "Lori Nelson," *Filmfax* No 118, 2008, page 61.

34. Ibid., page 118.

35. Don Vaughan, "Interview with Cindy Robbins," *Filmfax*, page 47.

36. Dennis Fisher, *Science Fiction Film Directors*, McFarland & Company, North Carolina, 2000, page 201.

37. Don Vaughan, "Michael Rougas Remembers Michael Landon," *Filmfax*, No. 188, 2007, page 107.

38. Don Vaughan, "Interview with Dawn Richard," *Filmfax*, No. 188, 2007, page 50.

39. Stephen Rebello, "Selling Nightmares," *Cinefantastique*, Vol. 18, No. 2/3, March 1988, page 52.

40. *Earth vs. the Sci-Fi Filmmakers*, pages 122-123.

41. Randy Palmer, *Paul Blaisdell, Monster Maker*, McFarland and Company, North Carolina, 1997, pages 130-131.

42. If *Machine Gun Kelly* had done *anything* for Charlie's career, he wouldn't have been available to play a supporting role in AIP's *Master of the World* three years later.

43. Michael S. Lottman, "Herman Cohen," *The Harvard Crimson*, March 23, 1961.

44. Bob Skotak, "The Angry Red Planet," *Filmfax* No. 17, 1989, page 46.

45. Richard Valley, "Three Ring Circus," Scarlet Street 36, page 30.

46. Larry French, *Video Watchdog*, pages 19 and 20.

47. This footage was used in just about every Poe film that followed.

48. Steve Brodrowski "Black Sunday: A Retrospective," *Cinefantastique* 2008.

49. Liner notes on the *Black Sunday* laser disc.

50. Tom Weaver, *Science Fiction and Fantasy Film Flashback*, McFarland & Company, North Carolina, page 178.

51. Pat Jankiewicz, "Stanley 'Batwriter' Ross," *Filmfax*, No. 16, 1989, page 48.

52. Actually, in *Beach Party*, Jody McCrea drinks a beer and Frankie Avalon smokes a cigarette in the sequel. It wasn't until the third entry in the series, *Bikini Beach* (1964), that a ban on smoking and drinking took effect.

53. Stephen J. McParland, *It's Party Time*, PTB Productions, Australia, 1992, page 21.

54. Ibid., page 14.

55. Edward L. Mitchell, "Jonathan Haze," *Filmfax*, No. 57, 1996, pages 37, 74.

56. Kim Holston, *Starlet*, McFarland & Company, North Carolina, 1988, pages 104-105.

57. William Vihard, "Being Deborah Walley," *Filmfax* No. 7, Feb-Mar, 2000, page 84.

58. Richard Valley, "Just an Average Joe (Hardy)," *Scarlet Street*, No. 10, 1993, page 69.

59. Chris Nashawaty, *Crab Monsters, Teenage Cavemen, and Candy Stripe Nurses*, pages 78-79.

60. Ibid., page 79.

61. Tom Weaver, *Science Fiction Stars and Horror Heroes*, page 171.

62. Ibid., page 313.

63. Greg King, "Count in *Yorga* Signifies The B.O., Not Nobility," *Variety*, April 12, 1971, page 4.

PART THREE

Roger Corman

ROGER CORMAN

"First and foremost I was trying to make a film that would be profitable. At the same time I was trying to make a film that would give some satisfaction to me. I put a lot of thought into those films. It may not look like it when you see them…"

This may come as a bit of a shock but I believe there is no other filmmaker who has been the subject of more books and documentaries than Roger Corman. What this has to say about the world in which we live I really don't know, nor do I care to hazard a guess.

The French critics took the lead in taking Roger seriously as a filmmaker when they lavished praise on *Machine Gun Kelly* in 1958. The U.S. critics didn't join in until the fourth or fifth Edgar Allan Poe movie. Then *Sight and Sound* magazine did a piece on him in the late 1960s and finally we had the first book about Roger called *Roger Corman: The Millennic Vision*, a collection of scholarly essays, written by a bunch of pontificating nudniks who found great significance in the directorial decisions that Roger had made for no other reason than to save a buck. Roger told me many years ago, long before he'd written his autobiography, that *The Millennic Vision* was the best book that had ever been written about him. I've always had the sneaking suspicion that he thought it was funnier than I did. Not that Roger doesn't take his films or himself seriously. Just not *that* seriously.

J. Philip di Franco's *Movie World of Roger Corman* was published shortly after *The Millennic Vision* and it was an unpretentious look at Corman's career. Like Chris Nashawaty's more recent *Crab Monsters, Teenage Cavemen, and Candy Stripe Nurses*, it linked together lengthy quotes from Corman alumni to tell the story of a guy who made movies as fast and as cheap as he possibly could, creating a body of work that was more interesting, intelligent and entertaining than anyone else working at his level. Both of these books are fun but only Beverly Gray's *Roger Corman: An Authorized Biography of the Godfather of Indie Filmmaking* (now in its third addition under its new title *Roger Corman: Blood-Sucking Vampires, Flesh-Eating Cockroaches and Driller Killers*) offers any real insight into Roger's character. Beverly Gray was Roger's assistant at New World and later his story editor at Concorde-New Horizons. After eight years of what she called 'loyal service,' Roger gave her job to one of her friends, a former employee who'd fallen on hard times and was willing to work for less money. I think Beverly wrote her book to get even with her boss. If that was her intention she jolly well succeeded.

Back in 1988 I wrote a listless book about Roger called *The Best of the Cheap Acts*. Before I sent it to the publisher I let Roger read it. He told me it was the worst book that had ever been written about him. By that I think he meant it was the least flattering book that had been written about him, although the caliber of my writing may have been in question as well. Well, the joke was on me for I had written that book as a way of getting my foot in Roger's door, hoping to wangle a writing assignment out of him, as Ed Naha had done a few years before me when he wrote a book about Roger called *Brilliance on a Budget*, a book that was more or less a retread of the di Franco book. So there I sat in Roger's office with egg dripping off my face, which was what I deserved for stealing someone else's game plan. "I'm sorry you feel that way," I said pathetically. "I was hoping to work for you." To a guy with Roger's moxie I must have looked a pretty sorry sight. After a quiet moment he said, "Maybe I was a little harsh. Come on. I'll take you to lunch."

During the course of writing my book I had interviewed Roger several times but I never felt at ease with him. My fault. Not his. He was always gracious and charming and for a guy who was as busy as he was, generous. He's a tall, broad-shouldered, good-looking guy with the charisma of a movie star. His voice is deep and authoritative and he delivers his stories with all the spontaneity of *Great Moments with Mr. Lincoln*. He seemed larger than life to me, which I found intimidating.

"What is it that you want to do?" he asked me over sandwiches and I told him that I wanted to write. And that's about all that I can remember about that lunch. Except that I offered to make changes in my book, to alter the text to his satisfaction, which hardly speaks well for me, but writing for the movies was something that I'd wanted to do since I was fourteen years old. And for reasons that I can't explain I really wanted to have my name on a Roger Corman movie. I've known a lot of other people who felt the same way. It was like a badge of honor.

Though he never said so, I believe it was the tone of my book that he objected to, which was not always respectful, but he had neither the time nor the inclination to go through it with a red pencil, and I doubt that he really cared all that much. It was almost an afterthought when he asked me to jettison the quotes from the critics, which were mostly favorable. Anyway, we returned to his office and I signed a contract to write *Sorority House Massacre II*. And Beverly Gray was given the task of working with me.

I had written a script for Joe Solomon who, like Roger, worked outside of the studio system and had made a lot of money with a picture called *Hells Angels on Wheels* (1967). But when I was working for Joe he hadn't made a movie for a couple of years and was hoping to make a comeback. For two weeks he and I sat in his office hammering out a script. We'd discuss a scene and then I'd write it. He read each page as it was coming out of the typewriter. It wasn't a particularly comfortable way to work but I have to say that at least I knew where I stood with Joe every step of the way. With Beverly Gray I was flying blind. She was more of a critic than a collaborator. She'd tell me what she didn't like, which was just about everything, but she never told me what she would like in its place. She spoke in generalities. Never specifics. My third draft was no closer to pleasing her than the first one had been. So when she asked for another rewrite I came to the conclusion that I would be writing *Sorority House Massacre II* for the rest of my life. Not knowing what else to do I called Roger to voice my concerns. I said that I was willing to do another draft but I needed more guidance than Beverly seemed willing to give me. He said that I had met my contractual obligation and sent me a check for my trouble. That script, like the one I'd written for Joe Solomon, was never produced.

A few months later Jim Wynorski asked me to work with him on a comedy for Roger called *Transylvania Twist* (1980). I'd known Jim for years, long before he went to work at Concorde in the publicity department. It was the perfect job for a guy who could well be the reincarnation of Baron Munchausen. After only two months on the job Jim created one of the most outrageous and fraudulent campaigns in ballyhoo history. Inspired by an old Arch Obler radio show, and unencumbered by any moral obligation to deliver what he promised, the posters and newspaper ads for *Screamers* (1981) read: "They're men turned inside out! And worse… they're still alive!" As there were no inside out men in the movie, angry customers ripped out drive-in speakers to show their displeasure at having been cheated, but Jim had turned what had been a box office dud into a box office bonanza.

Jim and I spent about a week cooking up gags for *Transylvania Twist* (gags that were used by the way) and then I got the bad news. Roger told Jim to get rid of me. I was 'difficult' to work with.

Uh oh! Two unproduced screenplays and the only thing I had to show for it was a couple of bucks and reputation for being difficult. Palookaville here I come.

A couple of years go by. I'm at a revival screening of *The 7th Voyage of Sinbad* (1958) and *Journey to the Center of the Earth* (1959). A lot of my friends were there including Jim Wynorski. A bunch of us were talking in the lobby after the show and out of the blue Jim offered me a job. If I hadn't been there that afternoon there is no doubt in my mind that the assignment would have gone to another writer. Come to think of it, I believe it had been offered to another writer. Jim is a man of impulse. I reminded him that I'd been tossed off the other project but he didn't seem to think it would be a problem. And it wasn't.

The script I was asked to write was a remake of a film that Jim had just made, a slasher movie called *Nighty Nightmares*. It had been secretly financed by Roger's wife Julie, and made behind Roger's back while the couple was away on vacation. Roger was so pleased with the film he wanted Jim to make it again. Same story. Same cast. Only this time, instead of having the buxom young ladies running around in their undies in a sorority house, pursued by a mad killer, Roger wanted to make use of the sets that had just been built for *Corporate Affairs* (1990), which as I recall consisted of one large reception area and a few suites. This change in locale presented Jim and I with a problem—how to get the women out of their clothes and into their underwear. (Try to imagine someone like David Lean or William Wyler wrestling with a dilemma like this.) Not that women would ever run around in their underwear regardless of the location, but it was a little easier to swallow when they were in a sorority house. I asked Jim if it would be too much of a problem to redress the reception area to make it seem like we're on different levels of a high rise instead of a single level office. Jim liked that idea because it opened up all sorts of possibilities for us. It not only gave the ladies more room to run and hide from the killer, it also meant (and this was the genius of the stroke) that they could discover a lingerie company on another level. The sequence where these ladies become so excited when they discover these frilly and sexy undergarments (and just can't wait to try them on) is as ridiculous and infantile as anything you can imagine. But half-naked women is just about all that a film like this has to offer. I should add that the women in Jim's films were never hired for their acting ability. I once fished a headshot of a very attractive young lady from Jim's trashcan. I asked if she could act and he told me she was terrific. "Are you going to use her?" I asked. "No," he replied rather blandly. "Her tits weren't big enough." This from the man whose favorite expression is: "Take 'em out and let 'em breathe." At one time Jim was touted as Roger's successor but time has proven otherwise. After an astounding one hundred directing gigs, Jim is *still* working for Roger. But at least he's still working, which is more than I can say.

So, now that we had solved the underwear problem, and had crossed the line into lunacy to do it, it didn't seem too outrageous to suggest that the ladies find a weapons manufacturer on another level. Jim liked that idea too because he loves machine guns. Unfortunately, there wasn't enough money in the budget for bullet hits, so what you got was a lot of noise and no payoff. (Feel free to supply your own analogy.)

I had a week to write the thing, five days of which I squandered because I couldn't believe that Jim really wanted a carbon copy of the first picture, which to my way of thinking was as crappy as it could possibly be. I went off in a different direction and had the weekend to make things right again.

Proving that it's a small world after all, the original *Nighty Nightmares* was given a new title—*Sorority House Massacre II*. For a brief time the picture I worked on was called *Tower of Terror*. It finally emerged as *Hard to Die* (1990). A more honest title would have been *Hard to Watch*. Whether it was an improvement over the original is *Hard to Say*. There were those who felt the first version was better and I would be the last person in the world to argue with them. They were both, to my way of thinking, miserable excuses for entertainment, but what mattered to me was that I finally had my name on a Roger Corman film.

More time goes by. I was at Fred Ray's house and who should call but Beverly Gray. Fred happened to mention that I was there and she asked to speak to me. To my surprise she was friendly and chatty, which she'd never been when I was working with her. She told me she was writing a book about Roger so naturally he was the topic of our conversation. I was in the middle of some grim tale about Roger and one of his children when she interrupted me. "Wait a minute," she said. There was a brief moment of silence before she told me to go ahead. "Are you recording?" I asked. She admitted that she was. The story I was about to tell her was hearsay and grounds for legal action if it wasn't true, which is why I hadn't used it in my own book and I told her so. I also reminded her that it wasn't good form to record someone without telling them first. I put a quick end to the conversation and that was my last encounter with Beverly Gray.

I wish I could report that her book is lousy but I can't. It is well-researched, well-written, highly informative and very entertaining. It's everything a good biography should be, which is to say that no one in their right mind would want to be the subject of such a book. I know I wouldn't. Beverly probably wouldn't either. Every temper tantrum, foible and blemish is there for all the world to read. At this point I think it would be safe to say that Roger no longer thinks that my book is the worst one that was ever written about him. I doubt that he even remembers it. Or me for that matter. But he won't forget Beverly Gray. She will be persona non grata in Corman world until hell freezes over.

Before Beverly's book, people kept the worst stories about Roger to themselves. Most of the people I interviewed had a tale or two to tell about how cheap he was, but Roger likes those stories. He's proud of his frugality. The only note of hostility I encountered came from Mel Welles, an actor who often worked for Roger. He and I met for lunch at some coffee shop on the Sunset Strip and after exchanging a few pleasantries he suddenly exploded. "Why do you want to write a book about Roger? He's crazy! He's a mad man!" I didn't know what to say but then I didn't need to say anything because he kept on ranting, giving me all of the reasons why I shouldn't write my book. After he'd had his say I turned on my tape recorder and the interview began. Before my very eyes he morphed into a completely different person. It was a remarkable thing to behold. Throughout the interview he was giving a performance. After we finished I turned off the recorder and asked him if he wasn't worried that I might print some of the things he'd said before the recorder was on. "I'm counting on your discretion."

"When you're writing this thing don't make Roger a villain," Jonathan Haze told me. "He gave chances to a lot of people and he was the only one doing it. I got the opportunity to play a lot of different kinds of roles in those pictures. Where else could you play a cowboy one week and a gangster the next? Nobody else was doing anything like that? The part I had in *Not of This Earth*, the sleazy chauffeur… That was a great part. I don't think there was anyone else who would have let me do a part like that."

Haze is best-known for his performance in *The Little Shop of Horrors* (1960). I spent one of the best afternoons of my life interviewing the writer of that film, Charles Byron Griffith. He had recently divorced his wife and was living in a small apartment building at the time, which he managed in lieu of the rent. Griffith had nothing but disdain for his film work and had little cause to celebrate the direction his career had taken. But he blamed no one but himself for being too lazy to peddle his talent to someone other than Roger.

"The trouble with Roger is that he inspires you to do good work and then he degrades it," Griffith told me. "After the first couple of pictures I realized what they were all going to look like. I couldn't think about that while I was writing them. It would have crippled me."

Griffith was chatty and witty and open, almost the antithesis of Roger. He made me feel very much at home. After four hours he said, "You have enough now, don't you?" I said that I did. "Good." He got out of his chair and disappeared into the other room. I was about to leave, assuming that he'd had more than enough of me, when he came back with a joint. He smiled.

"You do this, don't you?" He sat back down, took a hit and passed it to me. We both got high and carried on for another couple of hours, talking about anything and everything. I cherish that day.

Another writer who worked for Roger was my pal Randy Robertson. He wrote at least nine or ten films with Jim Wynorski including *Transylvania Twist*. Randy's whole life revolved around rock 'n' roll music and movies. His favorite T-shirt was the one that read: LIFE AT 24 FRAMES A SECOND. Randy loved to hang around the set. Sometimes he would play a small part but whether he did or not he wanted to be there. He told me on more than one occasion that when he died he wanted to be cremated and have his ashes scattered over the Warner lot, his favorite studio. He changed his mind about that and I didn't know why until I saw what had been carved on his tombstone. R. J. ROBERTSON, SCREENWRITER. More permanent than a poster.

One afternoon Randy and I were watching a documentary about Roger in which someone gleefully said: "We just love it when Roger comes to the set." Randy burst out laughing. "Oh yeah. Right. The temperature drops about 40 degrees."

The temperature did more than drop when Roger showed up at his Venice studio. The receptionist would sound the alarm the second she saw his car. Everybody scrambled to hide all of the equipment that Roger hadn't authorized and then hightailed it off the lot because if Roger saw too many people he'd want to fire somebody.

We just love it when Roger comes to the set!

What they *loved* was the opportunity that Roger gave them to work in the movies. While the studios did their best to keep hopeful young filmmakers out, the door to Roger's place was wide open. But there was a tradeoff. You were expected to work long hours for shamefully low wages. Roger got the money. You got the career. Maybe.

"I have to admit that Roger Corman, one of the most talented producers of any kind of film, is successful mostly because he lets people do what they could do best, and very often, fortunately for him, the chemistry worked," said composer Ronald Stein, who got his start with Roger.[1] Stein is just one of a legion who passed through the Corman Film School, a list that includes Alan Arkush, George Armitage, Timur Beckmambetov, Peter Bogdanovich, Barbara Boyle, James Cameron, Steve Carver, Francis Ford Coppola, Joe Dante, Jon Davison, Jonathan Demme, Tak Fujimoto, Dan Haller, Curtis Hanson, Jack Hill, Ron Howard, Gale Anne Hurd, Monte Hellman, Amy Holden Jones, Jonathan Kaplan, Irv Kershner, Gary Kurtz, Frank Marshall, Thom Mount, Jack Nicholson, J. B. Rogers, John Sayles, Martin Scorsese, Katt Shea and Robert Towne. Is it any wonder that so many of these people lobbied the Motion Picture Academy to give Roger an Oscar?

"I think to succeed in this world, you have to take chances," Roger said in his acceptance speech. "I believe the finest films being done today are done by original, innovative filmmakers who have the courage to take a chance and to gamble. So I say to you, 'Keep gambling. Keep taking chances.' Thank you."

Roger took more chances on people than he ever did on his films. Most of his films were in profit before he made them, having already been sold to the buyers based on the title and the concept. Before he opened New World Pictures the only time he really gambled on a film was when he made *The Intruder* (1962), a film about integration of the public schools in the South. He and his brother Gene financed that one out of their own pockets and put their lives on the line to make it. Despite the title of Roger's autobiography, *How I Made a Hundred Movies in Hollywood and Never Lost a Dime*, he lost money on *The Intruder* and was quite bitter about it. It was his one and only personal film. After that he retreated to the safety of the tried and true. "I do what Shakespeare did," he told me. "I give them entertainment."

He was born in Detroit on April 5, 1926, the son of an engineer and went to college to become one himself. But he didn't want to be an engineer. He wanted to make movies. He kicked around Hollywood for a while as a stagehand at KTLA and a reader at 20th Century Fox. While he was working at the Dick Irving Hyland Agency he sold a story to Allied Artists and became an executive producer on a film called *Highway Dragnet* (1954). He hooked up with a writer and actor named Wyott Ordung and together they made a truly miserable movie called *Monster from the Ocean Floor* (1954).

Ordung was the one who introduced Roger to Jonathan Haze, a fellow he'd met at a gas station. Roger gave him a part in the picture. Haze, in turn, introduced Roger to Charles Griffith, Dick Miller, Mel Welles, Bruno Ve Sota and R. Wright Campbell, who became part of Roger's stock company. Beverly Garland, a regular in Roger's early films, had been married to Campbell. Her second husband, Richard Garland, starred in two of Roger's movies. It was a pretty tight-knit group.

Gene Corman had become an agent and sold his brother's movie to Robert Lippert. Roger used the advance that Lippert gave him to make *The Fast and the Furious* (1955) which led to a three-picture deal with American International Pictures, a newly formed distribution and production company headed by James H. Nicholson and Samuel Z. Arkoff.

"He was [their] only supplier when they started," Mel Welles told me. "The deal was that upon delivery of the picture he would get fifty thousand dollars negative pick-up plus a fifteen thousand advance on the foreign sales. So he made every picture for under sixty-five thousand. In fact, every third picture he would send out and get it bootlegged for twenty-eight or thirty-thousand and deliver that one and get the sixty-five thousand. Not that he didn't share in further profits but Sam Arkoff was a pretty clever guy too, so you really never saw much later other than what you got up front."

Before television filled the airwaves with the cowboys every night of the week, the Western had always been 'a safe bet' and Roger made four of them for AIP. Two of them were generated by AIP, *Apache Woman* (1955) and *The Oklahoma Woman* (1956), while *Five Guns West* (1955) and *Gunslinger* (1956) were Roger's ideas. Even the trade magazines, which bent over backwards to say something positive about the films they reviewed, couldn't find much good to say about these weary Westerns. *Gunslinger* was probably the best of the bunch, if only for the novelty of having a female sheriff, but one of the things that all of these westerns share in common is they seem to take place in ghost towns because Roger didn't want to spring for any extras.

In his first six years as a filmmaker, Roger directed 22 features and had his hand in at least half as many more, all of them made in two weeks or less.

Lloyd Bridges plays the government agent who falls in love with half-breed Joan Taylor in *Apache Woman*.

Richard Denning manhandles *The Oklahoma Woman*, Peggy Castle, while Dick Miller watches in the background. Although there never seem to be any customers in this saloon, Miller is washing glasses every time we see him.

Somebody once said that Roger was the only guy in town who could make a movie in a phone booth for the cost of a call to New York and finish before his three minutes were up. He learned his craft on the job and his skill as a director improved with each picture, along with his ability to move faster and more efficiently.

"I think he was good with the camera, he knew how to move with it, but as I said I don't think I ever saw him work with actors," said screenwriter Richard Matheson. "He just cast them and assumed they knew what they were doing. He was good at making pictures quickly and on a budget, and he gave an interesting look to his films. They were always crisp and fast moving."[2]

Directors don't have time to work with the actors when they're shooting 45 to 55 set-ups a day. They function more like traffic cops, hustling everyone to the next spot, hoping the actors are prepared to deliver their lines on the first take. Things have to keep moving or the job won't get done on schedule. There's no time for nuance. But even if Roger had had the time it's doubtful that he would have had much to say to his actors. He didn't speak their language and he was a little in awe of them. He enrolled in Jeff Corey's acting class to help bridge the gap and some of the students became regulars in his stock company—Susan Cabot, Barboura Morris, Jack Nicholson and Robert Towne.

Roger's films were quirky, often gritty, and were more intelligent than the other films being made at his level. At a time when women were little more than window dressing, Roger put them front and center. When I saw *It Conquered the World* (1956) at a children's matinee, the kids went crazy when Beverly Garland took matters into her own hands and emptied a shotgun at the creature from Venus, telling it she'd see him in Hell before she'd let him make a slave of the world. We'd never seen a woman do anything like that before. It simply wasn't done in those days but Roger did it time and again.

Some people think Roger could have been a really good filmmaker if he'd had a little patience. I always suspected that if a project took too long it couldn't sustain his interest. He made a bet once that he could make a movie in three days. That was *The Little Shop of Horrors.* He completed the princi-

Susan Cabot is the sadistic Sabra Tanner in *Confession of a Sorority Girl*, an unofficial remake of Columbia's *The Strange One* (1957).]

Beverly Garland tries to convince Lee Van Cleef that
he's on the wrong side of the issue in *It Conquered the World*.

pal photography in two days but there was five or six days' worth of second
unit work left to be done. Nevertheless, he encouraged the myth that he'd
won his bet, as if speed was a perfectly good substitute for quality.

Obviously, the one thing you can't afford to waste on a short schedule
picture is time. As soon as Roger finished one shot he'd move his camera
to the next set-up without missing a beat. He knew exactly what he wanted
and he had to have a crew who could all but second guess him. Daniel Haller
joined the fold in 1958. His ability to design a set to make it look more expensive than it actually was made him indispensable to both Roger and AIP. One
of Roger's classmates, Jack Bohrer, became his assistant director. Bohrer said
Roger would be so focused at times that he had to shake him to get his attention. Chuck Hannawalt was the key grip. He was one of the few people who
could tell Roger what to do because Roger had a lot of respect for him. And
if he wasn't working on somebody else's movie, Floyd Crosby was Roger's

first choice for cameraman. They worked on twenty films together. And then there's Paul Rapp, whose official title was production manager but on one film he was a location scout, assistant director, actor, propman and chauffeur. Roger counted on these people, which is why they were paid a decent salary.

It wasn't until American International needed to upgrade their product that Roger was given three whole weeks to make a movie. That was *House of Usher,* which created an Edgar Allan Poe franchise that AIP was able to milk for almost a decade. Every now and then Gene Corman would negotiate a deal with United Artists and Roger was given as many as five or six weeks to make a movie. Those movies were pretty good. But the business side of Roger was always at war with the artist side of him and the business side was usually the victor. He was always tight-fisted, even when he was spending other people's money. Columbia became so concerned about his penny-pinching they threw him off a picture. The studio heads at 20th Century Fox were taken aback when he brought *The St. Valentine's Day Massacre* (1967) under budget. Roger hated working at Fox. The front office meddling and the waste generated by the studio overhead drove him nuts.

Most of the actors who worked for Roger during his pre-Poe period complained about how tight he was with a buck. Except for Beverly Garland. "Roger didn't really have any money to speak of when he made those pictures so you can't really fault him for trying to save wherever he could," she told me. "I mean, you knew up front what to expect so nobody really had any business complaining because you had to do your own stunts or your own makeup or because your dressing room was the nearest bush. Roger never forced anybody to work for him."

Beverly's right. To a point. But Roger didn't just cut the corners to bring his films in on budget. There were some corners he cut for no other reason than to keep more money in his own pocket. Forget about his temper tantrums. I've had a few of those myself. And forget about all of his other foibles that Beverly Gray happily documents in her book. Nobody's perfect. Forget about everything but his greed, which can't be glossed over just because he's given a lot of people an opportunity to work in the film business.

When you work people long hours for a nominal paycheck, the very least you should do is provide them with a decent meal. I'm not talking about a steak and lobster dinner but they deserve something better than a salami or Velveeta sandwich on plain white bread. That's what Roger gave the poor bastards who worked in below freezing weather in South Dakota when he was making *Beast from Haunted Cave* (1959) and *Ski Troop Attack* (1960). It seems to me that a hot bowl of soup wouldn't have been too much to ask. On *Big Bad Mama II* (1987), the food was so appallingly bad the film's leading lady, Angie Dickinson, took money out of her own pocket to feed the cast and crew.

Dick Miller told me that when Roger delivered *War of the Satellites* (1958) to Allied Artists two months after Sputnik was launched, studio head Steve Broidy was so pleased to have a headline hot movie he gave Roger $400 to throw a wrap party. "We're still waiting for that party," Miller said with a grin.

Roger is like the gangster that Edward G. Robinson played in *Key Largo* (1948). At one point he's asked what he wants and Robinson is stuck for an answer. Humphrey Bogart came to his rescue: "He wants *more*." Robinson is elated, almost overwhelmed at the simplicity of it. "Yeah," he confirmed, "that's what I want. I want MORE!"

Accommodation was another way Roger managed to hold onto his money. In South Dakota, he was able to get hotel rooms for a dollar a day by misrepresenting himself. He told everyone they were making a student film. And since he was able to put two people in a room, he was effectively housing everyone for fifty cents a day. And still all they got was a cold sandwich.

The cast and crew of *Swamp Women* were housed in an abandoned hotel in the middle of the swamp. Roger spent the night in town. Beverly Garland said the only time Roger ever went first class was when he shot a couple of pictures on Kauai. Everyone stayed at the only hotel on the island at the time, the Coco Palms. Then, according to Jonathan Haze, Roger got a deal on a Boy Scout Camp and all of the crew and some of the actors were taken out of the hotel and moved into the camp. Haze put up with it for a couple of nights then

Susan Cabot is having a close encounter of the worst kind
with Richard Devon in *War of the Satellites*.

got fed up. "Roger, I can't do this," he said. "If you want me to act in the movie then I gotta be in a hotel where I don't have eight grips snoring in my ear all night. I don't want to go to sleep at nine o'clock at night. I don't want to have to sit in the toilet to read my script. I want to live like a human being. If you can do this Roger you do it. You stay here. But I'm going back to the hotel."

Cameraman Jacques Marquette was led to believe he'd being staying at the Caribe Hilton when he flew to Puerto Rico to shoot a couple of movies for Roger. Roger met him at the airport and told him they were staying in a big mansion instead. The joint had five bedrooms with five army cots in each room. And one shower for twenty-five people!

"So everybody would come back and use the bathroom and the toilet immediately plugged up—that would always happen," said actress Betsy Jones-Moreland. "We were always out of hot water because there were twenty or twenty-five of us trying to take a shower!"[3]

Roger put a slightly different spin on this nightmare. He said that having everyone stay at this "large Mediterranean-style house on the beach" made the trip feel "like a vacation." But it wasn't Marquette's idea of a vacation. He refused to stay there. So Roger drove him to another place, a cabana with no bathroom and no place to eat. "Finally," Marquette said, "after all day looking at all these different horseshit places, he took me to the Caribe Hilton. Now what happened is that all the people that were staying at the 'mansion' came into town on the weekend. They'd come to my hotel and eat dinner with me, and I'd sign the check for all of 'em!"[4]

Marquette was headed for home when the hotel clerk informed him that he wouldn't be allowed to leave until the bill was paid. Marquette was under the impression that it had been paid. He placed an angry call to Roger, who assured him that he'd get right on it, but he didn't. Desperate, Marquette hid a reel from each movie.

"He *hid* them, because we didn't have tickets to get home, we didn't have money to get home, the crew wasn't getting paid," said Jones-Moreland. "We were truly stranded. Roger was going on to other things—and we *weren't*! Jack hid the film—he stashed it in a freezer or something—and he wouldn't let Roger have it until we not only got our checks, but we got our checks cashed and we had the money in our hot little hands, to do with as we pleased!"[5]

Clearly we see that morale isn't high on Roger's list of considerations, nor is the safety and welfare of the people who work for him. Actress Allison Hayes recalled an incident while she was working on *Gunslinger*. "That was in the be-

Tony Carbone and Edward Wain (Robert Towne) are both after
Betsy Jones-Moreland, *The Last Woman on Earth.*

ginning days of Roger Corman when his promise to himself was he would be a millionaire by the time he was 36 or 37. So he was shooting a gun off on the other side of the camera instead of paying to have it dubbed in. It spooked the horses. This was in rehearsal. John Ireland told him not to shoot the gun and Roger said okay. We did the shot. Sure enough, he shot it off. My horse went up in the air and off I went. He never even called to ask how I was."[6]

Miss Hayes finished the film with her arm in a sling. She asked Roger, "Who do I have to fuck to get off this picture?"

Roger wanted Betsy Jones-Moreland to jump into an ocean full of sharks and manta rays for a scene in *Creature from the Haunted Sea* (1961). They got into an argument that ended with Roger yelling, "Just do it! Just get in the goddamn water! I don't want to hear any more about these fucking fish!" Miss Jones-Moreland vowed that if a shark bit off her leg she was going to beat Roger to death with the bloody stump.[7]

Beverly Garland is the town marshal in *Gunslinger*. One exhibitor said it was the kind of 'hokum' his customers wanted.

Likewise, during the making of *Swamp Women*, the cast expressed concerns about deadly snakes when they were asked to wade through the Florida swamp. Roger jumped into the water and said, "See, this proves there are no snakes." To which Beverly Garland replied: "The only thing it proves, Roger, is you're an idiot."

There were so many incidents during the making of *Viking Women and the Sea Serpent* (1958) that the cast should have received hazardous duty pay. (For a detailed account see the entry in the Filmography section at the end of this chapter.) However, it has to be said that at the end of the day, most of the people that worked with Roger liked him. "You can't *not* like Roger," said Jones-Moreland. "You have to be *lured* by that wonderful, wonderful smile and that ability to make you feel important. *Anybody, anywhere* has got to respond to that—I don't care who you are, you have to respond to that feeling that he's taking you in and you're part of the family and your input is important. He just *generates* that, and I don't even think he works at it."[8]

"Roger is such a nice gentleman," said actress Jackie Joseph. "There's something elegant about him. I mean for all the wonderful, semi-trash that he grew up on and so cleverly made a living on, and the wonderful actors and directors and creative people and writers who grew through him... he has an air of nobility about him. He looks like a high society person. And he talks like one. Maybe he *is* one. I don't even know."

Having focused on Roger's stinginess, it's only fair to mention, as Beverly Gray does in her book, that he has a generous side. Here's a story that she missed that actor William Campbell had to tell. He and his brother, screenwriter R. Wright Campbell, worked for Roger several times. "[T]here was a time when my brother was first getting started and he needed money," the actor recalled. "He gave my brother a thousand bucks. If that had been a business deal, Roger would never have forgotten about the loan. But the fact that it was a simple loan to a friend, he never asked my brother for it. As a matter of fact, after my brother had written a screenplay and picked up some money, he went to Roger and handed him the thousand back. Roger said: 'What the hell is that for?' My brother said, 'You loaned me a thousand dollars, Roger.' He'd forgotten that!"[9]

But in business matters Roger is Ebenezer Scrooge. He's even stingy with himself. If he's given a first class ticket to fly somewhere to give a speech or something he'll exchange the ticket, fly coach, and pocket the difference. On one occasion, he threw his back out just as he was about to embark on a fourteen-hour flight to Manila. Everyone begged him to fly first class but he just couldn't bring himself to do it. Call me naïve but I always thought the reason to make a lot of money was for the security that came with it, along with freedom to live your life in comfort. Obviously that's not the way Roger sees it. Maybe to him winning the game is more important than what he's won. He has amassed a small fortune through hard work and innovation. And by taking someone else's share of the pie.

Roger says he's forty percent artist and sixty percent businessman. If that's the case then perhaps novelist and playwright J. B. Priestley may have inadvertently given us a perfect description of Roger in one of his essays about Hollywood. Priestley maintained that Hollywood was managed by business men pretending to be artists and by artists pretending to be business men. "In this queer atmosphere," he wrote, "nobody stays as he was; the artist begins to lose his art, and the business man becomes temperamental and unbalanced."

For sixteen years Roger worked closely with, though not exclusively for

Jim Nicholson and Sam Arkoff at American International. For the most part they had a good relationship. They'd come to him with a project or he'd go to them, but either way he was left alone to make the picture the way he wanted to. Still, he didn't control the distribution of his films and to that end he and his brother created The Filmgroup.

"I wasn't trying to be my own AIP," he said, "but I felt that I was making these films that *they* were distributing and *they* not only had certain controls over what I was doing but *they* were getting a disproportionate share of the proceeds. And I had a little bit of money to invest so I thought I could continue to produce and direct while I ran my own company."

Small town exhibitors were still suffering from a shortage of product and Roger thought that by offering the same kind of low cost, exploitable double feature packages that had made AIP such a success he could relieve some of their pain. "Make no mistake about it," he told the press, "such good pictures, because of rising production costs, are becoming increasingly difficult to make. But it can still be done."[10]

Apparently not. A cursory look at Filmgroup's inventory reveals a list of titles that would put the most undemanding viewer into a rage or a coma. Of the more than two dozen movies made for, or acquired by Filmgroup for distribution, the only one to make any kind of impact was *The Little Shop of Horrors*, which only gained an audience after it was sold to television. This $26,000 quickie became the basis of an award-winning off-Broadway musical in 1983 and a multi-million dollar movie four years later for which Roger was paid handsomely. "I can't think of any film that gave me a better return on my investment," he remarked.

Filmgroup's *Dementia 13* (1963) is noteworthy only because it was directed by Francis Ford Coppola. As a piece of entertainment it is woefully lacking. *The Wasp Woman* (1959) is remembered (if it's remembered at all) for its wonderful and completely misleading poster. And *The Terror* (1963) is notorious for being one of the only movies in Hollywood history to have no story whatsoever.

A friend of mine got his hands on a 35mm print of Filmgroup's *Ski Troop*

Attack and was kind enough to invite me to his place for a screening. I'd never seen it. There were two other people in the audience that night and as my friend carried the film to the projection booth, one of them noticed that the entire film was in one three reel can. "I didn't realize the film was so short," he remarked. "Wait until it's over before you say that," I cautioned. Fifteen minutes into it he was checking his watch. At regular intervals. It was a very long 63 minutes.

At one point Roger flew to Russia, which he thought might be a good place to make cheap movies. He was shown a science-fiction film called *Planet of Storms* (1962) which was loaded with special effects. After taking a tour of the production facilities, Roger had the impression that he might not be allowed to leave Russia. So he asked for permission to return to America to see if he could find a buyer for *Planet of Storms*. The second he stepped off the plane he phoned the folks in Russia to say that he wouldn't be coming back and then sold the movie to himself. He made three movies out of it—*Voyage to a Prehistoric Planet* (1965), *Queen of Blood* (1966), and *Voyage to the Planet of Prehistoric Women* (1967).

Francis Ford Coppola and Jack Hill were asked to create a new story and some new scenes for another Russian sci-fi flick called *Nebo Zovyot* (1959). Roger wanted a couple of monsters for the trailer, something 'phallic.' Coppola and Hill gave him more than he bargained for. One of the monsters resembled a giant penis with eyes. The other looked like a vagina with teeth. "Don't you think it's a little raw?" Roger asked. "Nobody will know," Coppola assured him. The film was released as *Battle Beyond the Sun* (1963), much to the displeasure of the exhibitors who booked it. "Indescribably bad," one exhibitor complained. "These flops are going to eventually discourage the most ardent fans," observed another.

Gene Corman quit The Filmgroup to produce pictures for Robert Lippert at 20th Century Fox. Running the company by himself proved to be more than Roger could handle. He threw in the towel and gave all of the films to AIP to distribute.

"The Filmgroup made money every year," Roger said, "but we never made

The 'phallic' monsters from *Battle Beyond the Sun.*

much money. I finally just let it drift away because I realized I could not produce, direct and run a distribution company at the same time. It was too many things."

Two years later Roger became the darling of the avant-garde when he produced and directed *The Wild Angels* and *The Trip.* Both praised and chastised by the critics, these two films took in more revenue than AIP had ever seen and marked the beginning of the end of the relationship that Roger had enjoyed with the company for twelve years.

In the past, Jim Nicholson had changed a few of Roger's titles but he never messed with the content. Nicholson made a minor change to *The Wild Angels* that was so silly Roger was able to laugh it off. But the addition of a disclaimer at the front of *The Trip,* and an alteration in the climax of *The Trip* turned what had been an objective film about LSD into a denouncement of drug use. Roger's relationship with Nicholson was further strained when he was sent to New York and Paris on an AIP promotional junket. When he found out that Nicholson planned to deduct his expenses from the salary he was supposed to receive for his work on *De Sade*, which he'd done as a favor, Roger fired off an angry letter to Sam Arkoff, taking the opportunity to remind Arkoff that they still owed him over $200,000 in profit participations.

Roger had been thinking about severing his ties with the company for years but he was haunted by a recurring nightmare in which AIP still owed him money for some picture but he couldn't remember which one. Things finally came to a head with the release of *Gas-s-s-s!* (1970), no pun intended.

"I turned in the final cut, left for Europe, and changes were made without my knowledge," Roger said. "When I saw what AIP did to my film, I realized we had come to the end of the line as a team."[11]

The film received mixed reviews from the critics. *Films and Filming* found that it had "a lightness of touch and controlled wit rarely encountered in U.S. parodies." *New York Magazine* said: "There's a cool overlay and a serious undertone to the fun and games that give one an insight into the youth level that has long been Corman's forte. It's worth seeing for this alone." But *Variety* was less than pleased. "Obviously aimed at the youth market, it will take some very tolerant youngster to sit through this poorest of the Corman films." One of the worst reviews came from the *New York Times*. "To the extent that Roger Corman's *Gas-s-s-s* is an end-of-the-world movie," wrote Vincent Canby, "you might—if you were taking leave of your right senses—describe it as both his *Weekend* [1967] and his *Shame* [1968], although it's far less funny than Godard and a good deal more pretentious than Bergman."

Viewed today *Gas-s-s-s, or It Became Necessary to Destroy the World in Order to Save It*, looks terribly forced and dated, the work of a director out of touch with the audience he'd hoped to capture. Ironically, using his playbook that same year, three of Roger's alumni—Peter Fonda, Dennis Hopper and Jack Nicholson—turned Hollywood upside down with the ultimate counter-culture picture, *Easy Rider* (1969), a film that had slipped through AIP's fingers because of Sam Arkoff's insistence on replacing Hopper as a director if he ran behind schedule. Not an unreasonable demand considering who he was dealing with, but it cost him a small fortune.

Gas-s-s had been a difficult film to make. The script was written as they were shooting and Roger was in a foul mood the entire time, snapping and barking at everyone, relieved when the ordeal was over. He'd already made the decision to quit directing so that he could take another shot at running his own company. This time he'd give it his full attention.

While Roger was in Ireland shooting *Von Richthofen and Brown* (1971) he got in touch with Larry Woolner, after Gene Corman had made it clear that he wasn't interested in being a partner in his brother's new company. Roger met Woolner back in 1954, when he and Jim Nicholson were making the rounds of the exhibitors and distributors in an effort to persuade them to invest in Nicholson's new company. Roger took the opportunity to cut his own deal to make two movies for Woolner and his brother Bernard, the owners of a string of Louisiana drive-ins.

Roger and Larry Woolner moved into the penthouse suite of a four-storey office on Sunset Boulevard, in the heart of the Sunset Strip, and opened New World Pictures. And on December 26 that same year, Roger married Julie Halloran, a dark-haired UCLA graduate who back in 1964 had applied for a job as Roger's assistant. Stephanie Rothman had better credentials so she got the job. Julie got the boss. On their first date Roger told her, "I'm on overload right now. My life is a little out of control but in about two weeks I'll have everything under control."[12] And he's been saying it ever since.

Eleven years later Julie gave birth to his first child, Catherine, after spending a full day producing *Crazy Mama* (1975). Apparently Julie was as driven as Roger. She produced *Moving Violation* (1976) while she was seven months pregnant with his second child, Roger Martin. She prided herself on being able to produce movies and children simultaneously.

Joe Dante told me he was in the screening room at New World, watching the dailies from *Grand Theft Auto* (1977), when Roger Martin, who couldn't have been much older than a year, began chanting "Money-money-money-money" while sitting on his father's lap.

The couple had two more children, Brian William and Mary Teresa. The two boys (especially Roger Martin) were quite rebellious and proved to be more than Roger and Julie could handle. Having raised a high-spirited step-daughter who seemed hell-bent on making a shambles of my marriage I can only say "Welcome to parenthood." (For a more detailed account of the boys' reckless and rebellious shenanigans please see Beverly Gray's book.) Suffice to say Roger and Julie survived the ordeal and remain happily married.

Not so the partnership of Roger Corman and Larry Woolner. After less than a year Woolner moved across the street and became Roger's competitor as Dimension Pictures, taking two movies with him—*Twilight People* (1971), *The Sin of Adam and Eve* (1973)—and one property, *Sweet Sugar* (1972). Roger said their breakup was friendly and always credits Woolner with the idea for New World's first release, *The Student Nurses* (1970), which was written and directed by Stephanie Rothman. Rothman told Henry Jenkins: "We made it while Roger was out of the country, directing a film of his own, *Von Richthofen and Brown,* so we were free to develop the story of the nurses as we wished, as long as there was enough nudity and violence distributed through it. Please notice, I did not say sex, I said nudity. This freedom, once I paid my debt to the requirements of the genre, allowed me to address what interested me—and continues to interest me today—political and social conflicts and the changes they produce. It allowed me to have a dramatized discussion about issues that were then being ignored in big-budget major studio films."

Roger made a string of nurse movies while simultaneously exploring the prurient possibilities of teachers, stewardesses and models. All of these pictures followed a formula: lots of action, lots of nudity (Roger isn't comfortable with sex), and a little bit of social comment, though Roger didn't want to stress it. To assure his male audience that they'd see plenty of skin Roger made sure these pictures received an R-rating. The best that one can say about these trashy movies is so long as an actress was willing to take her clothes off, she'd get a stronger role than she would have from a major studio.

One of Roger's competitors, Crown International, was having a lot of luck with biker movies, a genre that Roger had kick-started with *The Wild Angels.* So when Charles 'Beach' Dickerson[13] wanted to produce a biker movie, and had already raised half of the money, Roger gave him the balance on the condition that the film would be ready for New World's opening. *Angels Die Hard* (1970) gave Roger a good return on his investment so he continued to mine that genre as well.

The exploitation film was in its heyday when New World hit the scene. The drive-ins and grind houses were hungry for product and Roger gave it to them. He was no longer the maverick filmmaker taking on the establishment, in spite of the left-wing posters that lined his walls. He had become Nicholson and Arkoff rolled into one, and every bit as corporate. He was now 10 percent artist and 90 per cent businessman. The irony is that he'd left AIP because they'd tampered with his art (or, as Jim Wynorski once said in the throes of a blind rage, his "fucking art,"), but Roger did exactly the same thing to the young filmmakers who worked for him and probably never thought twice about it. To be fair, these young hopefuls didn't have his experience and most of them will admit that they learned things from Roger that served them well when they moved on to bigger and better things.

"The trouble with making a movie for Roger Corman is that he always insists on pissing on it before he releases it," said Angie Dickinson, the star of *Big Bad Mama* (1974). More than ten years later she was back for a sequel, *Big Bad Mama II*, which was written by my pal, Randy Robertson. I was sitting next to her in a small screening room when she saw the picture for the first time. Early on there was a particularly unflattering close-up of her and I heard her groan. She nudged my shoulder and whispered in my ear, "This is what happens when you hang around too long."

The high cost of shooting movies in and around Los Angeles forced Roger to look for new, less expensive locations. Actor/producer John Ashley had been making horror movies in the Philippines for a couple of years.

"While we were making *Beast of the Yellow Night* [1971], Roger Corman was forming New World Pictures," Ashley recalled. "He called me in the Philippines and said he'd be interested in handling the distribution on *Beast*. He flew over while we were shooting it and looked at some dailies and said he'd take it and gave us a little advance on it. He told me he was getting ready to do a picture called *The Big Doll House* [1971] and was thinking about shooting it in Puerto Rico. Well, the outgrowth of everything, after some conversation, was that Roger shot it in the Philippines."

Jack Hill described making *The Big Doll House* as a "fun nightmare." The

Big Bad Mama.

day he arrived a typhoon blew the roof off the film stage. There was also an uprising in the works so it wasn't strange to see fresh bullet holes in the hotel where he was staying, a converted mental institution where rats and cockroaches ran amok.

"The people are wonderful, and I love them, and they try so hard to please you," Hill remarked. "You ask, 'Can you do this and that?' 'Oh yes, sure, no problem'—they like to see you smile. Then, of course, they can't do any such thing at all. They had stunt men who'd get up to take a fall, and cross themselves and jump. If they want to have a man on fire, they just set a guy on fire who'll try and jump into the water as quick as he can."[14]

Roger didn't like *The Big Doll House* when he first saw it. He thought they'd gone too far with the sex and violence. But when Hill's $100,000 film grossed $4 million bucks, Roger tossed his scruples into the nearest waste basket, gave Hill a $20,000 bonus for a job well done, and sent him back to the Philippines to make another one just like it.

Shooting in the Philippines proved to be so advantageous that Roger negotiated a deal to build a couple of soundstages there, in exchange for some equally advantageous tax breaks. He hooked up with producer Cirio H. Santiago, a man who shared his disregard for the safety and welfare of his cast and crew.

These women-in-cages movies all followed the same formula. The women were raped and brutalized for the first half of the picture and then got even during the second half. The best that can be said of these sadistic little epics is they were the training ground for Pam Grier, the cinema's first female action star. After making a handful of pictures for Roger, this pretty, saucy, sexy and lethal woman went to work for AIP and became the queen of the Blaxploitation movies. Long live Pam Grier!

"The early days of New World were really exciting because the staff Roger assembled was highly intelligent and really enthusiastic," said Frances Doel. "Anyone would do any job to get the chance to get their foot in the door of the film business. There was a lot of energy. Anybody could have a good idea. He welcomes input, suggestions, ideas from everybody—in fact, demanded it. It was fun and exciting because he was very much hands-on, the leader, in charge, there all the time."[15]

Once New World was up and running, Roger became concerned about the company's sleazy image. His sales manager, Frank Moreno, showed him the way to upgrade it. Without consulting with Roger he bought Ingmar Bergman's *Cries and Whispers* (1972) for the U.S. market. Roger was delighted when it took in a million and a half bucks and received five Academy Award nominations. The distribution of high quality foreign films proved to be both profitable and good P.R.

"During the time that we were distributing foreign films, we won more Best Foreign Film awards than any other company in the business," said Roger. "I did it partially to make money but also because I really wanted to distribute those films. I loved those films and I thought I could do well by them. Major studios weren't geared to properly distribute them and the aficionados hadn't the clout to get good terms. I was able to give them more

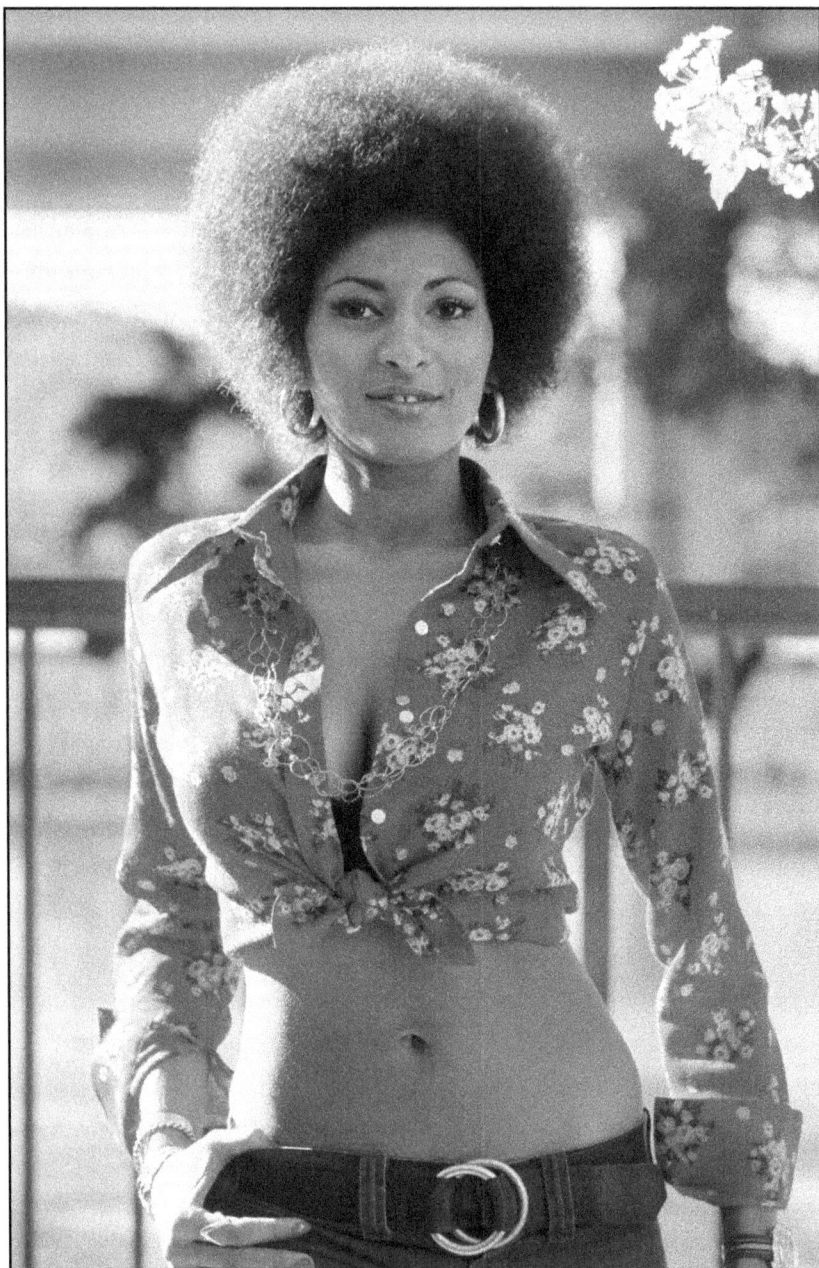

Pam Grier.

personal attention. For instance, there was a rose, I think a yellow rose that was significant to the plot of *Cries and Whispers*. We had a charity screening at one of the art houses in Westwood and two of my assistants, dressed in long gowns, gave a yellow rose to the women who attended the screening. Normally, we played off the art houses and that was the end of it, but we put *Cries and Whispers* into the drive-ins. Not many but a few. Everybody said we couldn't do that. Ingmar Bergman thanked me when I met him at the Cannes Film Festival. I'd given him a bigger audience for his films."

Of all of the films that Frank Moreno bought, only one failed to pay for itself, and for his efforts he was told that he'd get ten per cent of the earnings. But when it came time to collect Roger didn't want to honor the agreement. "I had to go up there and negotiate and settle my contract with him and get my participation," he said. "Behind me came Barbara [Boyle], and Paul [Almond] who each had a little piece. And Roger was very upset for about two weeks. His sense was that it was all his, and that we weren't entitled."[16]

And yet, like so many others, the two remained friends. Roger continued to seek Moreno's counsel in business matters and even invested money with him.

Foreign films aside, the heart and soul of New World Pictures was the crap. And nobody knew how to sell crap any better than New World's director of advertising and publicity Jon Davison. He got his foot in the door by doing a free rewrite of a picture called *Night Call Nurses* (1972). He was the one who brought Joe Dante and Alan Arkush into the fold to cut trailers. The two learned that what they *didn't* show was as important as what they *did* show. If the photography was lousy they'd crib scenes from other movies. If the sound was poor they'd let used car salesman Ron Gans carry it with his unbridled enthusiastic narration. With Davison's help Dante and Arkush created a series of salacious and campy campaigns that bordered on self-parody.

"*TNT Jackson* will put you in traction."

Cover Girl Models—"They're over-exposed but not under-developed!"

Darktown Strutters—"Better move your butt… when this lady struts."

Arkush walked into the editing room one morning with the catch line that had come to him while he was in the shower. "Ron Howard pops the clutch and tells everyone to *Eat My Dust!*" Without missing a beat Dante said: "Tells the *world* to *Eat My Dust!*" "Lennon and McCartney," Arkush said reflectively.

These two guys brought a spirit of fun and irreverence to the seedy operation. Their tongue-in-cheek approach to everything went so far as to infect the company's pressbooks. Exhibitors who booked *Eat My Dust* were encouraged to offer free passes to the patrons who had the most speeding tickets.

The suggestions in the pressbook for *Up from the Depths* (1979), referred to by its director as *Crap from the Dreck*, were even more outrageous. Here's a sample:

> Invite the local YMCA to stage a charity "Swim for Your Life" contest at the shark tank of the local aquarium. Coat the little boys and girls with bacon grease and throw them into the tank. For every minute that the little buggers survive get sponsors to donate money to the cause. Just in case none of the kiddies swim more than a minute, film the event and sell it to the local television station billed as "The Making of *Up from the Depths*... Don't forget to consult the local SPCA for approval before you do this one! Watch your grosses soar!"

This sort of tomfoolery wasn't confined to the pressbooks. Spurious items were often planted in the trade magazines. When Universal and Dino de Laurentiis were trying to beat each other to the punch with a big-budgeted *King Kong* (1933) remake, *The Hollywood Reporter* announced that Roger Corman would be entering the *King Kong* race. This was one time the joke backfired. Roger saw the item and thought it might not be such a bad idea and it took some doing to talk him out of it.

Jon Davison gave Arkush and Dante the opportunity to make a film of their own by betting Roger he could produce a picture for $80,000, which was half of the cost of the cheapest picture in New World's inventory. Roger took the bet but hedged it. He gave Davison $60,000, probably assuming the balance would come out of Davison's pocket, but who the hell would have any spare money working for Roger? Davison told Dante and Arkush to do their best. They concocted a comedy that parodied New World's operation and used massive amounts of action sequences from the New World library. They shot the picture during the day and continued to cut trailers at night, and still managed to bring *Hollywood Boulevard* (1976) in on time and *under* budget. These were the kinds of hoops you had to jump through for Roger, who told more than one frustrated director who'd come to the end of his or her rope, "Remember, if you do a good job you'll never have to work for me again."

Which was the whole point. You worked for Roger so that you could leave Roger. Arkush did it by making *Rock and Roll High School* (1979). He had a very successful career in television. Dante's breakout movie was *Piranha* (1978) after which he moved to Avco-Embassy to make *The Howling* (1981). Davison went on to produce the screamingly funny *Airplane* (1980).

"People are fond of leaving Roger and doing other things and talking about how Roger loused up their movie by interfering too much," Joe Dante told *Fangoria* magazine. "But then, if you really look back at it, if Roger made your rubber-fish movie a little worse, or your women-in-cages movie a little worse, whatever he did, in the long run it probably was more beneficial than you originally thought at the time, and was certainly worth the experience."

One of Roger's most popular films during this period was *Death Race 2000* (1975), primarily made to take advantage of the advance publicity generated by *Rollerball* (1975). Roger took an option on a short story by Ib Melchior and hired Robert Thom to adapt it. "It was really an awful script," director Paul Bartel told *Time Out*. "It was very long and by the end of page 45, the cars still hadn't left New York City." Charles Griffith was asked to take a crack at it. He and Bartel agreed that a film about a cross-country race, in which the drivers racked up points by running down pedestrians, had to be a satire. "There are many times when a Corman picture can only be a comedy," Griffith told me. "Roger didn't want it to be a comedy and felt we were in a conspiracy against him. Actually, we were in a conspiracy *for* him." Roger maintains that what he wanted was a smart comedy like *Dr. Strangelove* (1964); not a silly

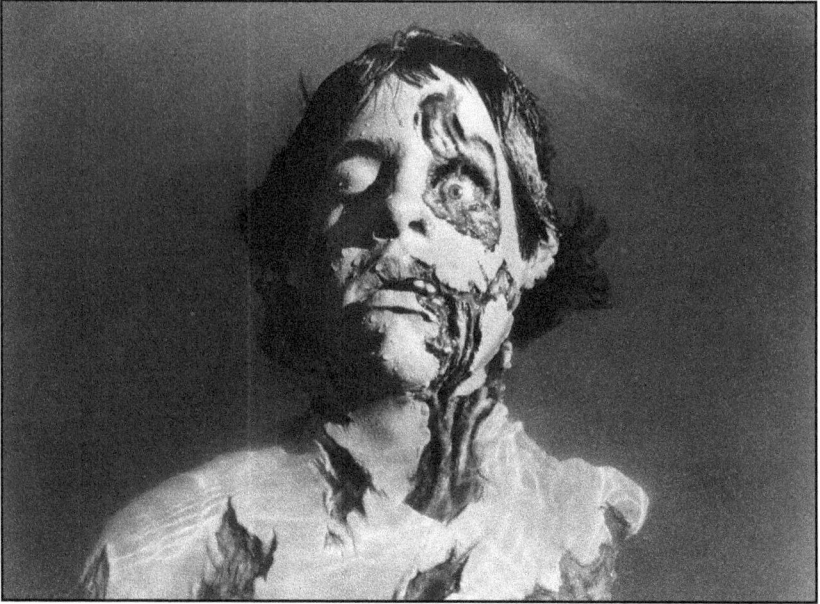

Piranha.

comedy. And though Bartel and Griffith insist that he ruined the film by cutting down the humor and increasing the violence in post-production, Chris Koetting, who wrote a book about New World, said he read the script and found that most of the humor, as well as the violence, was left intact.

Roger had to invest in some sound stages to make *Battle Beyond the Stars* (1980), his answer to *Star Wars*. His attorney, Paul Almond, negotiated the deal to buy a piece of property vacated by Hammond Lumber. "There's only one stipulation," Almond told Roger in a tone that suggested he was about to break some very bad news. "The locals are afraid of gentrification. They won't let you modernize the outside of the building." There was a short pause before the two men burst out laughing.[17] Of course fixing up the place would have been the last thing on Roger's agenda. He never bothered to take down the Hammond Lumber sign because somebody told him it would cost about $300 to remove. Years later Roger sold the property to a developer for $4.3 million. *Slaughter Studios* (2002) was made one step ahead of the wreckers.

According to the trade magazines, the budget for *Battle Beyond the Stars* was $3 million, split fifty-fifty between New World and Orion. Roger told the writer, John Sayles, that he wanted *The Magnificent Seven* (1959) in outer space and that's what Sayles gave him. Sayles couldn't deny that the film was cheesy but he thought everyone did some 'imaginative' work.

James Cameron was making models when he caught Roger's attention with his design for a spaceship with tits. "This is exactly what I want," Roger told him and pretty soon Cameron was designing all of the sets. He understood that Roger didn't care if the sets looked good. He just wanted them finished. Hoping to emulate the look of the multi-million dollar sets designed for Doug Trumbull's *Silent Running* (1972), Cameron hot-glued McDonald's Styrofoam trays to the walls and sprayed them with automotive lacquer and metallic paint.

The score by James Horner, and the special effects, were recycled for a half dozen more movies.

As Hammond Lumber, the fact that the property lay under one of the flight paths to the Los Angeles International Airport had been of no concern. It was, however, problematic for a movie studio. As the three small, make-shift stages were never sound-proofed, planes would routinely disrupt production. Besides that little inconvenience the joint leaked like a sieve every time it rained. People would be standing in two feet of water using power tools.

In such a shabby and potentially dangerous environment, where people were overworked and underpaid, one would have expected to find obscenities scribbled on the bathroom walls. Not so. After the word got out that Roger felt the title for a film called *Mutant* was a little weak, the team at the lumber yard let their creative juices flow every time they sat on the crapper. *Mutant on the Bounty*, *Gidget Goes Mutant*, *Dial 'M' for Mutant*, *Thoroughly Modern Mutant*, and *Make Mike Mutant* were among the hundred-plus suggestions scrawled on the wall. The film was released as *Forbidden World* (1982). At one point Roger thought he should have his own sound studio after a bill for dubbing nearly sent him through the roof. Normally he worked with Ryder Sound, a company that billed him in increments, but he had to go with

Forbidden World.

another company once that billed him in one lump sum. For a couple of days Roger had everyone taking measurements for sound equipment until he was informed what the equipment would cost. That was the end of that.

New World became the largest independent distribution network in North America, with offices in twelve U.S. cities, plus the New World-Mutual distributorship in Canada, making it a very attractive enterprise. Roger turned down several offers to buy it, one for as much as $15 million. He told *Variety*: "I can't conceive of anyone dumb enough to offer that amount. The company is simply not for sale."

But, of course, it was. He sold it for $16.5 million in 1983 to Harry Evans Sloan, Lawrence Kuppin, Larry Thompson and Bob Rehme. He did it to free himself from what he called 'the albatross of distribution.' He continued to make movies under his new umbrella, Concorde-New Horizons. New World agreed to distribute his films in exchange for Roger's services as a consultant for two years, and his promise to stay out of the distribution business. But when New World stopped releasing his pictures, and kept the profits from the ones that they had, Roger became a distributor once again, something he really didn't want to do. New World sued him. Roger patiently waited until the company was about to go public and then instigated a countersuit. New World quickly settled out-of-court and Roger was free to operate as he pleased. Plus he got his film library back as a bonus, which he was able to sell to Buena Vista for an ungodly sum. After releasing what one might laughingly call some of the 'primo' titles, Buena Vista realized they'd bought the Brooklyn Bridge so to speak and sold the library back to Roger for a fraction of what they'd paid for it.

A friend told me he was standing in a Blockbuster one afternoon, looking for a video tape to rent, when a little girl standing next to him plucked a tape off of the shelf. Her father gently took it from her and softly said, "Remember what I told you, sweetheart?" He pointed to the New World logo. "When you see this on the box you know the movie isn't any good."

If you're interested in learning more about New World, you couldn't do better for yourself than to pick up a copy of Christopher Koetting's *Mind Warp! The Fantastic True Story of Roger Corman's New World Pictures*.

In 1986, at a time when several of the major independents were biting the dust, Roger Corman enjoyed the highest profit he'd seen for ten years, his success due in no small part to Brad Kravoy, Concorde's head of business affairs, who urged Roger to jump into the emerging video tape market feet first.

The theatrical market for low budget films was dying. The main source of revenue for low budget films had always come from the outdoor theatres, which were paved over to make room for shopping centers. The grindhouses were replaced by multiplexes. Fortunately for Roger, the major studios didn't embrace the video revolution as quickly as they should have, leaving Roger to corner the market. He made video deals with Columbia Pictures, Embassy Pictures, Media Home Entertainment, MGM/UA, Vestron Video, and Warner Brothers. The movies would be given a limited theatrical play a few months before their release on video. Once the rising cost of advertising made it impossible to open a low budget film in theatres, Concorde became a direct-to-video company. The women-in-cages movies were replaced by stripper movies and slasher movies and Don 'the Dragon' Wilson movies. For a brief period Concorde indulged in some family-friendly movies. Roger went wherever the money was, following the lead of the major studios, making bargain basement versions of whatever it was that they happened to be making at the time.

In 1987 Michael Douglas and Glenn Close made a sex-charged suspense thriller called *Fatal Attraction* (1987), the first of what came to be known as erotic thrillers. Concorde had one of its biggest hits with *Body Chemistry* (1990). Three direct-to-video knock-offs followed. Concorde's *Carnosaur* (1993) beat *Jurassic Park* (1993) to the box office by a month. Critic Roger Ebert called it the Worst Movie of 1993 but it took in close to $2 million and spawned two direct-to-video sequels.

By 1990 Roger Corman had become a legend. People who had never seen one of his movies knew his name. (I don't think Beverly Gray had seen any of the movies Roger directed when I talked to her and I'll bet she still hasn't.) Name recognition may have been the reason that Thom Mount, who got his start in the business from Roger, was able to persuade 20th Century Fox to bankroll *Roger Corman's Frankenstein Unbound* (1990).

There were many reasons why Roger was reluctant to accept Mount's offer. For one thing it had been 20 years since he'd directed a film. Also, he'd been cut a lot of slack over the years for some of the short-comings of his films because of the short schedules and poverty budgets. There'd be nowhere to hide this time, not with an $11 million plus budget and a first-rate cast that included Raul Julia, Bridget Fonda and John Hurt. He may have had some other misgivings as well but he couldn't resist the money he was being offered: one million bucks. So off he went to Italy with Julie at his side, doing her best to bring out the artist in him and squelch the Scrooge. At one point Roger asked Mount, "If we finish early do we get to keep the money we save?" Mount told him to just spend the fucking money.

"He seemed throughout the experience to be less at ease with directing than I had hoped," said Mount. "On the other hand, there were times when it was worth everything, because you could just see Roger having a great time on the set. Certain sequences, certain actors, certain situations: Roger was just flying. He would actually smile."[18]

Frankenstein Unbound.

He may have been smiling then but the people who worked at Concorde at the time say that Roger was cranky and irritable when he returned to work. Alas, the film proved to be a major disappointment, both to the critics and to the public. As Sam Goldwyn once said, "They stayed away in droves." After a disappointing two-city domestic release, Fox sent it straight to video. Warners controlled the overseas market. They gave it to an independent distributor.

Back in 1957 a lot of exhibitors were shaking in their boots when Fox West Coast Theatres joined Paramount's Telemeter in petitioning the Los Angeles city council for a franchise to permit their cooperative participation in cabled video. The threat of pay-per-view television was seen as the last nail in their collective coffins and Roger Corman took their side. "Many exhibitors are still paying for their widescreen and stereophonic sound installations," he said. "These introductions, which were improvements, have become standard operational procedure now and would not even be mentioned in advertising if contractual obligations didn't require it." Roger believed that any innovation that didn't improve the quality of the pictures was not going save the industry as some had claimed, but rather it would prove to be a temporary solution to dwindling theatre attendance.[19] But it was cable-TV that saved Roger's bacon when the home video market had run its course in the mid-90s. He produced thirty-two films for Showtime's *Roger Corman Presents*. One of those films, *Black Scorpion* (1995), was turned into a series that ran 22 episodes. Now he's making junk for the Syfy Channel—*Dinoshark, Dinocroc vs. Supergator, Sharktopus* (all 2010) and *Piranhaconda* (2011).

Roger once said that the worst thing a filmmaker could do was set out to make a campy movie, but that's exactly what he's doing now because he's been backed into a corner. The movies he's making today, if you adjust for inflation, are probably cheaper than the movies he was making at the start of his career. He can't even pretend to make something that resembles a real movie anymore and maybe that's okay with him so long as he can make *something*. And it should be noted that *Sharktopus* was the Syfy channel's biggest hit.

Roger Corman and Vincent Price, taking a break
during the making of *The Pit and the Pendulum*.

There was a time when companies like MGM and Fox would ask Roger to make something because he could do it as well and cheaper than they could. But they aren't coming to him anymore. He has to go to them. And that's something that's been pretty hard to swallow.

A long time ago Roger told me movies were more fun to think about than they were to make. I can't imagine that the films he's making now are even fun to think about. And yet, though he's suffering severe back problems that require medication, like that little battery-powered bunny, he just won't stop.

Selected Filmography

MONSTER FROM THE OCEAN FLOOR (1954) with Anne
Kimbell, Stuart Wade, Dick Pinner, Jack Haze and Wyott Ordung. Written by William Danch. Produced by Roger Corman. Directed by Wyott Ordung. B&W 64 minutes. A Palo Alto Production. A Lippert Pictures Release.

Wyott 'Barney' Ordung was working at Alfonso's restaurant when he happened to run into Roger at General Service Studio. The two decided to pool their resources to make a low budget science-fiction movie. Roger raised most of the money from his friends. Barney kicked in the rest by selling his two-bedroom chicken coop in Sun Valley and by hocking his life insurance. Roger hoped to make the picture under the radar because he wanted to keep the labor unions off his back. So when someone from one of the trade magazines phoned to ask about the picture, Roger gave them a phony title, *The Sea Beast*, and said he was making the picture in Ensenada. Someone from the union eventually tracked him down at Malibu beach. After seeing what a small operation it was, the guy gave Roger a break.

Roger Corman: "I had seen a picture in the paper of a one-man submarine that the Aerojet-General Company had made, and I was trying to get started and thought this would be a good basis for a science-fiction picture. I called Aerojet and said if they would let me use it in the picture, I would give them a lot of free publicity. They said yes."

Jonathan Haze: "I was working the night shift at a gas station so I could go to auditions during the day. This little guy named Barney Ordung used to come in all of the time in a beat up old car, talking about how he was going to make a movie with a guy named Roger Corman. In those days everybody in Hollywood was going to make a picture. You didn't really think that much about it. One night he comes in, all excited and says, 'We're gonna do it. We're finally gonna make the movie. Come on. I want you to meet the producer.' We drove to the Cock 'n' Bull where Roger had his office. Roger said they were making a science-fiction movie. 'There's a party for you,' he says. 'A Mexican. But you'll have to grow a mustache. You'll also have to bring your own costumes, do your own stunts, and you won't be paid overtime. You still want it?' I said 'Sure.' Hell, I would've done it for free."

Anne Kimbell: "My mother and aunt were actor agents with the Sue Carol agency. I grew up in the agency. Roger rented his first office in the same building with my aunt and my agent, Jean Halliburton. When she heard that this charming, preppy newcomer Roger Corman was seeking an actress who could swim well for *Monster from the Ocean Floor*, she wanted to help him out and thought I should audition. So, Roger, my agent Jean and Wyott Ordung went out to my cousin's swimming pool as I remember; I did the length of the pool and it was a done deal. The unsung hero of *Monster from the Ocean Floor* was Al Hansen, a salvage diver who invented the first underwater camera who lived on Catalina Island where we filmed. Al's wife is the one fighting the shark! Not me. I wouldn't do it even though Roger assured me, in his own very special way, that it was an 'old' shark!"[20]

The Critics: "Good direction and performances…"—*Boxoffice*; "…it's a long way from a Grade-A product."—*Los Angeles Daily News*; "…a well-done quickie."—*Variety*; "…is distinguished by some magical undersea scenery, including swimmer Anne Kimbell…"—*Los Angeles Times*; "The monster in question resembles a huge, one-eyed octopus, but it is no more convincing than the plot."—*Los Angeles Examiner*.

The Exhibitors. "It kept the kids running to the lobby during the movie's exciting scenes."—James Wiggs, Jr., NC.

FIVE GUNS WEST (1955) with John Lund, Dorothy Malone, Touch Connors, Paul Birch and James Stone. Written by R. Wright Campbell. Produced and directed by Roger Corman. Pathecolor 78 minutes. A Palo Alto Production for American Releasing Corporation.

Roger Corman: "This was my first film as a director. I was sick to my stomach the whole time. I was so nervous I couldn't eat. It rained the first day. I was on my way to the location when it started. I pulled over to the side of the road and threw up."

Jonathan Haze: "He kept his eyes glued to the script the whole time until Bobby Campbell told him to forget the script and watch what the actors were doing. Bobby was a friend of mine and he wrote a good part for me and himself."

R. Wright Campbell: "Now, it had been established in the screenplay that I was a dead-eye; that I could pick off a fly at 300 yards. The cameras are rolling and [John] Lund (who wasn't at all athletic) is supposed to be crawling around under [the house] while I'm winging off shots. I must have shot six times and John never fired back. He was supposed to get me with one shot. Well, it looked silly as hell but of course Roger never re-shot because there wasn't any time. That was a take."[21]

Roger Corman: "*Five Guns West* was a breakthrough for me. With almost no training or preparation whatsoever, I was literally learning how to direct motion pictures on the job. It took me four or five of these 'training films' to learn what a film school student knows when he graduates."[22]

Jonathan Haze: "I staged all of the fights in it. And if I stage a fight, and I'm in it, I never lose. Which was funny because Mike Connors was in the picture only he was Touch Connors in those days, and he was this big guy, you know, and I was this little guy, but I'd lick him in all the fights and I think that kind of ticked him off."

The Critics: "At the outset we are told that [the five outlaws] must move through a land swarming with Comanches and Union cavalry. This raises audience expectations for excitement the picture fails to deliver. There are but two longshots of distant redskins and the fighting consists of a hand-to-hand struggle with one lone Indian. It's a good deal as though you tried to produce Ben Hur by talking about the chariot race."—*Hollywood Reporter*; "No matter at which point on the compass this quintet of shootin' irons is aimed, it is not going to blow any gaping holes in the cash-drawer records."—*Boxoffice*; "Scripter R. Wright Campbell's plotting is acceptable but he permits his character to talk too much. The result in that the pacing by producer Roger Corman … lags often enough to make the unspooling seem slow."—*Variety*; "The broader, plainer audience that has been the mainstay of the western melodrama … is quite likely to give this attraction substantial support."—*Motion Picture Herald*.

The Exhibitors. "… filled with quite a bit of action and a plausible plot… Had no bad comments on it."—I. Roche, FL.

Val Dufour and Allison Hayes from *The Undead.*

THE UNDEAD (1957) with Pamela Duncan, Richard Garland, Allison Hayes, Mel Welles and Richard Devon. Written by Charles B. Griffith and Mark Hanna. Produced and directed by Roger Corman. Black and white 75 minutes. A Balboa Production for American International Pictures.

Mel Welles: "If you're going to understand [*The Undead*] you have to go back to the events that were going on in the world at the time. That picture was based on the Bridey Murphy phenomenon. There was a woman (I don't remember her name) who was hypnotized and under hypnosis described her previous life as a person named Bridey Murphy. So Chuck Griffith wrote this marvelous script and all of the dialogue was written in verse."

Chuck Griffith: "I told [Roger] that by the time we got the thing out it would be a dead issue. Then the Paramount movie based on [Morey] Bernstein's book bombed so Roger changed the picture from *The Trance of Diana Love* to *The Undead* which is a zombie title. The whole thing was originally written in iambic pentameter, all of the stuff in the past. The scenes were separated by synclines done by the Devil. It was the best piece of writing I'd done up until that time or maybe since. I don't know. Roger loved it when he first read it. Then he showed it around and nobody understood it so he told me to translate it into English a couple of days before we had to shoot. And it was gone, you know. It was a mess then."

Richard Devon: [*The Undead*] was shot entirely in an abandoned market on Santa Monica Boulevard. Roger got some phony boulders and he filled the place with dead shrubbery and all of that. They had a bee-smoker to create the dreadful-smelling fog, and a camera and the whole thing was shot there."[23]

Dick Miller: "I was a leper. There was this old Australian make-up man and we worked out some effects with Kleenex… You wet it and it looks like skin. Like a bad sunburn. And it was great. But Roger shot the make-up in a master shot. And then when my face is cleared up, after I've sold my soul to the Devil, he shoots the nice handsome shot of me. Me with my be-bop haircut trying to play a medieval leper. It was unbelievable. He moves in for a close-up to show that my skin has cleared up. I said, 'You missed this fantastic make-up.' 'Well, we're not going to go back and get it. Forget it.'"

Chuck Griffith: "Allison Hayes was supposed to cut Bruno Ve Sota's head off with an axe. He was supposed to back up against the wall and she was supposed to swing an axe that went through the neck, right into the wall. Then the body was supposed to slide down the wall, spurting blood, and the head was to stay on the axe blade, looking surprised. No attempt was made to do that. Bruno was really dying to do it."

Richard Devon: "Anything that costs a penny over his minuscule budgets turns Roger Corman into a monster. He is a dual personality. You meet him in his office and he's absolutely charming. That boyish face of his. He digs his toe in the carpet. All of that jazz. You get him on the set, and he's Attila the Hun."[24]

Roger Corman: "It was a very strange film. I haven't seen it for a long, long time. I was maybe a little too ambitious for ten days and seventy or eighty thousand dollars. This is one of the things I learned over the long-run. We were better off making a small picture for a small amount of money than trying to make a big one and cheat it."

The Critics: "…a witch's brew that smells more than it scares."—*Hollywood Reporter*; "Roger Corman has packaged known ingredients of horror melodrama with enough deft touches to make *The Undead* boxoffice."—*Motion Picture Herald*; "The pacing is slow and the thrills at a minimum."—*Variety*; "…a complicated and often confusing storyline."—*Los Angeles Examiner*.

Pamela Duncan and Richard Garland.

ATTACK OF THE CRAB MONSTERS (1957) with Richard Garland, Pamela Duncan, Russell Johnson, Leslie Bradley and Richard Cutting. Written by Charles B. Griffith. Produced and Directed by Roger Corman. Black and white, 62 minutes. A Los Altos Production for Allied Artists.

This film has everything going for it, a good script, decent actors, a great melancholy score by Ronald Stein... even the titles by Paul Julian are fun. There's only one little flaw, one teeny-weenie glitch that fowls up the works. The Crab.

Chuck Griffith: "We all laughed when we saw it. The Dice Company made it. I think it cost Roger four hundred dollars. It was made of Styrofoam and the eyes kept peeling off."

Mel Welles: "They took it to Marineland and tried to push it underwater and the arms broke off."

Charles Griffith: "It was called *Attack of the Giant Crabs* when I wrote it. Roger wanted suspense or action in every scene which was his way of telling me he didn't want a lot of exposition."

Mel Welles: "From my standpoint it was the least colorful Roger Corman picture in terms of behind the cameras, because it went basically the smoothest. I don't

The crab.

remember Roger screaming much. Roger was like a skipper on a yacht where you really don't have time to baby people. [He] was a totally effective filmmaker in terms of the business end of it, not in terms of the quality factor because this conversation is not about that. As a producer, he executed his job of solving problems within the parameters of his authority with the greatest amount of efficiency."

Ed Nelson: "We were shooting a scene on the beach of Malibu where one of my men was killed falling out of a motorboat. And Roger had me yell to the other guys in the boat, over the surf, with emotion (because the dead guy was supposedly a friend of mine), 'Bury him!' I mean, the boat was sixty feet away and the surf was pounding, and Roger wanted me to holler, 'Bury him!' with emotion! How the hell…! Chuck Griffith played the guy who fell out of the boat: he also wrote the picture."[25]

Russell Johnson: "Believe me, everybody who worked for Corman in those years was doing two or three jobs. They learned their trade. This was when Roger was making films for around $75,000 and we were all making next-to-nothing. I remember one scene in *Crab Monsters* where I had to come up out of the ocean wearing some scuba gear and holding the girl in the picture. We were supposed to shoot the scene in the morning when the tide was supposed to be *out*. Well, Roger didn't get around to it until towards the end of the day, when the tide was coming *in*! And there were these big rocks underneath us. The girl and I were both scared to death. She grabbed a hold of me at one point to save herself because she thought some wave was going to pull her away. It really pulled at me. With the flippers on there was no way to stand up, so we had taken them off. And that's when I hit and broke my toe against the rock."[26]

The Critics: "…woefully wanting in its ability to raise goose pimples on anything but a goose."—*Boxoffice*; "It isn't necessarily believable, but it's fun…"—*Variety*; "Average… suffers from a limited budget so that the monsters that provide the chief horror… are not as large or menacing as they should be."—*Hollywood Reporter*; "A below average example of the current science-fiction vogue. The story is chaotic, the idea is wildly overexploited and the film in general verges on the lunatic, with remarkably poor playing."—*Monthly Film Bulletin*; "Acting is fair to go; direction… is about the same."—*Los Angeles Times*; "It's great!"—Mark McGee.

The Exhibitors: "One of the best Saturdays we've had in many weeks with 3 cheap pictures from Allied Artists. Not new ones either."—Art Richards, SC; "Played with *Not of This Earth* and this combination is okay. It did good business."—S. T. Jackson, AL; "This is one of the best horror double bills that we have seen in a long time—suspense, intrigue, adventure, with many a scary scene that frightens the daylights out of a person."—Dick Warner, Canada.

NOT OF THIS EARTH (1957) with Beverly Garland, Paul Birch, Morgan Jones, William Roerick and Jonathan Haze. Written by Charles B. Griffith and Mark Hanna. Produced and directed by Roger Corman. Black and white 67 minutes. A Los Altos Production for Allied Artists.

Paul Birch is an emotionless and brilliant vampire spy from the planet Davanna. He comes to Earth hoping to find a new source of blood. If our blood is acceptable, Earth will be turned into a blood bank. If not, Birch has been instructed to blow up the planet, making this one of Corman's bleakest and best films. Birch's performance is right on target. He never burlesques the role. His lack of social grace and directness is at odds with Dick Miller's street corner hustle as the salesman who tries to sell him a vacuum cleaner. It's a very funny moment.

Dick Miller: "I came up with the line 'If you want to purchase, purchase, if you don't want to purchase, don't purchase.' Roger wanted me to wear a bowtie. I told him I sold door-to-door in the Bronx and I always wore what I always wore. I told him I wanted to wear a black shirt. It was the only time I remember arguing about wardrobe."

Chuck Griffith: "I walked into Roger's office and told him we should make a horror movie about a guy with X-ray eyes that zaps people. He said, 'We're not making horror movies anymore. We're making science-fiction now.' It took me a month to write the script. My wife at the time was a nurse. She helped me make all of the medical gobbledygook more believable."

The Critics: "...leaves as many loose ends as can be found in a flop house carpet..."—*Boxoffice*; "It plays off at a regulation pace with attention to chills and thrills... Things get rather gory, but s-f fans won't mind. They should especially like the ending..."—*Variety*; "...slightly above average production for this kind of picture."—*Motion Picture Herald*; "This seems to be a slightly above-average production for this kind of picture... Miss Garland, especially, does very well by some surprisingly good humor that is part of the Griffith-Hanna script."—*Hollywood Reporter*.

The Exhibitors. "This is quite a hair-raiser. Will scare the kids and drive them out to the lobby to hide under the manager's wing."—Michael Chiaventone, IL.

TEENAGE DOLL aka **THE YOUNG BEBELS** (1957) with June Kenney, Fay Spain, John Brinkley, Colette Jackson and Barbara Wilson. Written by Charles B. Griffith. Produced by Bernard Woolner. Directed by Roger Corman. Black and white 68 minutes. A Woolner Brothers Production for Allied Artists.

"This is not a pretty picture," warned a pre-credit disclaimer. "It could not be pretty and still be true. What happens to the girl is unimportant... What happens to the others is more than important; it is the most vital issue of our time. This story is about a sickness, a spreading epidemic that threatens to destroy our very way of life. We are not doctors... We can offer no cure... But we know that a cure must be found." Most of the J.D. movies during this period had a prologue like this to make it appear as if the producers were not exploiting the subject but were simply raising concerns about it. *Teenage Doll* may have been the grittiest of the bunch. It is as grim and hopeless as any film noir and though it would be a stretch to call it a good film it has more than its share of good moments. It's one of Corman's most interesting efforts and yet it has all but disappeared from any discussion about his work. The only thing that Corman seems to remember about it is an encounter with the woman who delayed the shooting one night by turning on her sprinklers, hoping to be paid to turn them off.

June Kenney, the star of *Teenage Doll*, was also in Gene Corman's
Hot Car Girl, pictured here with Dick Bakalyan.

June Kenney played Barbara Bonney, on the run from a girl-gang called The
Black Widows for accidentally killing one of their members. Though she is 'introduced'
in the credits, Kenney had worked in television before Roger hired her for this movie.

Chuck Griffith: "The script I wrote was rejected by the Hays Office (or whatever it
was called at the time) so I had to rewrite it over the weekend, or should I say I had
to ruin it over the weekend."

Jay Sayer: "The scene in *Teenage Doll* where I turn into a raving maniac and attempt to accost June was quite good. I played it just the way Roger wanted me to. Roger said 'Give me all you have. I want to see how big you can get. I could always tone you down.' So Roger told me to do it exactly the same way on camera."

June Kenney: "I was leery because I wasn't sure of how much pressure I should apply in order to have it break... and we had to get it in one take. Roger and I consulted over it a few times and he saw how uneasy I was with having to hit this guy over the head and hope I didn't hurt him. Roger got me through it."

Jay Sayer: "When June hits me over the head with the bottle, even if it is candy glass, filling it with liquid gives it the same force as a regular glass bottle. Either someone else or the prop man put water in it. June was very apprehensive about it. But she did it and knocked me cold!"[27]

The Critics: "The overall result is that a batch of would-be dramatic screen tests made in some acting school for aspiring young troupers were thrown together with but scant regard for continuity, consistence or believability... a veritable marathon of unmitigated mugging."—*Boxoffice*; "The acting is uneven, but Corman has managed to sustain the initial motivation. The principals are young, hard-working, relative newcomers to the screen. Too much footage is concerned with the female shape and form, a matter that lamentably labels *Teenage Doll* adult entertainment."—*Motion Picture Herald*; "Unremitting unconvincingly downbeat tenor, clumsily executed, deaden b.o. chances for any audience outside of sex-and-sadism fanciers."—*Variety*; "... so much contrived effort for shock values went into the scripting that the weak attempt at moralizing was negated and audiences will be amused, rather than horrified, at luscious babes... acting tough, tough, tough when, with their perfectly made-up faces, they should have been attired in décolleté evening gowns rather than blue jeans and windbreaker jackets."—*Hollywood Reporter*.

THE SAGA OF THE VIKING WOMEN AND THEIR VOYAGE TO THE WATERS OF THE GREAT SEA SERPENT aka VIKING WOMEN AND THE SEA SERPENT (1958) with Abby Dalton, Susan Cabot, Brad Jackson, June Kenney and Richard Devon. Written by Lawrence Louis Goldman. Produced and directed by Roger Corman. Black and white 70 minutes. A Malibu Production for American International Pictures.

Jack Rabin owned a company that specialized in low cost special effects. He approached Roger with a script and some exciting drawings of a sea serpent attacking a ship full of Viking women. Rabin said that for $20,000, plus a percentage of the picture, he and his partner would bring those drawings to life. Roger showed Irving Block's drawings to Jim Nicholson and Sam Arkoff. They gave him $70,000 to make the picture. It was shot at Iverson's Ranch in the San Fernando Valley, Cabrillo beach, Bronson Canyon and ZIV Studios. Three days into production Roger knew he'd made a big mistake. Everything seemed to be going wrong and it started on the very first day when assistant director Jack Bohrer was waiting for a bus to take him to Paradise Cove. With him were four young ladies dressed in skimpy rawhide Viking outfits. One of those young ladies was Kip Hamilton. She was the star of the movie. She had her agent with her and he wouldn't let her sign the contract.

Jack Bohrer: "The girl and her agent probably assumed they could pressure Roger into more money. Big mistake. So I called Roger at the location. He was always there an hour ahead of everyone. I told him the situation and asked what we should do."[28]

Boxoffice, Aug. 31, 1957: "Abby Dalton moved into starring position, replacing Kip Hamilton, forced to withdraw from the cast because of a strep throat. Shirley Wasden [Abby's sister] was moved to first featured position but fell off a horse and had to be replaced by June Kenny."

Betsy Jones-Moreland: "Abby's sister pitched over the head of her horse… and plowed her head right into a rock… She was unconscious; she had to be taken away. And when Roger went to the hospital to see her—she was not even conscious yet— he tried to get her to sign a release, that he was not responsible or liable for any of this. (I was not there so I can't swear to this, but this is what I was told.) That was Roger to the core!"[29]

Jonathan Haze: "People did a lot of things for Roger. And sometimes he took advantage. Like when we made *Viking Women and the Sea Serpent*. He had all of these young girls in a boat and the tide came up and took them out to sea. A lot of people took a lot of chances."

Richard Devon: "We were all down there on the day when Roger shot the scene where the Viking women launch their ship. If you recall in the film, the rudder falls off the boat. Needless to say, that was not supposed to occur, but Roger is undaunted—nothing stops Roger. They just kept going. The girl who swam after the boat was swimming for her life, because of the undertow."[30]

Betsy Jones-Moreland: "We were all of a sudden on our way to Hawaii. We had no engine, we had *nothing*! We had no one to come get us! Roger is walking up and down on the beach and he is slamming his hat on the ground, then picking it up and walking a few more steps and slamming it down again."

Susan Cabot: "We started screaming at him, but the sound of the ocean drowned us out. Before we knew it, the bottom of our boat started to fill up with water, and we had nothing to bail out with… We spotted two surfers not too far off, and Abby Dalton and I started screaming and waving our arms wildly… The surfers finally heard us and came over. They took a couple of girls and headed toward shore, and Abby and I took Betsy Jones-Moreland. By the time we finally got to land… the tide was beginning to rise, fast, and the tiny strip of sand that was left began disappearing under the water. We couldn't just sit there, waiting for a miracle; we had to start climbing up the face of the cliff."[31]

Sally Todd: "So we're in the ocean, and the waves, which seemed to be like 30 feet high by then, started crashing down on us. Within minutes, the boat broke in half and all of us girls went flying into the surf. I got hit in the head by one of the barrels and actually broke one of my pinkies. The rip tide started pulling some of the girls out to sea and when Roger saw that, he hollered for someone to call the Coast Guard. Abby Dalton and I were the only good swimmers in the group. Somehow we got past the rip tide, but it pushed us sideways into this huge cliff that was jutting out into the water. By this time Abby and I are screaming and flailing our arms because we're both being body-slammed into the side of this mountain. We decided we should try to get out of there if we could, so we began climbing the rocks that were at the base of the cliff. You'd think that Roger Corman would know enough to film all this, right? I mean, this is good dramatic stuff. But instead, he turned all the cameras off, the jerk."[32]

Jay Sayer: "Sometimes Roger would have you do things that he knows little or nothing about. Like riding a horse. Roger thinks you step on the brakes and the horse stops… For goodness sake Roger wanted us, who were all on horseback, to stop at the edge of a cliff. Half of us were just actors and some were stunt people. At one point, Betsy Jones-Mooreland [grabbed a megaphone] and yelled across the canyon to Roger, 'We are not going to do this Roger. It's very dangerous and someone could get killed.' Roger was across the canyon doing the long shot and yelled back to Betsy, 'It's in your contract Betsy!' And Betsy yelled back, 'In your hat Roger!'"[33]

Abby Dalton.

Abby Dalton: "Roger, on his way to setting his record, set up shots so quickly in the canyons that one of the Viking girls in the background raced through a shot with her sunglasses on. No one even noticed."[34]

Roger Corman: "When we shot the girls at sea in a storm, in the studio in front of a process screen, I knew we were in trouble. The plates had been shot from the wrong angle. I couldn't match them. And the sea serpent was too small; a little hand puppet."

Abby Dalton: "The process shots were hilarious. They were rocking the boat in this cavernous studio, squirting hoses and tossing buckets of water at us in our wet Viking buckskins. Between every shot the crew plied us with brandy to keep us from freezing to death."[35]

Roger Corman: "I learned a very valuable lesson from this picture. Never be sold by a presentation."

The Critics: "The story line is not particularly outstanding, but such attractive femmes as Abby Dalton, Susan Cabot and June Kenney—dressed in primitive attire more seeworthy than seaworthy—provide good patron bait for the thrill seekers, not to speak of the huge sea serpent which is made chillingly real by clever special effects work."—*Boxoffice*; "Plentiful action and the scantily clad women are attractive and resourceful."—*Harrison's Reports*; "…a briskly-enacted attraction that should satisfy action aficionados."—*Motion Picture Harold*; "What other company would have the vision and daring to dress up and peroxidase a crew of sorority sisters as Valkyries, set them in an overgrown dory and dispatch them from the shore of Uttermost Thule (Zuma Beach?)… in regard to direction and script, suffice to say they make A-I's *Teenage Frankenstein* look like *The Brother Karamazov*."—*Los Angeles Times*.

TEENAGE CAVEMAN aka **PREHISTORIC WORLD** (1958) with Robert Vaughn, Darrah Marshall, Leslie Bradley, Jonathan Haze and Frank DeKova. Written by R. Wright Campbell. Produced and directed by Roger Corman. Black and White, Superama 65 minutes. A Malibu Production for American International Pictures.

Robert Vaughn: "I couldn't wait to do it. It was a magnificent script written in blank verse about the end of mankind."[36]

R. Wright Campbell: "The whole thing was an allegory… about the destruction of the world by atomic power. And here is mankind trying to struggle out of it, building all the myths, the taboos, doing all the things that were supposed to preserve the remnants of the race long enough for it to survive. And when Vaughn's character goes stumbling off into the lush forest, when he goes daringly out there—which is also allegorical, that somebody sooner or later is going to turn their back on the teaching of the elders and find out what was said was not true—he was supposed to come upon this spaceman in what I envisioned as a marvelous, elaborate spacesuit, you know, Victorian, sort of like the kind of stuff Disney did in *20,000,000 Leagues*

Under the Sea [1954]. Well, and this is why I say that Roger really had no artistic intent about most of what he did, instead of this, he came up with this lizardman suit he'd found."[37]

Beach Dickerson: "I was supposed to fall off a log into this water that was so filthy it almost made me throw up. So I held my breath and I jumped in… Then we went to Bronson Canyon and shot my funeral sequence… I was sitting in the wardrobe truck watching. Roger comes over to me and says, 'What are you doing here?' And I said, 'Well, I can't be out *there*. It's *my* funeral!' And he said, 'Bullshit. Who would recognize you anyway?'… A couple of days later Roger was shooting a sequence where this character called the Man from the Burning Plains rides into camp and gets stoned to death. They brought in this scroungy old horse and I look around and ask, 'Who's going to play the Man from the Burning Plains?' And then I saw them coming toward me… Then we went to Iverson's Ranch and they were going to do this scene where they hunt and kill this bear. I was waiting for the trainer to show up with the bear when I see this guy coming toward me with a bear suit."

Robert Vaughn: "The producer hired the worst actors in the world and changed the title to *Teenage Caveman*. That was me. It was one of the great bad pictures of all time."[38]

The Critics: "Production has been given adequate mounting in a restricted interior set and several location areas for chases."—*Hollywood Reporter*; "The title role is played with sincerity by Robert Vaughn. A similar approach to the original story and screenplay by R. Wright Campbell is made by producer-director Roger Corman, creating a modest budget film with some statue."—*Motion Picture Herald*; "This is obviously a low budget picture, and in theatrical terms it doesn't always sustain, but the message is handled with restraint and good taste, and gives substance to the production."—*Variety*; "…the ten cent title notwithstanding, this is an interesting motion picture and judged with the context of its intent, remarkably good."—*Los Angeles Times*.

A BUCKET OF BLOOD (1959) with Dick Miller, Barboura Morris, Antony Carbone, Julian Burton and Ed Nelson. Written by Charles B. Griffith. Produced and directed by Roger Corman. Black and white 66 minutes. An Alta Vista Production for American International Pictures.

Chuck Griffith: "Roger showed me the sets that had been built for *Diary of a High School Bride* (1959). There was a coffee house, a living room, an apartment, and a police office. 'You see these?' he said. 'They're going to be standing for an extra week. Write a horror picture for these sets. So I wrote something called *The Yellow Door* and I showed him the first 30 pages, and when he read it he became enraged. 'This is a comedy!' he said. 'You have to be good to do a comedy!' I said, 'Roger, you're gonna make it for thirty or forty thousand. How can you lose?' 'But I don't know how to shoot comedy,' he said. 'Just shoot it straight,' I told him. There was applause on the set after Julian Burton finished his speech. Roger got excited. He took me to dinner and said, 'We've got to do another one right away. I don't want a sequel or anything else. I want exactly the same picture. Just change the names and the locations.' The first script I wrote was called *Gluttony*, about a salad chef who serves up people. Cannibalism was against the production code at the time so we had to drop that idea."

Dick Miller: "*Bucket of Blood* wasn't meant as a satire or a slapstick comedy. It was meant to be dark humor. It was a very serious story. The only comedy in it was pretty much the attitude that I adopted. It was a strange part. I was playing a mental retard basically, and a murderer, and the only way to make these pieces pay off was to adopt a certain attitude and that became humorous. I think I played it intentionally that way. I don't think it was an accidental performance. I wanted more of the innocence and naivety of the character. I didn't want him to be a stark killer or a moronic killer, I wanted him to be an innocent killer. And I think that's where the humor came from. But it was basically a very straight story. It's an old French classic. It's nothing new. It's been done many times. *House of Wax* and things of that nature... I thought it was a classic picture in every way except the money. Some of the effects were cheats. If they'd only had some production money. Everybody's good. The story's good. They would screw up on things that wouldn't get laughs, but then they would show a mannequin and say it was a statue. Things like that. And they cheated a little on the end. They couldn't do what they wanted to do... I'm supposed to be covered in clay and things like that. It would have been a more startling effect than some gray makeup... None of these are great pictures understand, but I always thought if

Barbara Morris was a featured player in a dozen or
more Corman films. She was married to Monte Hellman,
who became a director after she introduced him to Corman.

Bucket of Blood had had another chunk of money in production it would have ranked with any of the top horror films. It's the best script Chuck ever wrote."

The Critics: "Director Roger Corman has set out to satirize both the horror film and the Beatniks. He succeeds rather well on a small budget."—*Los Angeles Times*; "Dick Miller gives a performance of sustained poignancy as the half-wit hero."—*Monthly Film Bulletin*; "A 66-minute joke compounded of beatniks and gore. It's too comic to be a typical horror film and the horror is too explicit for it to be a comedy, but for the youth market at which it is intended, the feature looks like a winner."—*Variety*; "It's Roger's best picture."—Mark McGee.

The Exhibitors: "Played *Bucket of Blood* on the bill with a much higher rated film from another company, but this one saved the night. They liked it, it's different." Arlen W. Peahl, OR.

THE LITTLE SHOP OF HORRORS (1960) with Jonathan Haze, Jackie Joseph, Mel Welles, Dick Miller and Myrtle Vale. Written by Charles B. Griffith. Produced and directed by Roger Corman. Black and white 70 minutes. The Filmgroup.

On December 21, 1959 the Dice Company delivered four strange looking plants to Roger Corman's office at Amco Studios for which they received $750. The next morning, at 7:45, the cameras started rolling on what was then called *The Passionate People Eater* and by 9:15 the following evening the majority of the picture was in the can. Charles Griffith, Mel Welles, Jonathan Haze and photographer Vilis Lapenieks spent six more days shooting second unit exteriors.

Jonathan Haze: "All that stuff was non-union. We shot all that on skid row. We had all of these bums in the picture for ten cents a shot. They'd save enough to buy a bottle of wine, drink it, and be back for more."

Dick Miller: "Roger offered me the lead in *Little Shop* but we'd just made *Bucket of Blood* and it was the same picture. The same part. I said 'Give it to Jonathan.' Now, I could kick myself."

Jonathan Haze: "It's the one everybody remembers me for. At the time it was just another job, just another Corman film. There was nothing special about it."

Dick Miller and Julian Burton from *A Bucket of Blood*. The plot for this movie was revamped for *The Little Shop of Horrors*.

Roger Corman: "At the time we made *Little Shop*, it cost as much to hire an actor for five days as it did for two days, so I rehearsed the actors for three days and shot them for two, using multiple cameras. On the first day, after shooting for only an hour, the assistant director announced that we were hopelessly behind schedule. Then John Shaner and Jackie Haze did a scene in a dentist's office during which they accidentally knocked over a chair. Dick Rubin, who was the property master, said it would take an hour to put the chair back together. I said, 'The scene ends with the dentist chair falling over.'"

Jackie Joseph: "I think Roger was pre-lighting everything. I don't think we had a dressing room. To save time I had the next outfit hanging in a carpenter's booth on the sound stage so that I could quickly change and run in to the next set."

Mel Welles: "The interesting side-line on *Little Shop of Horrors* is that after the picture was made, Roger wagged his finger at us for a long time with an I-told-you-so attitude because he had difficulty getting the film distributed. The exhibitors thought it was anti-Semitic. They thought it was anti-Semitic for two reasons. One, we had a character in it called Mrs. Shiva who had relatives that were always dying. In the Jewish faith, when someone dies and you mourn them, it's called sitting Shiva. And her name was Mrs. S. Shiva which was a *Mad* magazine play on it. That was one thing they thought was pretty irreverent. The second thing was I was playing a Jewish character and by the time I discovered that the plant was eating people, the place was full and the cash register was going and I decided not to call the police because of the money I was making. Exhibitors took that to be an anti-Semitic thing. The way the picture eventually got released was when American International bought Mario Bava's first horror picture, *Black Sunday*. It was an awful picture but it had the best campaign that I had ever seen up to that date on a low budget exploitation motion picture. They mounted a beautiful campaign. But they needed another picture because in those days you released everything in double features. So they agreed to take *Little Shop of Horrors*."

Roger Corman: "When I finished the picture, Bob Towne said: 'Now you have to remember, Roger, making a movie is not like a track meet; it's not how fast you can go.' But I thought *Little Shop* turned out rather well. And at a sneak preview, I discovered that it was much funnier than I thought it was. The audience really liked it. That's why I was surprised and a little disappointed at first when it was only moderately successful. Even a moderate success is a success, but a moderate success is something you make from a low budget mystery or western; something tried and true. Something as zany as *Little Shop* should either have been a big hit or a flop. Or so I thought."

Dick Miller: "Today everybody makes a movie and if it bombs they call it a cult film. They say there's hidden things in it that you don't see. To me that's bullshit. A cult film has to develop a cult. And you don't do that in the second year after it fails. We kept hearing it was showing here and there and the college kids were eating it up. This was five years after the thing was made. Normally we had a life run of six months on most of our pictures. You made it, you got as much money as you could out of it, and then it became, you know, mandolin picks. There was very little you could do with those films, which is why Roger never copyrighted them. That's why he almost lost the whole deal when they wanted to make it into a musical."

Jonathan Haze: "It was different. I think it surprised a lot of people. If it had been a bigger picture—if one of the big studios had made it—I don't think people would have treated it the way they have. It just wouldn't have been the same."

The Critics: "This is low comedy, to be sure, and the percent of parody is considerably less than 50-50, but the film comes up with several good laughs via its wild disregard for reality and its wacky characterizations."—*Variety*; "If Roger Corman intended tongue-in-cheek story treatment, he's admirably succeeded. The deft production-directorial touches of the resourceful, redoubtable Roger Corman are very much present and accounted for."—*Motion Picture Herald*.

The Exhibitors. "... a sleeper. Paper is real good and the movie is the most unusual one we've had in a long time. Gross good—and plenty of laughs. The plot is real screwy, but a lot of fun. Understand it was filmed in a couple of days, but it did better for us than the super-epics."—Ray Boriski, TX.

ATLAS (1960) with Michael Forest, Frank Wolf, Barboura Morris, Walter Maslow and Christos Esarchos (Indros). Written by Charles B. Griffith. Produced and directed by Roger Corman. Eastmancolor, VistaScope 79 minutes. A Beacon Film Production for The Filmgroup.

Roger was hoping to capitalize on the sword-and-sandal excitement generated by *Hercules* (1959) when he set out to make this picture. It was supposed to be a co-production between Filmgroup and independent producer Vion Papamichelis. It was touted as Filmgroup's first million dollar, color and scope reserved seat roadshow attraction, although the budget was actually set at $80,000. A week before the starting date, during a tearful lunch, Papamichelis backed out of the deal and took his 500 costumed extras with him. Instead of cutting his losses, Roger went ahead with the picture. Charles Griffith was flown to Greece and asked to scale down his script to accommodate Roger's $40,000 budget. The result was hardly what one would call a roadshow attraction. It was more of a road apple attraction.

Chuck Griffith: "I wrote it in a hotel room in Athens with Frank Wolff over my shoulder ridiculing me as I was doing it. He was saying, 'This is so puerile!' But there was no time to think at all. You had to type. I said, 'I can only do one thing! I can't think and type at the same time, so shut up.' It was really hilarious, the whole picture. I think I got $100 bucks for that. Roger picked up a girl in Berlin and she was the script girl, wardrobe and props—all kinds of things. I became associate producer because I was there. We had a Greek cameraman and a Greek crew. It was hysterical. Nobody knew left from right and nobody could march. The guys playing the guards wanted their relatives to recognize them so they tore the nose guards off

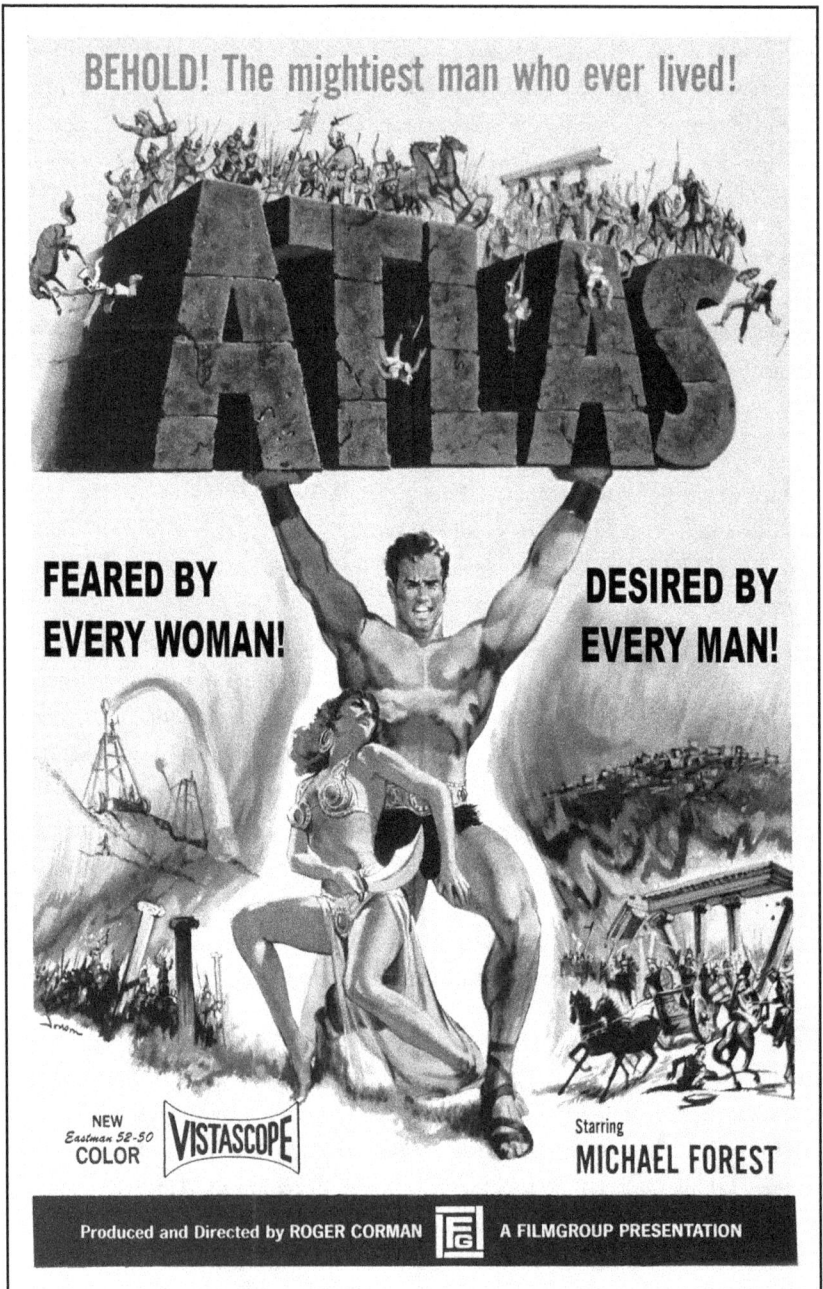

Artwork for *Atlas*, one of the most impoverished spectacles ever made.

their papier-mâché helmets so you had all this paper hanging from their helmets. The tips of their spears were made at a tire shop and they all drooped. We had to shoot in public buildings, of course, because there was no money. We had permits to shoot, but not with actors, so we were constantly being thrown out."

Roger Corman: "My crew struck in the middle of the three-week production. The budget was moving up toward $70,000. 'There's no way you guys can strike,' I said angrily. 'We're behind schedule and you've got to work. Look, work today, and tonight I'll buy everyone rounds of ouzo and retsina at a tavern and we'll work out your problems.' We did. Their real problem was that no Greek producers would recognize them as a legitimate union and give them any power. So I signed a document that, in effect, made me the first union producer in Greece."[39]

Roger called this film 'a total disaster.' Good performances from the three principals (especially Barboura Morris) couldn't save it. And the very least one should expect from a film like this is to have some body builder in the title role. Poor Michael Forest looks more like Steve Allen than he does Steve Reeves.

The main titles, patterned after *Spartacus* (1960), and the score by Ronald Stein raise expectations for a truly epic film, expectations that are immediately squashed by a cheesy and amateurish opening shot. Perhaps the title Griffith suggested would have been more appropriate: *Atlas, the Guided Muscle.*

In an effort to explain why Atlas would not be going out as a roadshow attraction, Roger told the press: "Exhibitors with box office acumen we respect indicate the dangers of pricing pictures out of the market. They admit the occasional success of roadshows but point out that they are interested in long-run attendance increase over extended periods instead of spot bonanzas. In effect, the roadshow oasis may be a mirage." Translation: "If we charge top prices for this impoverished piece of crap they'll tear the theatre apart."

The Critics: "...in Michael Forest's capable portrayal [Atlas] comes alive with a zestful vitality and youthful exuberance both refreshing and admirable to encounter."—*Boxoffice*; "Michael Forest, as Atlas, is earnest enough, but stacked up against Steve Reeves, he generates far fewer oohs and ahs!"—*New York Herald Tribune*; "Roger Corman produced and directed the activities, ostensibly on Greek location sites. They provide an additional source of nostalgia for the grandeur that was Rome."—*New York Times*; "A dreadful Grecian epic patterned after early Joe Levine."—*Show Business Illustrated*; "Producer Corman tries all the tricks he knows to create a muscleman mood on a pygmy-size budget, but director Corman is left with no elbow room for the imaginative effects which qualify him as a darling of the avant-garde.

The colors are limpid, there is some placid wrestling, no tortures, even the pitched battles are a bit cissy... One's interest is sustained from complete collapse by the film's touches of self-burlesque."—*Films and Filming.*

THE INTRUDER aka **THE STRANGER** aka **SHAME** aka **I HATE YOUR GUTS** (1962) with William Shatner, Frank Maxwell, Beverly Lunsford, Robert Emhardt and Jeanne Cooper. Written by Charles Beaumont based on his novel. Produced and directed by Roger Corman. Black and white 80 minutes. Pathe American/Filmgroup.

In 1958 Charles Beaumont wrote a novel based on an incident that took place in Clinton, Tennessee. A militant segregationist tried to rally support to thwart the Supreme Court ruling that outlawed segregation in public schools. Producers Ray Stark and Elliot Hayman took an option on Beaumont's book but let it lapse after a couple of years. Roger bought the book and hired Beaumont to write the screenplay. "I think the idea to do a film like this one came to me during the Little Rock crisis," Roger recalled. "I was down in Brazil at the time, scouting locations for a jungle adventure film and I was appalled by the bad reputation Little Rock gave us."

This was supposed to be the first of three pictures for producer Edward Small. A budget was set at $500,000 and Tony Randall was being sought for the lead. But Small put *The Intruder* on hold in favor of something that promised to be more commercial, *The Tower of London* (1962) with Vincent Price. Roger had made two successful Edgar Allan Poe movies with Price and though the actor had agreed not to make any Poe movies for anyone but American International, Small must have felt that having the actor parade around an old castle in a period setting was close enough. Roger didn't get along with Small. The old time producer was too meddlesome and the two men mutually agreed to call it quits. Roger went looking for someone else to back *The Intruder* but no one was interested. With no other options open to him he decided to bankroll it himself.

With Gene Corman acting as an executive producer, Roger took his cast and crew to Missouri. William Shatner was cast as the rabble-rousing segregationist. Shatner was a stage actor looking to break into the movies.

William Shatner: "He never told me why he wanted me for the part, but I'm sure it was because I was handsome, brilliant, and didn't need the money—because he didn't pay me! One night we were shooting a white-supremacy parade in the black part of town, and someone was knifed in the crowd. The shoot seemed to go on forever. It was very tense. I was glad to get out of there in one piece."[40]

William Shatner delivers one of his best performances in *The Intruder.*

Gene Corman: "It was important for us to film [in what was called The Badlands] so we had to have all the support of the black community… I met a white teacher from the high school who introduced me to a black pastor in the Badlands who became my conduit for the whole scene. And he thought I was a communist. He gave me a lot of help… I'm wandering around this place, meeting people, you know, what you do to set up a film—locations, deal making, casting. I met Charles Barnes. He had never acted before. He was, as I look back, braver than anybody. He was an honor student and an athlete. He'd just graduated high school and was looking to go to college. He'd been working with a road construction team. We had a couple of meetings and I gave him the script to read. This was the first time anybody had read the script by the way. I asked him to please respect what I was doing. He knew who Louis De Rochemont was and I said we were trying to give that immediacy to the film. I said we were going to bring in actors but that it would be wonderful if he would be in the picture. It was an important role and he was wonderful in the film. Terrific. And he read it and he was in awe of what he read. 'I think it's wonderful,' he said, 'but do you realize how dangerous it is to make this film?' I said, 'Charles, this is America. Nothing's going to happen.' Then he said, 'I'm going to have to show this to my mother.' I said, 'Fine. Please ask her not to discuss it.' And she didn't want him to play the role. There were a couple of rough days back and forth but at the end of it his mother agreed that he could do the film. And I still didn't believe anybody was going to get serious."

Leo Gordon: "They told us to pack up and get out with a police escort. Hard-nosed, goddamn people. The bartender wore a pistol in his belt and had a blackjack in his pocket. All of them looked and sounded like Slim Pickens."

Roger Corman: "The sheriff and local cops seemed to be shadowing us everywhere, trying to intimidate us. The only sequences in which I felt we got some tacit cooperation was the night we shot the Ku Klux Klan parade, the cross-burning, and the church bombing in the back section of town—or Niggertown, as they called it. For Klansmen we used some of the local boys who were hanging out at the bar; these guys needed almost no preparation or direction to get into character."[41]

Gene Corman: "The preview is the best part of the story. I phoned Bert Pirosh [the head of the Pacific Drive-In Theatres in California] and I said to him that I wanted to set up a preview. I asked for Baldwin Hills or a place that was on the cusp of the black and white scene… Five minutes into the picture the audience was bristling. We had a black and white audience. Mostly white. You shoulda heard the people in the lobby. I mean they weren't writing cards, they were ripping them up, throwing them down. 'Trashy Hollywood communists!' I mean, here I am, a dyed-in-the-wool Republican, you know. You have seldom heard what went on. I got a call the next day from Bert. He said, 'Gene, what the hell are you up to?' I said, 'Bert, I think we're on to something.' He said, 'Gene, this is very simple. There's no way we're going to play your film in any of our theatres… You're lucky that they didn't rip the theatre apart last night. And then the MPAA wouldn't pass it because we'd used the word 'nigger.' We fought it."

Roger Corman: "The major studios had used the word and I felt that because we were a small company we weren't given the same consideration. They finally agreed."

After a brief run in New York, Pathe-America Distribution Company gave up on the film and it languished until Cinema Distributors of America released it in 1966 as *Shame* and later *I Hate Your Guts*. "I don't know how many films I'd made before—ten, fifteen—and they'd all been successes," Roger said. "This was the first one that lost money. The reviews were wonderful. I can still remember after all these years one of the papers said: 'This motion picture is a credit to the entire motion picture film industry.' Which is very nice to have but as I say it was the first film that lost money."

A recent release on DVD finally put the film in the black.

The Critics: "Roger and Gene Corman's *The Intruder* comes to grips with a controversial issue—integration, and those who would defy the law of the land—in an adult, intelligent and arresting manner."—*Variety*; "The picture captures the true militant attitude of Southerners on the question of integration and it brings out the atmosphere of tenseness that prevails."—*Boxoffice*; "Some highly explosive material is handled crudely and a bit too clumsily for either conviction or comfort… But this must be said for *The Intruder*: it does break fertile ground in the area of integration that has not yet been opened on the screen. And it does so with obvious good intentions and a great deal of raw, arresting power in many of its individual details and in the aspects of several characters… [Corman] has caught, in one hideous little incident of a Negro family terrorized in their car by a mob of snarling hoodlums, the bestial temper of mob hysteria. And he has got in the stolid, handsome faces of many of his Negroes the lineaments of dignity and courage."—*New York Times*; "…an impeccable cast of performers led by William Shatner, who gives a superb performance."—*Motion Picture Herald*; "No masterpiece, this bold portrait of racial injustice has plot contrivances and occasional amateurish acting that are more than compensated by authenticity, plus a superb performance by William Shatner as a suave, slightly insane rabble-rouser."—*Los Angeles Times*; "A touchy subject… is handled unflinchingly and with dramatic insight and development…"—*Hollywood Reporter*; "Its lack of context, its irrelevant sexual excursions, its final falseness, its air of a daring descent into moral slums, insure that it will have little helpful effect on the appalling situation it depicts so vividly."—*New Republic*; "…an earnest attempt to deal with the problem of school integration in the South…"—*New Yorker*; "It was shot on location with an accuracy of detail and facial type this is downright scary… Despite a touch of patness in the windup, this agonizing tale of race hatred and exploited ignorance is a courageous work…"—*Playboy*; "There is so much good in this courageous, realistic and stirring documentary-styled story... that one regrets having to find fault with any of it—even though the fault is minor."—*Cue*; "Much of the strength of the film comes from the fact that it was shot on location, with the townspeople all too willingly playing themselves ... No studio set can quite convey the sun-drenched torpor and shabby meanness of a small Southern city, or the squalor of 'nigger-town,' or the sense of latent violence that throbs behind the fly-speckled window and flaking clapboard façade of such a community."—*Saturday Review*; "If Corman's film fails to match Cy Endfield's *The Sound and the Fury* or Losey's *The Dividing Line* it is partly because he has interested himself too much in the stranger (whose psychology isn't so brilliantly observed anyway), and the film ends on an anticlimax (this man's feelings of humiliation seem of little importance to me compared with other issues at stake).—*Films and Filming*.

THE TERROR (1963) with Boris Karloff, Jack Nicholson, Sandra Knight, Dick Miller and Dorothy Neumann. Written by Leo Gordon and Jack Hill. Produced and Directed by Roger Corman. VistaScope and Pathecolor. 79 minutes. A Filmgroup Production for American International Pictures.

Sam Arkoff came to the wrap party for *The Raven* and wondered why the sets weren't being dismantled and put into storage. Sensing that something was up, he returned the following day and found Roger filming another movie for his own company. Like a kid caught with his hand in the cookie jar, Roger grinned. The idea to make another picture had come to him during the second week of production on *The Raven*. He'd asked Boris Karloff, one of the stars of *The Raven*, to stick around for two more days for a small amount of money plus the promise of $15,000 *if* and *when* the film earned more than $150,000. (Karloff eventually got his money, but only after he agreed to work for two more days on *Targets* three years later.) Roger phoned Leo Gordon and asked him to write some scenes for Boris Karloff and Jack Nicholson. "He didn't have a story," Gordon said. "Just Karloff, a couple of actors, and the damn castle."

As the sets were being torn down around them, the actors raced from set to set, exchanging dialogue that had no meaning or motivation. Months later, Francis Ford Coppola was hired to write and direct the rest of the movie and hopefully make some sense out of it. He took Jack Nicholson and Sandra Knight (Nicholson's wife at the time) to Big Sur. Jack Hill went along to record sound.

Jack Hill: "Francis had this shot of Jack Nicholson and Sandy Knight coming down this hillside trail in the woods, and as they came around the corner of the hillside,

The Terror.

thousands of butterflies were going to fly up in front of them. So he had guys out catching butterflies all set to go, and he called action, they let the butterflies go, and Jack Nicholson comes around acting like a fag, y'know, flapping his arms. And he says, 'Oh, is that a take?'"[42]

Monte Hellman: "After five weeks of shooting, Roger fired Francis, and hired me to finish the picture. Jack Hill was hired to write a new script with me. A lot of what Francis shot was thrown out, except the stuff [with Dorothy Newman], and I finished the picture in five days of shooting. All of the interiors are Roger's (with the exception of Francis's witch's lair), and most of the exteriors are mine. To the best of my recollection, and contrary to legend, Jack Nicholson did not direct any of the film."[43]

Dick Miller: "I got a call from Roger. He said, 'We're going to finish the picture.' I didn't know what he was talking about. 'What picture?' I asked. '*The Terror*,' he says. It was hysterical. When you see the film you'll see me walk through a door and I'll gain twenty pounds. And my sideburns kept moving up and down. And, of course, my character kept changing because we never knew what we were supposed to be doing."

Jack Nicholson: "I throw Dick Miller up against this door, and Dick Miller now tries to explain the entire picture in one speech. It's the only film that I know of that has no story line that you can follow[44] ... I believe the funniest hour I have ever spent in a projection room was watching the dailies for *The Terror*. You first saw Boris coming down this long hallway in the Baron's blue coat. Then he'd move out of the shot. Then I'd come down the hallway and after I'd cleared the frame—Roger didn't even bother to cut the camera and slate the shots—Sandra [Knight, his wife at the time] would come down the hallway. Then it was Dick's turn, looking weird in his black servant suit. And then Boris would come down again, this time in his red coat. All of this shot as if in one take with no cut."[45]

The Critics: "... manages to project a goodly numbers of thrills and chills and presents an interesting well-plotted story as well."—*Hollywood Citizen News*; "No one believes in what they are doing, and it comes all too obviously across."—*Films and Filming*; "... an imaginative horror picture, done with sound production values that make it a class item in its field."—*Hollywood Reporter*.

The Exhibitors: "Doubled this with *Dementia 13* ... opened very good on Friday. Saturday was below average, as was Sunday. My 13-year-old daughter Pam (who is an authority on horror pictures) says that *Dementia* killed the deal and I believe she may be right. Play *The Terror* but put it with something else, sez Pamela."—Paul Wood, FL; "Okay for horror fans and horror situations. Average business for its type."—Terry Axley, AR.

THE HAUNTED PALACE (1963) with Vincent Price, Debra Paget, Lon Chaney, Jr., John Dierkes and Leo Gordon. Written by Charles Beaumont based on "The Strange Case of Charles Dexter Ward" by H.P. Lovecraft. Produced and directed by Roger Corman. Panavision and Pathecolor 85 minutes. An Alta Vista Production for American International Pictures.

Roger got the idea to make this picture while he was working on *The Premature Burial*. He intended to use the two leads from that picture—Ray Milland and Hazel Court—along with Boris Karloff. When Pathé caved to Arkoff's demand to turn over *The Premature Burial* to AIP, Roger went ahead with the picture under AIP's umbrella. Milland and Court were replaced by Vincent Price and Debra Paget. And Lon Chaney had to fill in for Karloff, who had taken ill while he was in Italy making *Black Sabbath* (1964).

Vincent Price is possessed in *The Haunted Palace*.

"Then, after the picture was finished, Jim and Sam changed their minds and decided they somehow wanted to integrate the picture into the Poe series," Roger recalled. "I always felt calling it a Poe picture made absolutely no sense. It was really something that was done simply for box office appeal, because all the Poe pictures had a made a lot of money for AIP."[46]

AIP changed the title from *The Haunted Village* to *The Haunted Palace*, the title of one of Poe's poems. When producer Irwin Allen unsuccessfully tried to stop them from using the title, Roger gave his secretary a list of Poe titles to register, *The Black Cat* among them. His secretary politely reminded him that he'd already made *The Black Cat* as part of his *Tales of Terror* (1961) trilogy.

Once the film was finished, AIP threw a wrap party at the Tahitian and sent the bill to Roger in the amount of $68.14. He returned the bill with a note saying it was the first time he'd been invited to a party and asked to pay for it.

The Critics: "...a well-made horror film, weirdly enough, a healthy specimen with black blood coursing through its veins. The perverse and yet persistent interest of the public in necromancy does not merely support a shoddy effort, but raises a competent work to inadvertent moments of lyricism."—*Newsweek*; "[Corman] has risen above the limitations of his medium to create a powerful and unified surrealist fantasy."—*Films and Filming*; "The moral is that you can't keep a keen warlock down—and who would want to, when he's so debonair a chap as Price, telling an unwilling but admiring visitor to his torture chamber 'Ah, yes, Torquemada spent many a happy hour here, a few centuries ago'... The Torquemada line is almost worth the price of admission—but not quite."—*New York Herald Tribune*; "Corman's direction takes full advantage of the big atmospheric sets (local) and gives... a lush feeling beyond even the respectable budget American International allows."—*Hollywood Reporter*; "Poe seems to be the favorite author of the horror merchants these days. Possibly because he isn't around to defend himself against the onslaughts of Hollywood screenwriters."—*Los Angeles Times*.

The Exhibitors. "Used this second run and did okay."—S. T. Jackson, AL; "Can't see how they got the whole story from one little Poe poem. Confusing ending. Should do good business for right type of crowd. Play it."—Chukk Garard, IL; "This picture did outstanding business and small towns should do okay on any playdate."—Terry Axley, AR; "Another business-getter from the company that has kept me in the black with this type of product. The house uptown reported that they outgrossed *The V.I.P.'s* with its second run."—Paul Wood, FL.

Edd Byrnes and Stewart Granger lock horns in *The Secret Invasion*.

THE SECRET INVASION (1964) with Stewart Granger, Raf Vallone, Mickey Rooney, Edd Byrnes and Henry Silva. Written by R. Wright Campbell. Produced by Gene Corman. Directed by Roger Corman. Deluxe Color, Panavision 95 minutes. A San Carlos Production for United Artists.

Gene Corman made a deal with United Artists to shoot this picture about five convicts who rescue an Italian general from a prison in Dubrovnik in exchange for their freedom. When the story was first being developed, the big-wigs at UA wanted the convicts to blow up an ammo dump, but that was too much like *The Guns of Navarone* (1961) as far as Roger was concerned so he suggested that it be a rescue mission instead. The picture was shot in Yugoslavia for $600,000.

Edd Byrnes was sitting next to Raf Vallone on the plane to Yugoslavia when he noticed a stack of books in Roger's lap. "There were titles like *How to Direct Motion Pictures* and *The Art of Motion Picture Directing* and things like that. I turned to Raf Vallone and said, 'This is going to be a great picture! We were really worried. But it came out pretty good.'"

Stewart Granger played the leader of the group, a role originally written for Bobby Darin. "They paid [him] fifty thousand," said Chuck Griffith. "I ran into him in the market a couple of weeks ago. He started ranting about Roger. He was a captain in the script and he said, 'I have to be a major!' I think he rationalized it by saying he was too old to be a captain."

'The Major' also felt he was entitled to any dialogue he took a fancy to and when he wanted to steal one of Byrnes' lines, the actor objected and Roger backed him up. Granger threatened to walk off the picture but as they were on a boat at the time, there was nowhere for him to go.

William Campbell was standing next to Mickey Rooney during one of the many shoot-outs in the film and one of Rooney's hot, ejected shells went down his shirt. "It gets lodged in my belly button," Campbell recalled, "and the casing is so hot—at first I tried to jiggle my leg to get it to go down, but it won't! And I'm doing a whole dance routine, and I hear Roger scream, 'Cut!' He said, 'What the hell is all that movement for?' I said, 'I've got a hot shell in my belly button!' Roger was an understanding guy, but the problem with Roger was, if you broke a leg, he'd say, 'Let's finish the scene.' There were things that he did sometimes that I would say, 'Roger I don't know how you get away with it.'"[47]

The Critics: "...a rather surprising amount of brisk muscularity and panoramic color, if not always credibility."—*New York Times*; "...a slam World War II adventure film..."—*New York Herald Tribune*.

The Exhibitors. "Plenty of action, a lot of suspense and good color."—Benny Leviton, GA; "A few women commented there was too much fighting, but most of the men and boys who saw it liked it better."—Lew Bray, Jr., TX.

THE MASQUE OF THE RED DEATH (1964) with Vincent Price,
Hazel Court, Jane Asher, David Weston and Patrick Magee. Written by Charles Beaumont and R. Wright Campbell from a story by Edgar Allan Poe. Produced and directed by Roger Corman. Pathecolor and Panavision 90 minutes. An Alta Vista/ Anglo Amalgamated Production for American International Pictures.

Roger has said time and again that this would have been the second in the series of Edgar Allan Poe movies if he hadn't been afraid that people would think he was ripping off Ingmar Bergman's *The Seventh Seal* (1956), as both stories took place in the middle ages and both had scenes of Death personified. Truth is he didn't want to make the picture for AIP. Roger met a wanna-be writer from Arkansas named John Carter while he was making *The Intruder*. He continued to correspond with

Carter by mail and with instructions to combine *Great Expectations* and *Psycho* with
a heavy dose of *The Seventh Seal,* Carter went to work on an outline. In the meantime
Roger made a co-production deal with Alfred Wagg Pictures in England. He hoped
to shoot the picture in Greece. While he was working on *The Pit and the Pendulum,*
Roger sent Carter a copy of Richard Matheson's script to use as a guide in writing dialogue with an archaic feel that didn't get bogged down by archaic speech patterns.
By November, Carter had completed a first draft. Roger gave it to Charles Beaumont
for an opinion. Beaumont was in the middle of writing *The Premature Burial* (1962)
at the time, a movie that was being financed by Pathé, the company that did all of
AIP's lab work. Beaumont hated Carter's 150 page script, which he found "scholarly,
complex, dull, undramatic, uninteresting and pointless." He promised Roger that
as soon as he was finished with *The Premature Burial* and Roger's next project, *The
Haunted Village,* which he estimated would take him a month and a half, he would
give Roger something that was "worthy of Bergman's best." Roger wasn't ready to
give up on Carter. He fired off a list of notes and asked him for a major rewrite.

Meanwhile, Nicholson and Arkoff heard that Roger was making a Poe movie
for another company from Roger's art director, Dan Haller. Haller was under contract to AIP and was afraid they might have a problem with him working on the picture. They told him to go ahead, then Sam Arkoff flew to New York and told Pathé's
owner, William Zeckendorf, he'd take AIP's lab work to another company unless they
gave AIP ownership of the picture. Roger was surprised to see Nicholson and Arkoff
show up on the first day of the shoot. "Welcome back to AIP," Arkoff told him.

Roger was in the middle of making *Tales of Terror* (1962), his fourth Poe movie,
when John Carter finished his second draft, which Roger sent to Alfred Wagg. Wagg's
readers didn't like it. "It's too much like a stage play," they said, and Wagg lost interest
in the project. Roger sent a letter to Carter wishing him well with a check enclosed.
Instead of giving Charles Beaumont a chance of making good his promise to write a
script worthy of Bergman's best, Roger wanted to see what Robert Towne could come
up with. But Towne was a slow writer and Roger grew impatient. He let actress Barboura Morris give a shot before he finally told Beaumont to go ahead. Still he wasn't
satisfied. He asked R. Wright Campbell to come to Europe with him to work on a
rewrite. Campbell introduced a subplot involving a dwarf from Poe's "Hop-Frog."

On November 19, 1963, *The Masque of the Red Death* went into production in
England as a co-production between AIP and Anglo-Amalgamated. Vincent Price
was once again in the lead with Jane Asher (who was dating Paul McCartney at the
time) and the wonderful Hazel Court in supporting roles.

"The scene in the film where I sacrifice myself to the devil gave me a very strange feeling," Hazel recalled in her autobiography, *Hazel Court Horror Queen*. "It really did give me a cold chill. Once I have sacrificed myself to Satan, I go into a trance-like state where I am floating, but even that scene, in which I have to writhe around screaming on a cold slab, did not affect me like stabbing my breast and giving myself to the devil."

The British Board of Film Censors would not release the movie until Miss Court's black mass sequence was cut from the film. It remained intact for its U.S. release.

Masque of the Red Death was the most lavish of the Poe pictures. Roger was given access to some fabulous costumes and the sets from *Becket* (1964), the photographer was Nicholas Roeg, and he had five weeks to make it.

Three days before the film was scheduled for release, Alex Gordon sought an injunction, claiming that Beaumont's script plagiarized a script he'd submitted to AIP back in 1959. His complaint was based on solely on Beaumont's script, not Campbell's rewrite which eliminated most of the similarities. The matter was settled out of court. "I don't blame Roger," Gordon said. "I don't think he ever saw my script."

The Critics: "Corman... has let his imagination run riot upon a mobile décor singular for its primary color scheme. The result may be loud, but it looks like a real movie. On its level, it is astonishingly good."—*New York Times*; "The film is beautifully costumed, the sets are lavish, the props exquisite."—*New York Herald Tribune*; "Corman may yet out-horror all the horror filmmakers."—*New York Daily News*; "Corman has devised a stylish excursion into demonology..."—*Newsweek*; "...dusts off a trifling Poe classic and adapts it to fit the collected smirks of Vincent Price."—*Time*; "...excessively talky at times and weirdly unbelievable, but it holds a strange fascination and winds up with a magnificent costume ball which ends with an orgy which turns into a veritable dance-of-death."—*Boxoffice*.

The Exhibitors. "This will please the horror patrons."—Harold Bell, Quebec.

Roger Corman and Bruce Dern.

Footnotes.

1. Randall D. Larson, "The Film Music of Ronald Stein," *CinemaScore* 1984, page 52.

2. Tom Weaver, *Science Fiction Stars and Horror Heroes*, McFarland & Company, North Carolina, 2007, page 310.

3: Tom Weaver, *Attack of the Monster Movie Makers*, McFarland & Company, North Carolina, 1994, page 184.

4: *Attack of the Monster Movie Makers*, page 206.

5. Ibid, page 193.

6. Beverly Garland saw Allison deliberately slide off her horse while Roger claimed her horse slipped in the mud and that's what caused her tumble.

7. *Attack of the Monster Movie Makers*, page 190.

8. Ibid, page 192.

9: Jan Alan Henderson, "William Campbell," *Filmfax* No. 75-76, 2000, page 108.

10: *Boxoffice,* June 27, 1960, page 29.

11: Roger Corman and Jim Jerome, *How I Made a Hundred Movies in Hollywood and Never Lost a Dime,* Da Capo Press, 1990, page 168.

12: Ibid, page 232.

13. Dickerson appeared in a number of Roger's early films as an actor while supplementing his income as an architect. He built Roger's two-story office building on San Vicente Boulevard and remodeled his 6,500 square foot Georgian home in Santa Monica.

14: Jeffrey Frenizen, "Not Just Another Cog in the Corman Factory," *Fangoria,* Vol. 3, No. 45, page 64.

15: Chris Nashawaty, *Crab Monsters, Teenage Cavemen, and Candy Stripe Nurses,* Abrams, New York, page 103.

16. Beverly Gray, *Blood-Sucking Vampires, Flesh-Eating Cockroaches and Driller Killers,* AZ Ferris Publications, California, 2014, page 111.

17. Ibid, page 132.

18. Ibid, pages 166-167.

19. *Boxoffice,* October 5, 1957, page W-3.

20. Paul and Paula Parla, "Our Teenage Living Doll," *Scary Monsters Magazine,* January 2010, page 65.

21: W. C. Stroby, "Pick a Genre, Any Genre," *Filmfax* 4, No. 32, 1993 pages 67-68.

22. *How I Made a Hundred Movies...* page 27.

23. *Sci-Fi Stars and Horrors Heroes,* page 54.

24. Ibid, page 54.

25: *Attack of the Monster Movie Makers,* page 234.

26. Jay Allen Sanford, "An Interview with Russell Johnson," *Filmfax,* No. 33, June-July, 1992, page 66.

27. Paul and Paula Parla, "Our Teenage Living Doll," *Scary Monsters Magazine*, January 2010, pages 56-57.

28. *How I Made a Hundred Movies…* page 48.

29. *Attack of the Monster Movie Makers*, pages 181-182.

30. Tom Weaver, *The Return of the B Science Fiction Stars and Horror Heroes*, McFarland & Company, North Carolina, 1999, page 59.

31. Ibid, page 67.

32. John O'Dowd "Sally Todd" *Filmfax* No. 124, 2010, page 42.

33. "Our Teenage Living Doll," page 66.

34. *How I Made a Hundred Movies…* page 47.

35. Ibid, page 47.

36. Phil Hirsch, *Hollywood Uncensored*, Pyramid Books, New York, NY, 1965 page 167.

37. W. C. Stroby, "Pick a Genre, Any Genre" *Filmfax* No. 32, page 71.

38. *Hollywood Uncensored*, page 167.

39. *How I Made a Hundred Movies…* page 110.

40. *Crab Monsters, Teenage Cavemen…* page 54.

41. *How I Made a Hundred Movies…* page 100.

42. "Not Just Another Cog in the Corman Factory," page 14.

43. Mike White, *Cashiers du Cinemart.*

44. *Crab Monsters, Teenage Cavemen…* page 51.

45. *How I Made a Hundred Movies…* page 93.

46. Lawrence French, "California Gothic," *Video Watchdog*, page 32.

47. "William Campbell," page 106.

Index

www.ingramcontent.com/pod-product-compliance
Lightning Source LLC
Chambersburg PA
CBHW060327100426
42812CB00003B/898